HUMAN CONSCIOUSNESS AND ITS EVOLUTION

HUMAN CONSCIOUSNESS AND ITS EVOLUTION

A MULTIDIMENSIONAL VIEW

RICHARD W. COAN

authorHOUSE®

AuthorHouse™
1663 Liberty Drive
Bloomington, IN 47403
www.authorhouse.com
Phone: 1-800-839-8640

Published by AuthorHouse 5/8/2013

ISBN: 978-1-4817-3626-8(sc)
ISBN: 978-1-4817-3625-1 (e)

Library of Congress Control Number: 2013905927

Table of Contents

Preface

The subject matter of this book is vast and fundamentally important. It would be presumptuous of anyone to attempt to deal comprehensively with it in a book, and it would be preposterous to pretend that one has the final solution to all the puzzles that it poses. I confess to being a bit presumptuous, but I have tried to avoid being preposterous. Many others have written about the evolution of consciousness, but they have left unsaid some things that I believe need to be said. In the pages that follow, I have endeavored to offer a fresh and broader perspective. On some issues, I have tried to suggest avenues that need to be explored further. There remain many gaps in my own understanding, and I trust that other authors will supply some of the insights that are missing from the present account.

One cannot write such a book without combing through an extensive literature and borrowing ideas from many people, and this work has left me with a heavy burden of outstanding intellectual debts. I am indebted not only to those who share many of my views but also to those with whom I have most sharply taken issue in this book. The latter would include, in particular, Julian Jaynes, Ken Wilber, Carl Sagan, and Jacob Bronowski. If I have expressed fundamental disagreements with them it is partly because they have stimulated my thinking sufficiently to evoke dissent. I am impressed with their work and regret that I have not actually met any of these gentlemen.

I also owe a debt to the many people who have shared their ideas with me in personal contact—including Laurens van der Post, P. L. Travers, Aniela Jaffee, and John Mattern. I am indebted as well to many people who have provoked insights that they did not necessarily intend to provoke. Thus, I have learned from James Hillman, who sees elaborate excursions into theory as a way of playing the old science game and evidence of a failure to awaken to post-modern consciousness. I have learned from Hans Eysenck, who sees enterprises such as this as a waste of time, by virtue of the impossibility of applying rigorous scientific methods. I have learned still more from Raymond Cattell, who accused me of wandering in search of the Holy Grail when I could have devoted my time to systematic gathering of valuable psychometric data.

I am indebted to the many students who have served as a soundingboard and occasionally as a panel of critics for my ideas. I have also learned much about the nature of human consciousness from the many people I have known who, for one reason or another, have stubbornly refused to accept the roles, pathways, or patterns of thinking dictated by convention. These would include a few friends who have undertaken the psychotic journey through hell and sometimes gotten stuck along the way.

Human Consciousness and Its Evolution

1

The Roots and Presuppositions of Evolutionary Theories

> In the beginning God created the heaven and the earth. And the earth was without form, and void; and darkness was upon the face of the deep. And the Spirit of God moved upon the face of the waters. And God said, Let there be light; and there was light. And God saw the light, that it was good; and God divided the light from the darkness. (Genesis 1:1-4)

Thus begins the account of creation in the first chapter of Genesis. To say "Let there be light," of course, is tantamount to saying, "Let there be consciousness, or mind," for it is by means of light that we become aware and can distinguish one form from another. Creation myths in general are concerned with our origin as aware beings. They deal with the great mystery of human consciousness and offer a symbolic account of its onset in the remote past within the species as a whole and within each individual in the early stages of life.

In this Hebraic myth, matter and light are created from nothing. In other creation myths, the original condition is not nothingness but chaos, or formlessness, and the process of creation consists of the conversion of nonform into discernible form. In still other myths, forms that exist already emerge into the light—from the womb of the earth, from the sea, or from the great world egg. Yet another theme is that of the world parents, heaven and earth, who have long been joined in sexual union and finally become separated. As a product of their conjugal act, light and individual beings now appear between them. There is a limited number of these basic metaphors of creation, and each of them is widely distributed in the mythologies of mankind. One basic idea runs through all of them: Long, long ago at a very special moment, there were discernible forms, and there was light with which to see them.

In Genesis there is also a description of a subsequent moment in the emergence of human consciousness. At the suggestion of the serpent, Adam and Eve eat of the fruit of the tree of knowledge. The serpent assures them that their eyes will be opened and that they will be like gods. In eating the fruit, Adam and Eve are indeed claiming as their own a godly prerogative, the right to choose deliberately, rather than following automatically the dictates of God, nature, or instinct. The act presupposes a fundamental discrimination between two conflicting urges and a choice between the two. As a consequence of the act, Adam and Eve can distinguish more generally between good and evil and, being aware for the first time of their nakedness, they can distinguish between male and female, or between the masculine and the feminine. Here we have another basic motif that has been widely employed to describe the origins of human consciousness—the creation or recognition of a duality. It is a motif that is shared by ancient creation myths and modern psychological theory, for we still tend to regard consciousness as a process of discrimination.

The great mythologies of the world abound with additional stories of gods and great heroes, and many of the recurring themes can be understood quite readily as further stages in the unfolding of human consciousness. The very existence of the mythologies attests to the fact that people have wrestled with the puzzle of their awareness from a very early time, and perhaps human consciousness and the myths that symbolize it have evolved together. If so, mythology may well provide the best available evidence for the actual course of our psychic development.

The Contemporary Crisis of Meaning

As old as the basic questions here may be, they seem to have a current urgency that they have not often had in the past. There is a growing interest these days in achieving a better understanding of our psychic evolution, and I think the reason for this is not hard to find. As many writers have noted, we live in an age in which there is a crisis of meaning. This condition has been described in many ways, but the central idea is that we have lost the vital symbols, myths, and religious images through which our ancestors derived a sense of meaning. With the aid of these symbols, one could feel securely rooted in one's family, society, and the universe. One had a clear sense of right and wrong, and there was an orderly plan to follow in moving through all the major transitions of a lifetime.

It may seem paradoxical that we suffer a loss of meaning at a time when an explosion of information is taking place, but the two processes are undoubtedly linked. The explosion of information is undeniable. We live at a time of unprecedented scientific and technological development. We have seen dramatic developments in methods of storing and retrieving information, as well as major improvements in the means of communication over vast distances. There has been an accelerated mingling of cultures, and we have grown accustomed to getting in touch with events on all parts of the globe with the flip of a switch and a twist of a dial. We have rapid access to a surprising array of facts, products, and ideas, and a brief trip can bring us face to face with a totally different climate and people whose cultural background, lifestyle, and traditional standards are entirely different from those to which we are accustomed. Many of the benefits of this new world are obvious, but as Alvin Toffler (1970) noted in *Future Shock*, the increased diversity, the rapid change, and the mounting pressure to make all kinds of choices have combined to become a source of severe stress.

The rapid change, diversity, and explosion of information are not the source of the crisis of meaning, though they undoubtedly aggravate our experience of it. Perhaps they are best viewed as concomitant effects of the conditions that have brought about the crisis of meaning. It is folly to think we can identify any simple underlying cause for all these developments. Industrialization, the spread of commerce, and accompanying changes in our political systems have each played a part. The growth of science over the past few centuries has been both cause and effect. The churches have played a role to the extent that they have insisted on dogmatic adherence to the symbols and imagery of the past, instead of permitting the natural evolution of religious images that grow and remain alive through a succession of generations. Whatever the causes, we have entered an age in which people have come to worship at the altar of science and technology. We have tried to rid ourselves of symbols, for we have grown suspicious of meanings that grasp us emotionally but cannot be spelled out fully for intelligent scrutiny. We have turned from symbols to signs with a clear literal message, and we look for the solutions to our ills and discomforts in the realm of cold, hard facts. As a reward for our devotion, we have secured a curious array of material honoraria: antibiotics, transistor radios, microwave ovens, computer systems that eliminate a lot of drudgery, chemical pollutants that poison our air and water, and nuclear weapons with which we can destroy all life on the planet.

It is difficult to adjust to such a mixture of material blessings. In particular, now that we have created a means for rapidly annihilating the human species, we shall certainly never succeed in subduing our constant fear that the means will be used.

Perhaps the least we can hope is that the material comforts we have amassed at the same time may bring a bit of joy into our lives. Yet for the most part, we do not seek to experience life to the full, nor do we rejoice at being alive. We consume alcohol, tobacco smoke, aspirin tablets, and tranquilizers in order to turn off unwanted sensations. We gorge our stomach with meals over-rich in fat and refined sugar, and we feast our eyes with hours of mindless pabulum packaged by the television studios. Rather than seeking to experience life fully, we are obviously trying to avoid experiencing too much, because there is something about our experience that we find unsettling. There is something about our own lives and about our relationships with one another, with other living beings, and with the planet we all share that seems badly awry. We cannot rejoice in being alive because we do not feel in tune with life. We are aware that something is missing, and we may not have a clear idea of what it is. We do have a growing sense that what we lack is not going to be found in our mounting collection of inanimate things, in the next phase of computer technology, or in the next breakthrough in the field of biochemistry.

Coping with the Crisis

While many people attempt in various ways to blot out the malaise that comes with a loss of meaning, there are others who seek a solution to the problem. Their search for meaning has all the earmarks of a spiritual quest, even though such words as *spiritual* and *religious* are used only occasionally in conjunction with it. Theodore Roszak (1975) speaks of this contemporary spiritual quest in terms of an Aquarian Frontier and sees evidence of the quest in such varied forms as the ecological movement, new forms of healing and psychotherapy, and the revival of all sorts of occult disciplines. According to a Gallup poll in 1983, the quest is also reflected in an increasing revival of traditional religious beliefs and practices—despite the fact that the crisis in meaning may be ascribed in part to a failure on the part of our churches and religious traditions. Within the church there is a growing realization that the institution has failed and that something fresh is needed. Thus, people in the church turn to Carl Jung and Pierre Teilhard de Chardin for new understanding, and they turn to the charismatic movement for a more vital experience of their faith.

Our focal concern in this book is yet another consequence of the crisis of meaning. The recognition that something is out of order in our experience of ourselves, other people, and the world around us has occasioned a good deal of obsessive introspection. This inner probing was expressed in the nineteenth century in the writings of philosophers like Kierkegaard and Nietzsche, and it led to the beginning of the psychoanalytic movement around the turn of the century. It has yielded the work of Freud, Jung, and a host of other theorists, and it has added a characteristic flavor to the novels and poetry of the twentieth century. Some of the questions we keep asking are: "What is the nature of the current stage in our development as conscious beings?" "By what course did we arrive at this stage?" and "What is our future destination?" Thus, we live in a time when the issues pertaining to the evolution of consciousness assume a salience and an urgency that they have not had in the past.

BASIC MODELS FOR A THEORY OF EVOLUTION

As we seek a better understanding of the evolution of human consciousness, we should keep in mind some basic characteristics of the enterprise of theory construction. We are attempting to answer a question for which we shall never find a final answer. People outside of science tend to think of scientific theories as statements of hypothesized fact, statements that must ultimately be proven true or false. While this conception may apply to some of the ingredients of theories, generally speaking it is a very erroneous view of theories as such. In the usual case, the set of ideas that we label a theory represents an effort to capture in a systematic way our current understanding of a given realm of human observation, in the light of available information and our present modes of conceptualizing. The theory takes recognized facts into account and may be viewed as an attempt to organize them, but the theory as such is not a statement of fact. It makes use of images and abstract concepts that are currently fashionable, and the fashions may depend on currents of thought that extend through a realm that is far broader than the limited province embraced by the given theory.

The Nature of Theory

In a sense, a theory is more akin to a work of art than to a scientific discovery, for it is something we create or construct. It is a set of ideas that we impose on our observations as a way of construing them and being able to think about them in an orderly way. In principle, there is an unlimited number of ways in which we might do this. There are many potential sets of ideas that would serve the purpose. By this, I do not mean that any possible theory is just as good as any other. Obviously we choose one theory over another because we believe that in some way it works better, but we have a rather loose set of criteria for making this decision. In general, we prefer a theory that uses few concepts in a logically coherent way and employs simple formulae, while at the same time it takes all known observations into account, enables us to generate predictions, and stimulates our thinking. Within the social sciences, we frequently disagree on the application of any one of these criteria and on the relative weights to attach to different criteria, and the criteria rarely prevent us from gamboling off on whatever theoretical path we choose. Ultimately we choose a theoretical explanation because it feels right, because it yields some of the sense of understanding that we are groping for, and more often than not, we invoke the criteria of theory evaluation after the fact, to rationalize a choice we have already made.

This may all seem rather slipshod, but it is really the way science has always operated. Science has never been the tidy enterprise depicted in elementary textbooks. It is an ever-shifting and often confusing succession of intellectual products of people who endeavor to make orderly sense of what they observe in the sky, in the earth around them, in other people, and in their own images and dreams. This succession is not altogether chaotic, of course, for there are three kinds of constraint that serve to ensure that our explanations will display a moderate amount of continuity and consistency and that certain basic ingredients will recur over and over again. One obvious constraint is the body of observations that prompt our efforts to explain. A second constraint is the one I have characterized in terms of fashion. We employ ideas and forms of explanation that are in vogue. In the terms of Thomas Kuhn (1970), we employ the major paradigms that currently pervade the thinking within our science.

A third constraint is that in constructing scientific theories we can never transcend our limitations as human perceivers and thinkers. For better or worse, we seemed designed—or, in contemporary computerese, "programmed"—to conceptualize in a limited variety of ways. For this reason, every major idea that appears in scientific theory—no matter how original it may appear at first glance—can be shown to have a long history. We may suspect that the theorist borrowed it from an earlier thinker, but then the same can be said of the apparent predecessor, and in an exhaustive historical search our efforts to find the first expression are frustrated ultimately by an absence of the necessary records. We often stop with the classical Greek philosophers because we lack the means to go further. In some sense the basic idea that keeps recurring often appears to represent an archetypal mode of experiencing. In some way, it is built into the very fabric of our experience. It is somehow inherent in our genetic makeup, and hence in our nervous and sensory systems, or it is bound up in the very nature of consciousness itself.

Many of our basic ways of thinking about matter, space,

causality, and time are so characteristically human that it rarely occurs to us that it is even possible to think in a different way. Human beings rely heavily on visual images, and most of our abstract words, examined etymologically, readily reveal a covert reference to positions, sequences, and simple actions in three-dimensional space. All theories of change, growth, development, and evolution make use of simple spatial metaphors, such as expansion, contraction, horizontal succession, circular movement, or vertical movement through a series of steps or levels. They also reflect our basic ways of thinking about time, which in turn are tied to these spatial metaphors.

The Cyclical View of Time

Mircea Eliade (1954) notes that an archaic view of time as cyclical is found throughout the world. The cycles encountered in nature play a part in the formation and elaboration of cyclical concepts: the twenty-four-hour diurnal cycle, the cycle of lunar phases, and the annual cycle of seasonal changes. The lunar cycle in particular plays a prominent role in the thinking embodied in mythologies. In the archaic view of things, the world is created over and over again, and many rituals devised by human societies contain formulae for the regeneration of the cosmos and humanity. Such an idea is widely incorporated into the ritual treatment of birth, marriage, and the installation of new rulers. In this way, such events are experienced as regenerations that annul the past and reinstate the beginning of a cycle.

Generally, in the archaic view of time, the beginning of the cycle is regarded as an ideal point, a Golden Age whose virtues have been gradually lost and whose ultimate return is ever welcome. There is a common tendency in modern Western society to see the cyclic view as a rather primitive perspective that we have outgrown, but in taking this stance we tend to overlook the extent to which our own thinking is still governed by a cyclic scheme, and we fail to realize that the alternative schemes to which we turn have no greater claim to absolute truth.

Alternative Models

In any case, the idea of a recurring cycle of events is one of the basic models in terms of which we can view all basic changes in the universe, including such human concerns as the evolution of consciousness. What are the alternative models? The clearest contrast to the cyclical model is a model that presupposes continuous unidirectional change. Several variations on this essential idea are possible. One possibility is a model of pure progress: a continuous, or monotonic, upward movement from origins that may be characterized as chaotic, formless, primitive, or unenlightened, to a condition marked by virtue, order, intelligence, enlightenment, or such. Subvarieties of this model are obviously possible. In one variation, there is a basic upward trend, but it is uneven. The upward movement is saccadic—it occurs in occasional jumps, and in between there are periods of stasis or minor recessions toward a more primitive state. In another variation, an eventual end or future plateau is forecast for the upward movement. Once we have made the right discovery, once the revolution has been fought and won, once we have achieved nirvana, there will be eternal bliss, peace, harmony, or unity with the godhead or brahman.

Opposite to the progress model is a model that presupposes steady deterioration or degeneration. Again the movement may be regarded as steadily proceeding in the same direction, this time downward, or it may be seen as subject to some fluctuation and possibly as leading to an ultimate chaos. This model usually assumes an original Golden Age, from which it was possible to move only in a downward direction. Such a model has not often been applied to the evolution of consciousness, but it has certainly been applied to many other human affairs, including the character of society as a whole.

In principle, if time and change are viewed as unidirectional, movement could be upward, downward, or simply horizontal. In the last case, we have continuous change, but it is neither progressive nor regressive. Changes of one sort tend to be balanced by comparable changes of a different sort. This is basically the model underlying the steady-state hypothesis of cosmological theory, but it is a model that has not found much application in biological or social science. I know of no one who would insist on applying this model to the evolution of consciousness.

In general, the other possible models may be construed as variations on the cyclical and linear models or as combinations of these two basic types. Simply curvilinear models assume a combination of upward and downward trends. One such model assumes that there was early progress at some time in the past but that change has since been downward. This is essentially a variation on the deterioration model. A slightly different model would assume that the ideal moment, the Golden Age, is now, that we live currently in the best of all possible times. In the past there was been progressive movement toward this peak, and unless we can retain all that we have accomplished, the only possible future is one of decline. The reverse of this model would be one in which the present is seen as a low point, the condition farthest removed from both an early Golden Age and the Golden Age possible or inevitable in the future. If the early and future Golden Ages are seen as equivalent, this model is not really distinguishable from the cyclical model.

A combination of the cyclical and linear models is clearly evident when change is regarded as helical, that is, when the course of development is likened to an ascending spiral staircase. In this model, steady progress is assumed, but at the same time, there is continual cyclical recurrence of certain qualities, phenomena, or events. In the simplest application of this model, there is just one great cycle, but the terminal point is at a higher level than the starting point. This idea can be found in both Eastern and Western thought. In the West, we find it notably in the work of Carl Jung, where the psychic development of the individual, or course of individuation, is said to start with an amorphous condition. Development proceeds from this via differentiation of specific psychic functions and contents, which emerge selectively into consciousness. As contrasting or conflicting functions and contents become differentiated and consciously utilized, they tend to become reconciled or integrated into a higher unity. The logical goal of the total process is a total integration of the psyche.

The basic model employed by Jung was formulated most clearly by Herbert Spencer, the great philosopher and theorist of the nineteenth century. Spencer believed the model to be of very wide applicability, and he was particularly interested in its application to biological and societal evolution. Spencer's model assumes a movement from simplicity or formlessness to complexly integrated form via the joint operation of processes of differentiation and integration. The idea was given extensive psychological use in this century not only by Jung, but also by Arnold Gesell, who regarded it as the key to development in the embryo and child. A trace of the idea is apparent in much of the literature on creative thinking and in the work of Teilhard de Chardin.

Evolution and Involution

We may conclude this brief survey of basic evolutionary models by noting a subtle variant that appears in the writings of Sri Aurobindo (1970) and Ken Wilber (1980, 1981). Aurobindo and Wilber speak of a progressive course of psychic development that proceeds from a preconscious condition to higher levels of consciousness that culminate ultimately in the unity consciousness of Hindu philosophy, but they both argue that the process of evolution presupposes a prior process of involution, in which the true condition of unitary being is enfolded or disguised. Involution may be regarded either as a prior process or as a process that operates along with evolution, since unitary being is not only a prior reality but also an implicit reality, ever-present and needing merely to be realized consciously.

Underlying the two-process doctrine advanced by Aurobindo and Wilber is a view of reality derived from Vedanta philosophy. This view assumes that behind the world of appearances composed of familiar objects and our individual identities is a hidden, implicit, and more basic reality. Views of this kind have been propounded recurrently through the ages by mystics in all cultures. In such views, the familiar, apparent reality may be regarded either as sheer illusion, as a lesser, more temporary, and relative reality, or as a reality that shares equal status with the implicit, absolute reality that lies behind it. Such ideas have long been regarded as rather absurd by Western scientists, but scientific thought in this century has been moving in a direction that seems to be remarkably consistent with that perspective on reality. We have grown more and more accustomed to the notion that our theories are as much human constructions as faithful maps of reality, and we have reached a stage at which a physicist like David Bohm can speak of an implicate order, hidden beneath the web of things and relations that we observe, without being expelled from the scientific community. A number of writers have claimed that there is a growing rapprochement between modern physics and Eastern mysticism.

Both Aurobindo and Wilber argue that the concept of evolution logically implies involution or that the one process requires the other. Perhaps the conceptual pairing is a matter more of psychological than logical necessity, for there appears to be something archetypal about it. The idea that a process of upward growth (evolution) requires a balancing process of death, destruction, or disordering (involution) may well be universal. It underlies a host of rituals in which a life (of a king, or the consorts of a goddess, for example) is sacrificed as a condition for the renewal of life. This ancient motif of compensatory destruction underlies the symbolism of the crucifixion in Christianity. One might argue that the compensatory motif needs no archetypal roots, that it appears universally in human thought simply because it fits so much of our common observation. It operates in an obvious way in the biological realm, for everywhere plant and animal organisms are consumed for the sake of the continued life and growth of other organisms. Within the individual organism, constructive and destructive processes (anabolism and catabolism) operate throughout life. The Freudian notion of life and death instincts may be viewed as a simple extrapolation of this observation into the psychological realm. It is possible in general to describe creative development, wherever it occurs, in terms of the joint operation of a process that is constructive, ordering, or integrative and a process that is destructive or disintegrative. Whether or not this notion is ultimately rooted in an archetype, it has been resurrected many times by theorists concerned with creative thinking, individual growth, biological evolution, and the transformation of cultures, societies, and political and economic systems.

THE MEANING OF UP AND DOWN

I noted earlier that in formulating abstract concepts we make extensive use of spatial metaphors. The metaphor of verticality plays a key role in the evolutionary models I have just discussed. We think of evolutionary change in terms of movement toward a condition that is higher and better or toward one that is lower and worse. But how do we decide what constitutes a higher and better condition or a lower and worse one? Often theorists who advocate different models appear to be arguing over the direction of the change that is occurring or has occurred, when in fact their basic difference is one of values. This is especially true in the realm of human affairs, because the social condition, societal structure, or psychological state that seems ideal to one person may be viewed with abhorrence by someone else.

Complexity and Adaptation

Herbert Spencer, endeavoring to formulate a concept of evolution that would apply to creative change in all scientific domains, attempted to sidestep value questions and to identify universal features of creative process. He eschewed the word *progress* because he felt it had limiting, anthropocentric connotations. He characterized evolution in terms of an integration of matter and dissipation of motion and a change from incoherent to coherent form, from homogeneity or uniformity to heterogeneity or multiformity, from the indefinite to the definite, from simplicity to complexity, and from confusion to order. He captured much of this description in a definition of evolution as a change from "a relatively indefinite, incoherent homogeneity to a relatively definite, coherent heterogeneity" (Spencer, 1912).

Defined in this abstract manner, the concept of evolution obviously fits processes that we observe in many different fields. In fact, Spencer sought to apply it to physical and chemical processes, to the evolution of the solar system, to the geological history of the earth, to the evolution of organic forms, to changes in social systems and societies, and to the development of languages, sciences, and arts. It is obviously not the only kind of process we observe: it is essentially the opposite of the disorganizing processes we characterize in terms of death, decay, erosion or entropy. Spencer recognized this and contended that we find everywhere two processes in an antagonistic relationship: evolution and dissolution, or disintegration. Each of these processes, he said, tends to follow the other. Hence, uninterrupted evolution over a long period is rare.

In dealing with biological evolution, Spencer allied himself with Darwin and saw complexity or heterogeneity as the key to successful adaptation and self-preservation in the face of various kinds of threats. He also spoke of biological evolution in terms of constant progress toward a higher degree of skill, intelligence, and self-regulation. It was Spencer who introduced the phrase "the survival of the fittest" as a way of expressing a key idea in Darwinian theory and an equivalent to Darwin's term "natural selection." In the position shared by Darwin and Spencer, biological evolution necessarily entailed an increasing ability to cope successfully with environmental demands. In equating the higher and better with successful adaptation, they adopted an essentially utilitarian stance.

This outlook still underlies most current thinking about biological evolution, and it is consistent with the importance attached to science and technology in our society. From such a perspective the shift in human thought from an emphasis on myth, religion, and symbol to an emphasis on science and signs is a progressive movement. A sharply contrasting position is presented by writers like Aurobindo and Wilber, who see the realization of spirit as a goal toward which we are heading. Our current intellectual focus is merely a necessary detour along the path that we must follow.

Surmounting the Needs of the Body

Probably many thinkers would agree that the mental evolution of the human species has entailed a movement from a preoccupation with the body and bodily needs toward a greater concern with matters in which the body plays a rather incidental role. The movement may be described in terms of an emphasis on the intellect or on spirit, and it is possible to rationalize it either as Aurobindo and Wilber do or on utilitarian grounds. Those who favor the utilitarian view, however, will tend to focus on the growth of realistic and analytical thinking, while the others may focus on the experience of a unity with universal spirit. It is also possible to emphasize the full realization of all the modes of experience that lie within the range of human potential, be they practical, aesthetic, spiritual, or social. Such a view is still consistent with the Spencerian conception of evolution as a progression toward greater organized complexity, but the complexity would appear to serve aims that go beyond mere self-preservation.

Societal Levels

A totally different approach to the question of levels of human psychic attainment is one that focuses primarily on the culture or social system and assumes that those features of mind and consciousness that accompany a more advanced culture or social system are superior to those found in a lower culture or social system. This obviously raises a new question: How do we decide what is higher or lower in the cultural or social realm? This is usually answered in terms of historical sequences, on the assumption that what comes later is better. The sequence most often noted in human societies is from a group that practices hunting and gathering to one that settles for a longer period in one locale and engages in agriculture and then to one that engages in commerce with neighboring groups. Perhaps we could agree that in moving from one state to the next, a society has improved in most respects. It does not necessarily follow, however, that every accompanying change in mentality or consciousness is an improvement. Something valuable may be lost in the process.

The issue gets even more complicated when we compare one contemporary society with another and make inferences about differences in levels of consciousness on the basis of a difference in their economics. Social theorists have often arrived at judgments on such a basis, but more often than not the result has simply been a specious defense of a bias present before any effort was made at systematic comparison. When they compare differing contemporary societies that have all advanced beyond hunting, gathering, and rudimentary forms of agriculture, they tend to assume that the present state of their own society represents the most advanced condition yet attained anywhere and that any society that has developed along a different path is obviously inferior in some respect. Only when confronted with an overwhelming body of dazzling evidence are we likely to admit that, at least in some minor respect, another society has reached a higher level than our own. Perhaps our thinking will continue to be tinged with ethnocentric bias until we reach a state at which our identification with the species as a whole becomes more important to us than our membership in a specific ethnic, national, religious, or racial segment of humanity.

The question of what is strictly higher or lower in the realm of human consciousness and mind remains unresolved. Within the broad spectrum of human consciousness, there are many possible modes of experiencing and information-processing. It is not at all clear that any one of these is superior to the others in any absolute sense, but the values that we attach to different modes will determine the way in which we view the changes that have occurred, that are occurring, and that are likely to occur in the future. In the chapters that follow, we shall have occasion to consider this issue in greater depth from a variety of standpoints.

VIEWS OF TIME, CHANGE, AND EVOLUTION IN INDIA AND CHINA

The basic ways in which we conceptualize the evolution of consciousness are related to the ways in which we think of development and change in the physical universe, animals and plants, and human society. I have suggested that the most basic models we employ in thinking about these things tend to be archetypal, that they represent a limited number of ways in which we are able and prone to view the nature of change. If this is a valid contention, then we may expect to find the same essential ideas appearing independently in different cultural settings, but we may also find some cultural variation in emphasis.

Hindu doctrines

One of the most elaborate developments of the cyclic model is found in Hindu cosmology, wherein a complete cosmic cycle, or mahayuga, is viewed as composed of four consecutive ages, or yugas. A mahayuga lasts a total of 4,320,000 years. This is not considered the total extent of time, for Hindu texts contain references to still longer cycles composed of various numbers of mahayugas. The four ages of a mahayuga represent a succession of increasing deterioration in the condition and ways of the world. They start with the Krita Yuga, an age of peace and serenity, and culminate in the Kali Yuga (our present age, alas), which is characterized by increasing human corruption, hunger, fear, disease, and calamities.

Such a view of the nature of time and natural events can encourage a kind of fatalism, since we appear to be stuck in a cosmic course of inevitable degeneration. The prospect of an ultimate rebirth of the universe in a state of perfection is of little consolation when we note that the Kali Yuga alone lasts almost half a million years. Yet for the individual being there is a way out. Within this grand cosmic cycle there occurs as well a cycle of *samsara*, or successive incarnations, that each individual passes through. According to Hindu doctrine, each of us reaps the consequences of all his or her actions, and the consequences, or *karma*, carry over into successive lifetimes. The penalty for a corrupt life is rebirth into more miserable circumstances. We can choose to work off the karma accruing from our misdeeds, however, by living morally responsible lives. In this way, we may succeed in achieving *moksha*, or release from the samaric cycle, and remain united with the brahman, or universal soul. The traditional Indian view accords little value to history in the Western sense, much less to Western ideas of social progress. The spiritual evolution of the individual, if it is to occur, runs counter to the trend in the world as a whole, and it can best be accomplished if the individual withdraws from the world.

Chinese Concepts

Chinese thought developed for many centuries in apparent isolation from Indian thought, and though it is also the product of a very complex culture, it differs profoundly in many respects from Indian thought. Yet the same motifs that underlie the Indian view of change and evolution are evident in Chinese thought as well. Through most of the known history of Chinese thought, a cyclic view of change predominates, but the idea of progressive evolution can also be found at times.

The most distinctly Chinese expression of the cyclic view appears in that ancient work, the *I Ching*, or *Book of Changes*. Here cyclic change is seen to lie in the nature of the tao, the essential pattern or way of the universe, and it is regarded as basic to the progression of the seasons and other facets of inanimate nature, as well as to the affairs of people. It is viewed as a necessary result of the continuous interaction of the two principles that underlie all events: yang (the masculine, positive, active, light principle) and yin (the feminine, negative, passive, dark principle).

Like Indian thought, the Taoist tradition of China embraces a notion of an early age of Perfect Virtue, or Golden Age, from which the ways of people and nature have declined. This early age, when people lived in paradisiacal harmony with one another and the rest of nature, has commonly been dated as the reign of the legendary Yellow Emperor, Huang Ti, who is said to have lived about five thousand years ago (Blofeld, 1978). Taoism has traditionally rejected the idea of progress, stressing instead the idea of a general decline in morality and in the quality of life from that early age.

In the *Tao Te Ching* of Lao Tzu, perhaps the most important classic work of Taoism, another basic motif for describing change also appears: an initial dualistic split and subsequent differentiation. Blofeld quotes one translation of the key passage and offers his interpretation of it:

"The Tao gave birth to One, the One to Two, the Two to Three, the Three to all the myriad objects which carry the *yin* and embrace the *yang* harmoniously intermingled." This seems to mean that the Tao, in giving birth to the potentiality of forms, produced the One; that the One's passive and active principles, *yin* and *yang*, are the Two; that these two in combination produced "three treasures," the three; and that from these are born all the myriad objects in the universe (Blofeld, 1978, p. 4).

James Legge (1962) offers a slightly different translation of this passage, but he concurs with Blofeld in interpreting the "Two" in terms of the complementary principles of yin and yang, and the theme of differentiation is still quite evident.

In Taoist literature one can find descriptions of a second sequence of changes that runs in the direction opposite to that of differentiation—a movement from the myriad objects to the three, from the three to the two, and from the two to the one. Blofeld notes this sequence as the essence of the unification sought by Chinese adepts of yogic alchemy. The basic aim of yogic alchemy would appear to be much the same as that of the various forms of yoga practiced in India: a psychic merging with the source of all being, or in Hindu terms the realization of identity with the brahman.

The two major traditions of Chinese thought are Taoism and Confucianism. Over the centuries these have interacted in various ways, each has influenced the other, and a variety of schools have emerged from the interaction. Joseph Needham (1956) notes that for centuries the neo-Confucians have for the most part accepted the idea that the universe has passed through alternating cycles of construction and dissolution. Whatever the original sources of this idea in earlier Taoist and Confucian thought, Needham suggests that it was first systematized by Shao Yung in the eleventh century and was elaborated in various ways by later thinkers. The neo-Confucians of centuries ago contended that the universe began in a state of chaotic unity and underwent a process of differentiation and construction over a period of thousands of years. Wu Lin-chhuan of the thirteenth and fourteenth centuries described successive stages in which first the celestial bodies were formed, then the various constituents of the earth, the finally human beings. This evolutionary progression is quite compatible with the views of modern Western science. In general, the neo-Confucians view such progressions as followed by periods of dedifferentiation, destruction and retrogression. Such descriptions from the early part of the second millennium may not agree in detail with the accounts of contemporary scientists, but the basic concepts have a familiar ring. The two underlying processes are essentially the same as the ones described by Herbert Spencer.

VIEWS OF TIME, CHANGE, AND EVOLUTION IN WESTERN CULTURE

The idea of progress has long played a more prominent role in Western thought than it has in Oriental thought, but the cyclical model also has a respectable history in the West. In Greece the cyclic view of change was expressed in many forms by different people. For the followers of Pythagoras it was bound up with the idea of a Great Year—actually a period of many ordinary years defined by the combined movements of the sun and the moon, a period in which a number of seasonal cycles would correspond to an exact number of lunar-phase cycles. Later Greeks, such as Plato, attempted to identify such a period in which the planets, as well as the sun and the moon, would all return to the respective positions they had occupied at an earlier moment in time.

Philosophers like Plato and Aristotle saw such a grand cosmic cycle as governing an endless repetition of natural events, but they believed that progress in human affairs could override the cycle. They also differed from their Eastern counterparts in having no clear idea of an ideal point, or Golden Age, within the cycle. The cyclical view of events has been resurrected many times in subsequent Western thought, and some people, like Machiavelli, have even contended that it applies in a general way to human history.

Astrological Cycles

The most persistent expression of the cyclic view is the one that runs through astrology. Most of the astrology known in the West can be traced to ancient Mesopotamia, but the ultimate roots lie beyond the beginnings of recorded history. Various forms of astrology have undoubtedly arisen independently in all parts of the world from the efforts of people to make orderly sense of the mysterious and complex pattern to events occurring on earth. Perhaps the effort starts everywhere with the observation of some undeniable correspondences. There are obvious connections between the position of the sun when it rises, the length of the day, and transitions in the weather, and animal and plant life. If we live near the sea, we can note a striking relationship between the tides and the phases of the moon. The more precarious life appears to be, the more vital it is to understand regularities of this kind and take note of all the cycles of cosmic events that may affect our welfare. Thus, astrology has long flourished in several forms in the West, just as it has in India, China, and other parts of the world.

If we do not regard astrology as a characteristically Western mode of thought, the reason may simply be that there has been more organized opposition to astrology in the Western world than there has been elsewhere. Over the past two thousand years, most of the active opposition to astrology has come from the church, which has seen an inconsistency between astrological concepts and Christian beliefs. In recent centuries, after long acceptance as a respectable branch of science, astrology has received stronger opposition from the scientific establishment. Astrology may re-emerge in a more scientific form as we gain more knowledge about relationships between celestial cycles and various biological and social events.

Modern Scientific Cosmology

Meanwhile, the hint of a great cosmic cycle keeps intruding into speculations about the most intriguing question in the realm of modern cosmology, the question of the ultimate fate of the universe. We have come to accept the idea that the universe as we know it is expanding and that it began in the distant past in what we like to call the Big Bang. That initial explosion is estimated to have taken place almost fourteen billion years ago. Whatever the correct figure may be, the big question that remains is whether the expansion will continue forever or whether the universe will ultimately start to contract and collapse upon itself. At present, the answer is uncertain, but scientists have attempted to gather relevant information. One pertinent factor is the average density of matter in the universe. Another is the rate of an apparent deceleration of the current expansion, which can be determined in principle by comparing the speed of recession of very distant galaxies with that of nearby galaxies. So far estimates of these factors cannot be made with sufficient precision to resolve the issue. Perhaps the universe will indeed continue to expand forever, but there is something intriguing about the idea that it will ultimately collapse and then, perhaps after the gods have had a few billion years to rest, another Big Bang will launch the whole magnificent sequence all over again. This would be the great cosmic cycle par excellence, and it would be one that occupies a time span of an order not previously imagined in the West (but consistent with the speculations of ancient Indian philosophers). Human history cannot extend through more than a minute fraction of one round of expansion and contraction. We are a fairly new species and, unless we mend our ways, we are not likely to last much longer. But what of the next great turning of the cycle? Will we return? If so, will our current history simply repeat itself, or will we follow a course more conducive to the continuation of life on this planet? Such is the stuff of science fiction, but for the same reasons, of course, it is the stuff of mythology, religion, and science.

Paradise Lost

The cyclic model of change, then, is quite evident in the West, as it is in the East. So too is the idea of an early Golden Age from which there has been subsequent decline. The term "Golden Age" is commonly taken as an allusion to the work of the Greek poet Hesiod, who spoke of four ages of mankind in terms of the metals gold, silver, bronze, and iron. It is uncertain whether this idea actually originated with Hesiod, for similar ideas have been found elsewhere in ancient texts (cf. Eliade, 1954). The four ages described by Hesiod are marked by differences in the quality of life and differences in the quality of people. The first people were a "golden race" of high moral character who lived in a bounteous worldly paradise. The succeeding ages culminated in the race of iron (which includes you, me, and Hesiod himself), people wicked in character and condemned to toil, weariness, and pain.

This sequence is reminiscent of the fate of Adam and Eve as depicted in Genesis, and the underlying theme of an earthly paradise succeeded by a life of misery and sin is a central thread in the world-views of the older cultures of the West and Near East. We find it expressed among the Jews, Christians, and Persians. In classical Greece it was expressed in so many forms by different writers that J. B. Bury (1960) contended (incorrectly) that the ancient Greeks had no concept of progress (cf. Guthrie, 1957, and Nisbet, 1970). In recent centuries, the idea of a decline from a lost Golden Age has appeared in such forms as the sentimental primitivism of the Romantic movement and the literary notion of a Golden Age of the North (Greenway, 1977).

The Myth of Progress

In any age in which there is widespread dissatisfaction with current conditions, people are likely to entertain an image of a preferred, ideal condition. It is possible to project this image into the past and to lament the loss of the paradise that once existed. It is also possible to project the image into the future and see any possible change as tending to lead toward the desired condition. To accept the myth of progress is to perceive the most essential ongoing processes and changes as providing a present that is an improvement over the past and as leading to a still better future. Surveying the expressions of the idea of progress over the past 2,500 years, Robert Nisbet (1970) notes that there have been two major emphases, one being intellectual in content and the other moral or spiritual. The first focuses on the gradual accumulation of knowledge, while the second focuses on progress with respect to morality, spirituality, happiness, serenity, and freedom from torments imposed by nature or society.

In classical Greece and Rome, the idea of progress was interwoven with the ideas of cyclic change and degeneration. We can see a variety of stances with respect to the application of these models in the writings of Anaximander, Plato, Aristotle, and Lucretius. In the writings of the early Christians we find a blend of Greek ideas of progress with Jewish millennialism. While a diversity of views was evident among the early sects, there was a widespread belief in a gradual spiritual evolution of humanity as a whole that would lead ultimately to a coming age of peace and happiness, when Christ would return to the earthly realm to serve as ruler. This version of the progress theme focuses on a future Golden Age, rather than indefinite development into the future. Over the past two thousand years, it has inspired a variety of Utopian remedies for the ills of humanity and society. We can read this influence even in the work of Karl Marx, but the more distinctly Christian elaborations of the theme stress the spiritual, rather than material, nature of the future age.

The myth of progress has been a pervasive theme in Western thought during the past three or four centuries, and during this period the major concepts of progress have focused more on the nature of the society than on the nature of the individual within it. Though various blends can be found, they have also tended to emphasize rationality more than spirituality. History was interpreted in terms of a general movement from myth and religion to science and rationality in the writings of Auguste Comte, Giambattista Vico, and the Marquis de Condorcet, and this outlook is now commonplace.

In descriptions of past and future changes in society, there is one fundamental issue on which the views of the historians, philosophers, and advocates of progress are divided. Some of them attach particular importance to the advancing freedom of the individual to make choices and follow a path of personal fulfillment. In sharp contrast to this group are those thinkers who attach little or no importance to individuality or individual freedom, who see a need for fundamental changes in the structure of society and in our collective ways of thinking, working, and interacting, and who see a need for the exercise of power (absolute, if necessary) to bring about these changes. The first group would include such individuals as Adam Smith, Immanuel Kant, John Stuart Mill, Herbert Spencer, and the founding fathers of the American republic. In this century, it would include many American political figures who have adopted such labels as *liberal* and *progressive*, and it would include most psychologists who identify with the humanistic movement.

Most (but not all) prescriptions for an ideal society have been formulated by advocates of autocratic power, who assume that the ideal blueprint can best be implemented by an elite group of people like themselves. Thus Plato's republic was to be ruled by philosophers. In the 1930 and 1940s, the movement known as Technocracy drew the support of many prominent engineers. They pictured an American society of unparalleled efficiency and prosperity ruled by a group of technologists. A more recent case in point is provided by B. F. Skinner (1948), whose *Walden Two* has been taken by many people as a serious model for a better society. The community described in Skinner's novel is ruled by a group of behavioral engineers, who relieve everyone else of the need to make any important decisions. They devise instructions and procedures calculated not merely to promote communal harmony but to reshape the thinking and behavior of all its inhabitants for their own good. To the advocates of freedom, the prospect of a society run autocratically by men who believe they have a thorough understanding of human nature and the ideal mode of living poses the greatest threat of all. The author of *Walden Two* is perhaps the century's leading authority on principles and methods for the alteration of behavior, but at the same time, he is a man who believes the concepts of freedom and dignity are outmoded, who considers conscious experience to be a mere epiphenomenon, and who has written a novel in which the characters are all lacking in psychological depth.

Faith in the myth of progress may have reached its greatest heights in the eighteenth and nineteenth centuries. Robert Nisbet (1970) believes that the basic premises underlying this myth have all come under attack in this century and that there has been a growing disenchantment outweighing our earlier faith. To be sure, we can find much evidence in this century of an alienation and a loss of meaning that make it more difficult to conjure up an ideal condition that we can project into either the past or the future, and the anti-Utopian novels of Aldous Huxley, George Orwell, and William Burgess depict a grotesque extrapolation of ongoing trends into the world ahead of us. Nonetheless, the progress model is still with us. It appears along with all the other basic models for conceptualizing change in our attempts to deal more focally with the evolution of consciousness. That is not an isolated enterprise, and the values previously expressed in our treatment of society and the world continue to color our thinking in this special area. If we keep hearing echoes of the past and echoes of ideas sounded in other spheres of thought, the reason may be that we keep trying to make sense of the world we experience in terms of a small set of very ancient myths, even though, for the sake of appearance, we keep dressing them up in novel, modern disguises.

SOME FUNDAMENTAL ASSUMPTIONS

In this chapter I have not yet dealt in a direct way with theories about the evolution of consciousness. I have argued, however, that such theories are based on the same models that we have employed for thousands of years for conceptualizing change in general in the world and in human affairs. I have also noted the relevance of our basic values to the characterization of change. Our views of progress and history depend on what we view as the desirable and undesirable conditions of life, and our views of changes in human consciousness depend on what we regard as desirable and undesirable modes of experience.

At this point, we should note some additional questions whose answers affect theoretical positions in a very fundamental way. One question is whether there is a universal sequence in the evolution of consciousness. Very often the idea of a universal sequence has operated as an unspoken premise, and in regarding people of their own society as the most highly evolved theorists have viewed the mental qualities of other peoples of the past and present as manifestations of earlier stages in the sequence. Given the obvious differences in development between Eastern and Western cultures, however, the premise seems overly simplistic. If we do not discard the idea of a universal sequence altogether, we must at least allow for variations in emphasis within the sequence.

A closely related question is whether something in the way of a sequence is inevitable. Even if we allow for some variation along the path—some possible alternative routes—is there something in the way of an overall direction that is unavoidable? This is almost tantamount to asking whether the sequence is governed by a final cause or goal toward which we are inevitably drawn, since those who conceptualize such a goal are most likely to argue that there is just one direction in which change must logically proceed.

The Immanent Goal

Aurobindo (1970, 1973) and Wilber (1981) regard an ultimate unity consciousness, the realization of identity with the atman and brahman, as an implicit goal underlying the evolution of consciousness, and they both argue that evolution presupposes a prior involution wherein the goal of Spirit toward which we are drawn becomes enfolded or hidden. Evolution, as they see it, cannot avoid making explicit what is already implicit. Wilber offers the additional argument that the time span allotted by scientific evidence for the evolution of various life forms and for the human species on earth is not sufficient to permit adequate explanation on purely Darwinian grounds. According to the Darwinian position, evolution depends on the accidental occurrence of a large number of mutations in genes and chromosomes. Mutations that enhance adaptation tend to be preserved and those that interfere with adaptation tend to be discarded in the process of natural selection. Wilber contends that to account for the rate at which evolution has actually occurred, particularly at the human level, we must assume a relatively rapid holistic pattern of growth that can only be possible if the sequence is guided in some way by an inherent growth plan. Wilber appears to be quite certain he is correct, but his position rests on a statistical issue that cannot be resolved with present information. The overall rate of evolution logically depends on a host of variables that are difficult to estimate—such as the number and nature of the mutations occurring at a given time, the probability that a given mutation will be beneficial or detrimental, and the selection pressure operating in a given environment. There are some species that settle into environmental niches to which they are so well adapted that little change occurs over periods of millions of years. Apparently Wilber assumes that there is something special about the human species, and the divine plan to which he refers may not apply to any other organism.

Alternatives to Predestination

I think we must grant that there is an open issue here. It is quite possible that the Darwinian explanation of evolutionary progress is not sufficient to account for the relatively rapid growth of the human brain, intelligence, and consciousness, though it is reasonable to accept it as a partial explanation. If so, we are still not compelled to join Wilber's camp, for there is an unlimited variety of ways in which we might account for rapid holistic evolution. We might assume, for example, that there is greater interdependence among cellular components within the adult organism than biologists have traditionally assumed. Thus, it is conceivable that certain changes in the cells of the nervous system will induce corresponding changes in reproductive cells. Hence, learning may affect heredity in ways not yet suspected, and an updated version of Lamarckian theory may yet prove creditable. Furthermore, if we respect the integrity of the total organism, we must allow for the possibility that conscious processes will have some effect on our genes—we know well enough that they can have all sorts of other effects on the body that are hard to explain in terms of conventional physiology. A corollary to this idea would be that mind and consciousness can evolve more rapidly once they have reached a certain minimal level of development.

Unlike the positions of Aurobindo and Wilber, explanations of this sort in no way presuppose an inevitable sequence or an immanent evolutionary goal. Darwinian theory assumes that there is uniformity in evolutionary progression only to the extent that environmental demand operates as a source of guidance. Adaptive change is feasible, and maladaptive change is not. There are different ways of adapting to a given environment, however, and there is no known limit to the variety of mutations that can occur by chance. The mutual isolation of subgroups of a given species results in increasing divergence and ultimately the emergence of separate species. Biological diversification is a fact of life for which Darwinian theory, in principle, accounts admirably. If we apply the same basic logic to the evolution of consciousness, we will assume that certain demands of life impose constraints on the course of that evolution but that, within the limits imposed by those constraints, evolution can proceed along many possible lines. The greater the mutual isolation of different peoples, the greater the likelihood that they will display different patterns of psychic evolution.

Unidimensional versus Multidimensional Views

Most of the conspicuous views on the evolution of consciousness appear to be alike in one respect: They are basically unidimensional theories. Each assumes that there is one particular kind of development that is important. There is progress so long as change serves to enhance a particular mode of consciousness. The progress model fits the theory in so far as evolution is thought of in terms of a more or less steady increase in that mode. To be sure, the theories may (and, in fact, do) disagree with one another with respect to the nature of the desired mode. An alternative position might assume that there is one ultimate goal but that there is more than one possible route we can follow to reach it. This is the position Wilber would be forced to take if he made a greater effort to account for cross-cultural evidence. As it is, he presents a unidimensional position.

I believe it is time to acknowledge the possibility of a more genuinely multidimensional position. I would argue that there is more than one possible goal and no clear reason to contend that all of us as individuals must develop toward the same common psychic end, or that humanity as a whole must continue to evolve in such a way that all its members eventually manifest alike some common ultimate mode of consciousness, or that the evolution of consciousness in the other complex organisms on this planet (e.g., the whales and dolphins) should head in the same direction—or directions—as our evolution is heading. I would argue, then, that we can distinguish a number of possible goals in the evolutionary process and that we probably need to recognize a still larger number of pathways leading to them.

2

The Goal of Human Psychic Development

In the preceding chapter, I contended that what we perceive as progress or regress, as positive growth or deterioration, in consciousness depends on what modes of consciousness we value. Since our characteristic and available modes of consciousness are rather central to everything we do, views regarding desirable modes of consciousness are closely linked to views regarding ideal modes of psychological functioning in general. In earlier work, I surveyed ideal-person concepts and analyzed many pertinent personality variables (Coan, 1974, 1977). I concluded that the major views could be described in terms of relative emphasis on each of five modes of fulfillment: efficiency, creativity, inner harmony, relatedness, and transcendence. While these modes provide a way to classifying the possible goals of personality development, they can be understood quite readily in terms of conscious modes and attainments of conscious functioning.

A theorist who emphasizes the mode of efficiency stresses the cultivation of physical, social, or intellectual capacities and the effective use of these capacities in dealing with all the problems of living. The mode of creativity involves the discovery or creation of novel form or novel experience, and the expression of this mode would seem to depend on the presence of such related qualities as spontaneity, flexibility, and openness to new ideas and experiences. The concept of inner harmony implies the resolution or absence of inner tensions or conflicts, as well as related effects that may be described in terms of inner peace, serenity, and emotional adjustment.

The mode of relatedness is concerned with the individual's relationship with other people, and in a given formulation we may focus on the capacity for intimacy, the ability to love, or a sense of community with humanity as a whole. The mode of transcendence is concerned with experiences in which one loses a sense of individual identity or separateness and realizes an identity with a larger whole. Many of the experiences embraced by this mode may be characterized as either aesthetic or mystical, but the experiences as such are not necessarily dependent on any specific set of beliefs or form of intellectual interpretation.

Sensory Awareness

Within the realm of conscious experience there are many capacities that we can cultivate and learn to use effectively. We tend to do this selectively, cultivating some capacities and neglecting others. There are many possible patterns of development and underdevelopment. On such grounds we might argue that efficiency is not really a single mode of fulfillment, but a host of possible modes. One kind of variation we can discern here, both within an individual over time and among different individuals, concerns the overall level of awareness. Perhaps we could better describe it in terms of the extent to which one gives attention to all the contents of consciousness. On the whole, a high level of awareness is stressed more often in Hindu and Buddhist cultures than in Western culture, and this is particularly true in the branches of Buddhism where the use of vipassana meditation is recommended. This is a form of meditation in which one attends fully and uncritically to whatever enters the field of awareness.

It is difficult to convey to Westerners the effect of such practices because we are so accustomed to a rather low level of awareness. Typically in our waking lives, we glance about us with glazed eyes, noticing only the few features of our surroundings that interest us at the moment. We attend to a few significant sounds and ignore the rest. We give little heed to most of the odors that pass through our nostrils, and we remain largely unaware of the stream of dreams, fantasies, memories, and images that flows constantly through our minds. If someone suddenly asks us what we were thinking or feeling five seconds ago, we cannot give an honest answer. We cannot remember because we were not paying close enough attention. If you are sitting in a fairly quiet room at the moment, you can gain some impression of the contents that you habitually ignore by closing your eyes for ten or fifteen seconds and noting during that interval all the sounds that occur in your surroundings. You may be surprised by their richness and variety, and yet these sounds are only one ripple within the total stream of impressions that we tune out nearly all of our waking lives.

Most people rely heavily on vision for orienting themselves to the world around them and for gaining information and understanding, but we have a number of additional exteroceptors, or sensory systems that provide information about the environment or about substances coming from the environment. These include audition, the chemical senses, and the various cutaneous senses. Besides these, we have systems of receptors located in our joints, muscles, and internal organs and on the surface of our mucous membranes. These yield sensations of pressure, tension, high and low temperature, and pain, and they provide all sorts of information about the state of body tissues and internal organs and about the position and movement of the body. In addition, we know that there are receptors located in the vestibular sacs and semicircular canals of the inner ear. These may not yield conscious sensations in a direct way, but they are responsible for initiating reflex adjustments to rotary motion and changes in the position of the head.

We respond to most of the input from these various sensory systems in a rather automatic way, paying little conscious attention to their contents. The automatic adjustments we make may be adequate and appropriate, but often they are not. A host of "psychosomatic" disorders may arise simply from a failure to respond properly to sensations from inside the body. We ignore certain sensations and end up fainting or applying avoidable stress to certain tissues and organs. We attend inappropriately to sensations that we have habitually ignored, because we do not know how to read them. We misconstrue their messages and sense nonexistent dangers in the wrong places. In some forms of yoga practiced in India, people manage to cultivate a level of control over bodily processes that seems astounding to Westerners. They may be able to slow the heart beat to one or two beats per minute, create a temperature difference of several degrees between nearby points on the skin, or control the flow of blood from an open wound. The basic prerequisite for the kind of bodily control manifested in such feats is simply tuning in closely enough to the experience of the body that one can take voluntary charge of the processes that are operating within it.

As I have noted, we usually do not pay much closer attention to the sensations provided by our exteroceptors than we do to the sensations arising within our bodies. If we are trained as artists, musicians, or wine tasters, we learn to make finer discriminations of certain kinds than most people do, but such training is always very selective. As a matter of fact, the practices of our culture encourage us to operate at a certain distance from the raw sensory level of experience. We do not dwell long with the sensation itself but take a step away from it by a process of abstraction and relate to our surroundings though a filtering network of ideas. There are advantages to doing this, but it means that in many ways we are not in as close touch with the world around us as are animals of other species and people of other cultures. If we at least recognize our shortcomings—and usually we do not—we can find ways to compensate for them. My aunt once told me a story that highlights our situation. When she and my father were very small, they moved with their widowed mother and their uncle from Missouri to the Oklahoma Territory, where they lived in a dugout on a large plot of land. One evening they went to a community meeting at a church. When the meeting ended, they set out for home in a horse-drawn wagon. Normally this would have been a short trip, but it is difficult to navigate in near-total darkness over an expanse of flat land lacking trees, fences, visible buildings, or well-defined roads. After an hour of driving, Uncle Bill decided he was hopelessly lost, and he hung up the reins and lay down in the wagon. The horse, finally freed from human interference, took them all home in a matter of minutes.

It is a well-known fact that, compared with other animals, human beings can boast of only fair sensory equipment. Many animals have far more sensitive noses and ears. Nocturnal animals, such as cats, can see better in very dim light, while the birds of prey have better visual acuity in bright light. When it comes to locating objects by sound, we possess only a minute fraction of the skill with which all bats and marine mammals are well endowed. If we excel in any one capacity, perhaps it is the sensitivity of our fingertips. There may be still other senses that we know little about because of our own deficiency. There is now considerable evidence for a magnetic sense in snails, bees, turtles, several species of birds, and several species of fish. R. Robin Baker (1981) reports evidence that humans, too, possess such a sense and can use the earth's magnetic field to navigate over short or long distances. Undoubtedly there are other species that can make far better use of such a capacity. On the other hand, it is also likely that we lack "horse sense" simply by virtue of our failure to use the capacities that we do possess.

Extrasensory Forms of Perception

There is still another kind of perception or apprehension that we need to consider, but one that may not depend on the use of senses as these are usually understood. I refer to what is commonly called extrasensory perception, ESP, or simply psi. I realize that many psychologists continue to question the reality of ESP, but the resistance comes almost entirely from those who are not sufficiently familiar with the large body of pertinent evidence. It is common to distinguish three main forms of ESP—clairvoyance, telepathy, and precognition—though it is not at all clear that we are dealing with more than one underlying process. For that matter, various other classifications are possible, if we take into account the nature of the apprehended content, associated imagery, and the circumstances under which the individual receives impressions.

If we think of ESP as one class of expressions of the mode of efficiency, it is interesting to note that it depends on a relinquishment of functions that are necessary for the full expression of certain other cognitive and perceptual expressions of this mode. It works best in states in which the individual is exerting little active control over the flow of images and impressions, or is at least open to irruptions of unexpected content. In fact, some of the most interesting evidence for ESP comes from research on telepathic dreams (Ullman and Krippner, 1973). On the other hand, the ability to make efficient use of ESP may depend on the disciplined cultivation of nonrational states through the extensive practice of meditation or active imagination (see Motoyama, 1978). Very often a great natural sensitivity for extrasensory impressions appears in individuals who lack much development along either spiritual or rational intellectual lines. Such people may regard their special talent as a curse, since it is frequently expressed in unpredictable invasions of unpleasant and uninvited impressions, with only an occasional bit of information that can be put to good use.

Clairvoyance and telepathy have often been developed to a high degree by practitioners of Hindu and Buddhist disciplines in the Orient. In the West, gifted individuals who have cultivated such abilities to an unusual level (Emanuel Swedenborg, for example) have often been regarded with great suspicion and dismissed as psychotics. In Western scientific circles there has long been great resistance to the acceptance of any form of ESP, and I see two major reasons for this. One reason is the great value we attach to modes of consciousness that tend to preclude the operation of ESP. Our educational practices are designed to encourage the organized and systematic use of rational thought processes, and the people who enter the various fields of science usually master this lesson better than anyone else. Thus, the natural conditions for the cultivation of psi ability tend to be neglected or avoided by people in our society, and this is particularly true for people who rise to prominence by virtue of manifest intellectual ability.

The second major reason is that ESP defies explanation in terms of the processes and mechanisms with which we are most familiar, notably the kinds of mechanisms (such as transmission and reception of electromagnetic energy) that would have been demanded by nineteenth-century physics. The solution to this difficulty may depend on a shift in our thinking to a different model of the universe. We still cling to the notion of a universe composed of isolated chunks of matter separated by empty space, a universe in which one chunk can affect another only if they come into contact or something moves between them. Gravitation and other field phenomena forced physicists long ago to accept the reality of action at a distance, but psychologists remain wary of the idea. Twentieth-century physicists think increasingly in terms of models of the universe in which all events are interdependent and each bit of matter somehow mirrors everything else in existence. Psychologists may come to accept ESP as a matter of course and cease to regard it as something that is obviously impossible once they realize that they are not as separate from the rest of the universe as they like to think they are.

Cognition and Human Intelligence

We have dealt so far with various kinds of perception or ways of attending to basic conscious content. Theorists who stress the mode of efficiency, however, are more likely to formulate developmental goals in terms of certain ways of processing basic content—in terms of modes of cognition rather than modes of perception. One of the most influential formulations in contemporary personality theory is Freud's concept of a strong ego, which essentially denotes a capacity for realistic and rational thinking. Definitions of *intelligence* commonly capture related ideas about ideal modes of cognitive functioning, and they usually have implications for idealized modes of consciousness. For this reason, the contemporary literature and research on human intelligence are quite relevant to the issues of this chapter.

Concepts of intelligence are subject to cultural variation, for what is needed for sound mental functioning in one setting may be much different from what is needed elsewhere. What the Kung bushman needs and values is not the same as what the middle-class American suburbanite needs and values. Within our own society, the definition of *intelligence* may depend on the values and orientation of the individual who defines it. The biologist may stress adaptation to the environment, while the educator stresses the ability to learn, and the philosopher stresses the ability to manipulate abstract concepts. Psychologists have never come close to a consensus on the constituents of intelligence. In constructing tests, they tend to stress those abilities in which they themselves excel. Thus, they devise more verbal-reasoning items than items that require spatial visualization.

Whenever psychologists have deliberately varied item types to tap many different expressions of intelligence, another constraint has become apparent, for what is measured depends on the ingenuity of the psychologist and the inherent ease or difficulty of devising items to assess a particular kind of performance. For better or worse, it is far easier to assess an individual's ability to memorize a series of digits than to assess his or her ability to discern the emotional dispositions of people. Reasoning and discriminative abilities are more easily evaluated than are intuitive and creative abilities. Even when we do not explicitly define intelligence as "what intelligence tests measure," we still judge an individual's overall intelligence according to a test performance, and our thinking about the nature of intelligence is subtly guided by the test operations with which we are familiar.

The individual who has done the most extensive analyses of intellectual factors using the greatest variety of item types is J. P. Guilford (1967; also Guilford and Hoepfner, 1971). In the course of his work, he has developed the structure-of-intellect model, a system of cross-classification of factors that identifies or predicts a total of 120 separate abilities within this domain. Though many other psychologists would argue that his factors are not all as independent as he claims, he has effectively argued that there are many more separate abilities here than we tend to assume. In Guilford's model, ability factors are classified simultaneously in terms of three basic aspects: the kind of mental operation executed by the individual, the content or kind of information to which the operation is applied, and the product, or formal nature of the result of the operation.

Guilford has shown that such traditional concepts as induction, deduction, and reasoning are not as simple as people think. They embrace a variety of distinguishable abilities and processes. On the other hand, a limitation of his system is that most or all of his factors seem to involve something in the way of rational or analytical thought. Modes of thinking that proceed by a more subtle route, modes that have been called intuitive or holistic, are more difficult to assess. It is easiest to devise a scorable item when all the information clearly required for a solution is provided in the item itself or in sources that all psychologists might accept. Intuitive modes of thinking, however, are likely to operate in their most nearly pure form in rather ambiguous situations where the information utilized may not be very obvious even to the individual utilizing it.

A distinction between concrete and abstract thinking is often encountered in the literature on the evolution of consciousness. It is not altogether clear that this is represented in the structure-of-intellect model, but Guilford suggests that it may reduce to contrasts in content that correspond to one of his modes of classification. If we direct our attention to possible test operations, it is not too difficult to think of possibilities that have not been tapped by any ability researcher to date. In general, intelligence-test constructors have confined their efforts to verbal, numerical, and spatial content. Guilford's main innovation has been in the use of verbally presented behavioral content. His symbolic-content and semantic-content items tend to be either verbal or numerical. His figural-content items are essentially spatial. They involve visual patterns, but it is obviously possible to make use of nonvisual patterns. We could devise items that employ rhythmic or tonal patterns. In principle, many other patterns could be used—e.g., patterns of odor or body movement—but much more ingenuity would be required to incorporate them into a test.

It may be more important to ensure that all important kinds of mental operations, or systems of conscious processing, have been assessed, and this is not easy to determine. The terms that Guilford applies to his five operation categories are broad enough to cover any mental operation we might think of, but it seems unlikely that all the modes of understanding that logically fall under his rubrics have been effectively captured in test items. The structure-of-intellect model is very illuminating as far as it goes, but there are probably many additional abilities that will be revealed by future research, and there is probably much in this domain that will forever elude all efforts at psychometric manipulation. Life itself is far more complex than the materials that can be employed conveniently in any psychological test, but as Guilford has shown us, the abilities we can assess with tests form a rather complex system. If the efficiency ideal for the development and evolution of consciousness amounts to a capacity for dealing intelligently with life, we must recognize that this is surely a multifaceted goal.

THE MODE OF CREATIVITY

Intelligence tests have traditionally done better at predicting an individual's ability to perform tasks that require an ability to learn rapidly, to understand complex principles, to derive logical conclusions, or to apply a body of knowledge than at predicting the ability to come up with valuable new ideas. The early constructors of intelligence tests probably neglected creative ability because there was a more pressing need to identify mentally deficient children and to identify individuals who could profit from a certain course of instruction or carry out assigned tasks in the army. Creative ability was rather tangential to these more immediate concerns. In the succeeding years it was neglected because it seemed inherently more difficult to measure. Guilford, however, made an effort to include it in his systematic analysis of the domain of intellectual performance.

In one phase of his research, Guilford developed a number of hypotheses regarding the ingredients of creative ability and planning ability, and he strove to devise test materials that might tap such variables as sensitivity to problems, penetration, fluency, flexibility, and originality. All of these concepts led to the isolation of factors that are now included in the structure-of-intellect model. The concepts of fluency and flexibility were particularly fruitful and led to the set of twenty-four factors that involve the divergent-production operation category. In any divergent-production item, the subject is asked to generate a number of relevant alternatives on the basis of information provided. Responses may be scored for variety, quantity, and in some cases originality.

Guilford's work has shown that many different abilities may be involved in creative performance, and there are probably many such abilities that remain to be uncovered in future research. It is also likely that personality variables and the social setting play a large role in determining whether creative production occurs. In our society males are given much more encouragement than females to be creatively productive in their work, but it is possible that the factors that operated in the artistic community of Florence during the Italian Renaissance are nonexistent now in any part of our society. Translating creative potential into creative production requires many things. It requires a certain independence in thinking and lifestyle. One must be able and motivated to look at problems and life situations in fresh ways. One must be able, at least for a significant moment, to set aside traditional values, customs, and standards and dare to entertain a perspective that to others may seem strange, crazy, shocking, or perverted. Having given audible or visible form to one's novel outlook or insights, one must be prepared to withstand negative, as well as positive, reactions from other people.

The Creative Process

The inner process that underlies creative production of a high level always requires a delicate balance of certain needs and tendencies that go in opposite directions. I have described this balance elsewhere in terms of an attitude directed toward openness and an attitude directed toward order and control (Coan, 1974). On the one hand, creativity requires a willingness to let go of established order, form, or procedures and entertain alternatives ranging from the bizarre to the chaotic; a willingness to think the unthinkable; and the courage to abandon one's store of knowledge and discipline and act naive, stupid, and childlike. On the other hand, it also requires an urge to establish order and produce meaningful form. We see this balance in the creative processes of nature and in the evolution of societies, as well as in individual creative production, for the creative process per se requires the abandonment, destruction, or disintegration of existing form combined with the emergence of new form to take the place of old form.

This balance has often been noted in an alternation or succession of states during the process of creative thinking. Graham Wallas (1926) spoke long ago of the four stages of preparation, incubation, illumination, and verification. The stage of incubation is of particular interest, since it is a stage in which one is not working in an organized way on the material or problem for which the creative idea (the illumination) subsequently emerges. During the state of incubation one may be asleep or one may be occupied consciously with something totally different. Other accounts of the creative process are even more explicit in their descriptions of a stage in which one lets go of preexisting ideas, forms, and systems and perhaps lets go of organized thinking altogether. Such a stage must be balanced, of course, by a later stage in which the ideas that emerge are worked through, edited, and assembled into a new system. Sometimes, the stage of incubation involves a vacation of many months from a project one has started. At other times, it consists of a period of disorganization lasting for several hours. In some kinds of creative endeavors there is an alternation of conscious states that can best be measured in seconds.

Whether or not we must think in terms of stages in the creative process, it seems necessary to recognize an interplay of different modes or states of consciousness. Theorists influenced by the psychoanalytic tradition usually speak of these modes in terms of Freud's concepts of primary and secondary processes. According to Freud, the primary process is the earliest kind of mental activity, and it consists of the production of hallucinatory images of gratification or of objects required to relieve the need tension. The primary process affords an experience of pleasure and temporary relief, but since the underlying source of the tension has not really been eliminated, the tension soon returns. Learning to deal realistically with needs requires the development of the secondary process, which consists of mental activity oriented toward objective reality. The secondary process enables the individual to perceive the actual state of affairs and take effective action to change it.

Freud considered primary-process mentation to be infantile in character. For him, personality development was essentially ego development, and its goal was to be understood in terms of the predominance in maturity of realistic and rational thinking. In the arts as in science, it takes an individual with a strong ego to be an authority or a learned historian or a sound critic. To do something creative, whether one produces a painting, a symphony, or an original scientific theory, requires a knack for tapping a flow of ideas and images that does not conform to the specifications of the secondary process. In Freudian terms, this implies a capacity for making good use of the primary process. One of the best known theoretical accounts of the creative process is that of the ego psychologist Ernst Kris (1952), who speaks of "regression in the service of the ego." The implication of this phrase, of course, is that the ego is still in charge of things but that it elects to stand aside for a given period for the sake of creativity. For this period, with the secondary process held in abeyance, the individual regresses to an infantile level of mental functioning, and the primary process holds sway, producing a loose flow of images that the ego can sort out and use once it steps back in to assume control.

This analysis agrees with the Freudian outlook in according higher status to the organized secondary process. To utilize the primary process is to function for a time on a lower and more primitive level. To speak of creative thinking in terms of regression is clearly to imply that the really significant achievement of psychic growth is organized, realistic thinking, not creative thinking itself. Whether or not we accept the values underlying such terminology, we may question whether the Freudian concept of the primary process is an adequate way of conceptualizing the open, free-flowing, disordered side of the creative process. In the Freudian view it is a process that does not undergo development in the way that the secondary process does, and it is a process that may be present most of the time in a small infant but appears in pure form in an adult only in dreams or in profound psychotic deterioration.

Recognizing some of the shortcomings of Kris's formulation, a few other theorists have offered minor modifications of it. Silvano Arieti (1976) believes we should recognize the development of a tertiary process, a process concerned with the "matching" or "combination" of the primary and secondary processes. Though Arieti does not articulate the nature and operation of the tertiary process in more than a sketchy way, the concept suggests a more adequate way of accounting for creativity without abandoning the psychoanalytic framework.

Another View of Imaginal Thought

Another possible way of surmounting the limitations of the Freudian concepts, obviously, is to abandon those concepts altogether. After all, an account of psychic development in terms of Freud's primary and secondary processes is inherently biased in favor of one particular developmental path. From the standpoint of Carl Jung, Freud's emphasis on rationality and accommodation to objective reality amounts to an overemphasis on the extraverted attitude and the functions of thinking and sensation. By granting equal status to introversion, feeling, and intuition, Jung allowed for more diverse modes of conscious processing. For Jung, giving heed to the inner reality of the archetypal realm was as important as attending to the outer, objective reality. He felt it was important to listen to the language of dreams, images, and symbols and to relate to the meanings that could never be brought into the full light of consciousness. He realized that one must relate to the dream, the symbol, and the vast unconscious realm to which it points as one does to a poem, knowing that when we try to reduce its message to simple operational prose there is always a loss of vital content.

For Jung, the ideal condition is one in which one has learned to live in creative harmony with the unconscious realm, allowing it to express itself in ways not strictly dictated by consciousness. He still saw the ego as the center of consciousness and a center that had a major role to play in life adjustments, but he noted that there was much in the total psyche that could never be integrated into consciousness, and the wise course was to be open to the calls from the depths and not maintain a rigid control.

While Jung did not always use the term *ego* in quite the way Freud did, he did not undertake a fundamental revision of the concept. It remains essentially the agent of conscious will, and despite the distortions of Freud's ideas in English translations, this is not too far from Freud's notion. James Hillman (1972), however, believes that it would be more consistent with what actually happens in Jungian psychotherapy to revise the concept or to recognize the need for a different kind of ego. He sees a discrepancy between Jung's espousal of the imaginative side of life and his continued use of the Freudian ideas of ego and analysis. He believes the Freudian outlook represents a perseveration of nineteenth-century views of development as a progressive, Darwinian march leading to the triumph of controlling, reality-coping consciousness.

Hillman believes we need to recognize the possibility of an imaginal ego, and he claims that this is the kind of ego that Jungian psychotherapy tends to cultivate. Rather than an ego concerned primarily with will and reason, the imaginal ego would be attuned to dreams and fantasies. It would be able to grasp symbols more directly and not seek to translate them into a more mundane language that cannot give full voice to meaning. In responding to one's full nature, the imaginal ego would follow a course that would seem at times discontinuous and in the long run rather circular, descending at times into conditions we are accustomed to labeling as psychopathological. An individual with a well-developed imaginal ego would lead a richer and more spontaneous existence than most of us and would probably not be particularly concerned with a progressive movement toward greater and greater achievements. Creativity is not Hillman's primary concern, but I believe his concept of the imaginal ego captures rather well some of the essential qualities required for a style of consciousness that permits the creative process to flow.

THE MODE OF INNER HARMONY

The mode of inner harmony is intertwined with the other four modes of fulfillment, since it implies a resolution of whatever urges there might be to seek fulfillment along divergent paths. It is also possible that inner harmony is a prerequisite for advancement very far along some of the other paths of fulfillment, particularly the path of transcendence.

It is possible to achieve a superficial kind of inner harmony with the aid of vigorous repression. An individual may have a well organized and logically coherent self-concept, act in a manner that is highly consistent with this self-concept, fit in smoothly with the surrounding social milieu, and report a high level of personal satisfaction and happiness, while at the same time maintaining this state of affairs at the cost of very limited awareness. With a sudden change in life circumstances, the illusion of perfect adjustment may vanish.

A more comprehensive inner harmony would require a genuine unity of purpose and of self-experience. This means a resolution of conflicting impulses and tendencies. Sometimes this is achieved by the elimination of a need that no longer serves any purpose. More often it would involve a reconciliation of conflicting urges into a larger whole that embraces them both or a recognition that features of the personality that appeared to be at odds with each other are actually necessary complements. We all have qualities that seem to run in opposite directions. We want someone else to protect us and take care of us, but we also want to be independent and self-sufficient. We want to be active, and we want to be passive. We want to achieve a loving intimacy with people, and we want to attack and destroy them. We have both a tough side and a tender side. We tend to achieve a clear and simple self-image by identifying closely with one side of each polarity and denying that the other side has anything to do with us. For a high level of inner harmony, however, we must recognize both sides as parts of our total being and develop a pattern of living and consciousness that permits a reconciliation. To the extent that we do this, we will appear more genuine to other people. There is something about the lover who denies hate, the macho male who denies his sensitivity, and the aggressive entrepreneur who cannot lean on anyone else that always rings a bit hollow.

The inner harmony that rests on total acceptance of whatever lies within one's own psyche will obviously affect other modes of fulfillment. As I have suggested, it may be necessary for transcendence, for one cannot reach a sense of unity with all being if one is still wrestling with parts of oneself. Inner harmony also eliminates the fundamental barrier to intimacy with other people, because we most often clash with people on whom we project the qualities we cannot accept in ourselves. It is also clear from the points raised in the preceding section that creativity requires an acceptance of content that emerges when one is not exerting active control over the flow of ideas and images. This content tends to be linked in various ways to the subconscious parts of our own being. If one insists on repression or denial of those parts, the creative flow is not possible. To be highly creative, one must either achieve an inner reconciliation or be willing to tolerate the conflicts. From the lives of creative geniuses, we know that there are both agony and ecstasy.

THE MODE OF RELATEDNESS

Like inner harmony, relatedness can be expressed in both superficial and profound forms. We see the superficial expression in the individual who proclaims an altruistic concern for humanity and hides deep resentments, in the individual who feels worthless and devotes himself or herself ascetically to the service of others, and in the individual who plunges into the interpersonal realm to escape the personal experiences that arise in solitude. A more profound relatedness is possible only if there is a profound acceptance of a total self that can be brought into a relationship with other people. This condition permits a genuine exchange of feelings, rather than an exchange in which some needs are revealed and others carefully covered up. It permits a genuine dialog, for this requires both an openness to whatever the other person expresses and a willingness to reveal one's own ideas, feelings, and needs.

On a still more profound level, relatedness ceases to be clearly an exchange between one self and other selves, for the boundary we commonly experience as dividing us from others tends to dissolve. We no longer feel entirely separate and individual, for in the relationship the narrow sense of personal identity expands to an identity that includes the other. We live in a society that attaches great importance to individuality. We tend to develop elaborate notions of personal identity, and we fear a loss of our identity. To gain a clear sense of who I am as an individual, of course, I must know how I am different from others. To reinforce the sense that I am a distinct individual, I must reinforce the boundary line that separates us. I do this by identifying closely with the qualities I regard as "me" and projecting outward onto other people whatever qualities I am unwilling to claim. It is ironic that in operating this way I am just like everyone else. We all start learning from an early age to guard our individuality and to reinforce the boundary by maintaining a critical attitude toward others. We are prepared to judge them for all of our unacknowledged sins.

It is refreshing to let go of the boundary and experience genuine intimacy with another person. On a few occasions I have discovered what it is like to do this in a large group. The first time was a number of years ago in a large encounter session involving over a hundred people. As other people shared facts and feelings from their own lives, I felt inhibited. I could see the flaws, the weaknesses, the naiveté of the people who spoke, and I knew that I, too, could be judged if I spoke up. And yet the moment finally came when someone spoke directly to me, and I responded with feelings and facts of my own, revealing the bits and pieces of my life that I had been hiding so carefully. At that moment, I was surprised at the ease with which I spoke, for my fears and tension had vanished. My being was permeated with a deep calm. Or was it the group that was so permeated? I could not tell because I was no longer separated, and I could no longer view any of the people around me with critical detachment. Whatever they revealed about themselves, I experienced them as part of a larger me that included all of us. Their flaws and their feelings were my flaws and feelings.

Each time I have had an experience of this kind, I have wished I could maintain it. It may linger for days, but then it eludes my grasp, and once again I am cut off, a very separate individual surrounded by people with various problems and quirks of their own. It is possible to maintain a sense of community with others that pervades much of one's life. This is the goal that Alfred Adler spoke of in terms of *Gemeinschaftsgefühl,* and many people are able to go far in this direction. To maintain the more profound sense of an experienced identity that embraces others, a sense of being always at-one-with-others, is rare. Perhaps a few Western and Eastern saints have done this. In our time, perhaps Mother Teresa, who has devoted her life to the diseased, the dying, and the poor of Calcutta, is an outstanding example.

One of the clearest historical examples is Saint Francis of Assisi, whose life is often viewed as the clearest expression of Christian love. Humble as he was, Francis was also a scholar, and his writings reflect his concern for others. Perhaps the best known of his writings is a prayer:

> Lord, make me an instrument of Thy
> peace.

Where there is hatred let me sow love;
Where there is injury, pardon;
Where there is doubt, faith;
Where there is despair, hope;
Where there is darkness, light;
Where there is sadness, joy.

O Divine Master, grant that I may not so
much seek
To be consoled as to console;
To be understood as to understand;
To be loved as to love;
For it is in giving that we receive;
It is in pardoning that we are pardoned;
It is in dying that we are born to eternal
life.

In another of his writings, variously known in English as the "Canticle of Brother Sun" and "The Song of the Creatures," he expresses a sense of kinship with all other creatures and with the various parts of nature, including sun, moon, stars, wind, water, fire, earth, and even death.

Saint Francis is an outstanding example of one form of mysticism. *Mysticism* in general refers to a spiritual path that emphasizes the value of an immediate experience of the spiritual, rather than an understanding mediated by ordinary perception, reason, or other intellectual means. I think it is useful to distinguish two main mystical paths. One is an introverted path, whereby one seeks the vital experience through prayer, meditation, or the sudden inspiration facilitated by quiet and solitude. The other is a more extraverted, or outward-oriented, path, in which one seeks the experience through interaction with others. It may be facilitated by more active, communal modes of meditation, such as Sufi dancing. The introverted path is the traditional path of

Eastern mysticism, and its primary goal is transcendence. The outward path is exemplified by Saint Francis, by Baal-Shem-Tov and other representatives of Hasidism, and by a few outstanding Hindus and Buddhists of recent centuries. In many respects, the two paths ultimately converge, but the outward path leads a little more clearly to an expression of the mode of relatedness.

THE MODE OF TRANSCENDENCE

The aim of the quest for transcendence is an experience of being that takes us beyond the confines of individual identity. This is the primary goal of traditional Hindu and Buddhist practices, though there is much variation in the form of these practices and in the precise way in which the goal is conceptualized. In general, the Hindu seeks a realization of the atman, the true individual soul or self that underlies our present, more shallow and temporary sense of conscious identity. A still more profound realization is that the atman is identical with the brahman, which we might define as the soul or mind of the universe, or the ground of all being. Thus, the Hindu mystic moves from the experience of separate individual identity to an experience of oneness with all being. The aim of Buddhism is similar, though Buddhists dispense with the concepts of atman and brahman. They focus instead on the importance of letting go of the ego identity, recognizing its illusory character, and giving up the attachments and desires bound up in the false identity.

Meditation is a common ingredient of the spiritual practices of both Hindus and Buddhists. Though there are many forms of meditation, nearly all of them involve procedures for moving from organized, rational consciousness to other modes of consciousness that are more spontaneous and governed less by active will. I noted the importance of such states for creativity and for ESP. I suggested that ESP might be considered a special case of efficiency, but it is often accompanied by dramatic changes in self-experience that might be regarded as expressions of relatedness or transcendence.

Paranormal abilities such as ESP emerge so frequently in the course of Eastern spiritual practices that Hindu and Buddhist literature contains many descriptions of such effects and some fairly detailed descriptions of the means for achieving them. It also contains many warnings about the dangers of becoming too fascinated with paranormal powers, since the quest for heightened self-esteem and admiration may lead away from the spiritual path of ego-transcendence. To a rationalist, mysticism represents a movement toward to a more primitive level of consciousness. Freud regarded the Buddhist quest for nirvana as an effort to retain the blissful unawareness of infantile or intrauterine existence. Contemporary psychoanalysts still stress the secondary process and rationality, but they may see some value in the occasional regression to more primitive modes of consciousness. Arieti (1976) describes the overall course of religion as a progression from gods directly experienced to gods abstractly conceptualized, but he believes that the occasional direct experience of the mystic may be needed to sustain the concepts and values of religion at its advanced levels. From the standpoint of the mystic, however, religion is realized fully only in the direct experience, and the concepts of the theologian can render it inadequately at best.

Carl Jung had a far greater appreciation for mysticism than Freud did, and he derived many insights from a study of Eastern thought as well as from the writings of Western mystics like Meister Eckhart and Swedenborg. While he appreciated rationality, he did not assign it the preeminent place in human experience that Freud did, and he found much value in other forms of consciousness. He understood the Buddhist and Hindu positions, however, as an advocacy of nonconsciousness, and he insisted that the ego, as the center of consciousness, must not be abandoned. Rather, we must seek a proper balance between the ego and the self, the center of the total psyche. I have suggested before that the difference between Jungian and Eastern thought is more apparent than real (Coan, 1977), and Martin Kalff (1983) has provided a still more lucid treatment of the matter. Common to both the Jungian and the Buddhist positions is a recognition that we need to overcome identifications that misrepresent our nature and to give heed to that part of our nature that lies beyond the reach of full conscious realization and egoic identification.

It is difficult to describe the modes of consciousness attained by way of the path of transcendence, for the best we can do with words is to liken the experience to the contents of ordinary perception, and something is always lost in such a rendering. The mystic either avoids any effort at description or resorts to concepts drawn from his or her religious and philosophical background in labeling and interpreting the phenomena experienced. The concepts may be drawn from Christian theology, Vedanta philosophy, Buddhist literature, or Judaic thought. Within any one tradition there is room for various descriptions of what is basically the same experience. The mystical experience is probably best understood in the East, and in the literature of Hinduism and Buddhism we find a variety of rich descriptions.

States Recognized in Buddhism

Daniel Goleman (1975) has provided a valuable summary of the states of consciousness described in the Visuddhimagga, a Buddhist work of the fifth century. He notes that three major kinds of training or discipline are attributed in that work to the teachings of Gautama. These include: sila, the cultivation of virtue or moral purity; samadhi, the path of concentration; and prajna, the path of insight. They are not three strictly independent paths, for they have a common purpose, and progress along any of the three facilitates progress along the other two. The path of sila begins with adherence to a code of moral discipline and includes ascetic practices and the limiting of possessions. Its aim is a death of the ego and the cessation of worldly desires and attachments.

The path of samadhi utilizes concentrative meditation, and its goal is to break and steady the thought continuum. A variety of possible subjects for meditation is employed, and with each one chosen the meditator seeks to penetrate it and become one with it. Goleman describes nine levels through which one may pass on this path. Each level is characterized by the kinds of experience that emerge at that stage and are then modified or eliminated as one moves on to the next stage. The experiences include, in succession: an assortment of hindering thoughts, sensations, body states, emotions, and images; feelings of rapture, bliss, and one-pointedness; feelings of equanimity; consciousness of infinite space; objectless infinite consciousness; and awareness of no-thing-ness. The final stage is said to be characterized by a still more subtle equanimity and one-pointedness, and there is "neither perception nor non-perception."

In the path of prajna, one proceeds not by concentration but my mindfulness. In this practice, one attends to what actually happens in successive moments of perception without imposing interpretations on the events. Our usual tendency, of course, is to move rapidly from raw sensory experience to abstract ideas that represent our expectations and preconceptions, without realizing the extent to which we are actually constructing the world around us in the very act of perceiving it. Mindfulness enables us to break this habit, and it leads into vipassana, a meditative practice in which one attends to every thought, image, or impression that arises. In the course of this practice, one passes through a succession of cognitive realizations. The first is that the phenomena contemplated are distinct from the mind contemplating them. Having experienced the duality of mind and object, one then realizes that there is no abiding entity or self to be found in the mind's functioning, and the duality is recognized as a misconception. In later stages, various changes occur in the experience of the objects and events passing through consciousness. They are observed to appear in rapid succession, but at a certain point they are seen with great clarity, and the beginning and end of each object of contemplation are perceived. A variety of feelings accompanies this clear perception: rapture, tranquility, vigorous energy, etc. As insight deepens, the experienced world seems to be in a constant state of dissolution, and all phenomena come to be seen as faulty and unsatisfactory. This realization paves the way for the ultimate realization of nirvana, a state in which mental phenomena cease and, in the arrested flow, the mind takes as its object the "signless, no-occurrence, no-formation." There are four levels of realization of nirvana, and the final one is that of the arahant (or arhat), a fully realized being. Such an individual is free from suffering, free from hatred and greed, and free from any desire for approval, fame, or pleasure. The acts of the arahant will be purely functional, serving either for the maintenance of the body or for the welfare of others.

The goals of the three paths are not quite identical, but they are obviously compatible, and the paths tend ultimately to merge. Effortless, choiceless action, the aim of the path of sila becomes inevitable with nirvana. One who has achieved nirvana can easily achieve the higher levels of samadhi, while one who has passed through the higher levels of samadhi can easily achieve nirvana. All these paths lead to a transcendence of ordinary egoic consciousness.

A Contemporary Indian View

The meditative practices of the yogis of Indian lead to similar effects, and they are intended to lead from the experience of individual separateness to a realization of atman and identity with the brahman. Haridas Chaudhuri (1975) describes ten kinds of authentic mystic experience that have been reported by yogic meditators: (1) the experience of the self as transempirical subject, as a detached center of awareness of the cosmic whole, (2) the experience of the self as pure transcendence beyond subject-object, (3) the experience of the creative ground of all existence, (4) the experience of the oneness of all existence, (5) the experience of Being or of the higher self as an eternal Thou, (6) the experience of the transpersonal Being-energy, (7) the experience of Being as the superpersonal spiritual mystery, as God beyond God, or an infinite existence-consciousness-bliss, (8) the experience of Being as the absolute void, as something empty of all describable determinations, (9) the experience of Being as cosmic energy, and (10) the experience of Being-energy as creative evolution.

These descriptions obviously correspond to some extent to the differing concepts of different traditions. Thus, the eighth accords with Buddhist concepts, while the ninth fits the descriptions of those who practice kundalini yoga. Chaudhuri believes these ten experiences represent an approximate order of increasing profundity. As a discipline of Aurobindo, he regards the tenth as the most profound. He also notes three inauthentic experiences that are often mistaken for valid mystic experiences. Two of them are simply regressions to pre-egoic conditions—to the oceanic feeling of the infant in one case and to the *participation mystique* of the primitive in the other. The third inauthentic experience is an experience of ego inflation or omnipotence that results from an identification of the ego with God or Being. The first two experiences amount to a failure to realize the ego, while the third represents a failure to realize the limits of egoic consciousness and a failure to transcend the ego. These three inauthentic experiences correspond to some common Western misunderstandings of the very nature of the mode of transcendence.

3

The Origins of Consciousness

If it is difficult to discern the future course of human consciousness, it is no less difficult, looking backward, to perceive the source of the path that led us to our present condition. When we ask about the origin of consciousness, we cannot avoid dealing with issues that concern the very nature of our subject. Is consciousness limited to human beings? If so, at what point did they become conscious? If it is not so limited, then where else does it exist? To take an extreme panpsychic position, we might assume that consciousness, or mind, exists throughout the universe, or that it is present wherever there is matter or physical energy. Alternatively, we might assume that it is confined to living forms and that it arises at an early stage in the evolution of organic matter. We can assume still narrower limits and suppose that it is found only in animals and not in plants, or that it is confined to animals above a certain level of complexity—perhaps only mammals or only mammals with brains of a certain size and complexity.

There is no easy solution to this issue, and the methods of science are of little avail in our efforts to resolve it. It is clear that a wide range of answers can be defended on rational grounds and that the answer we choose serves in part as a definition of consciousness. Perhaps the least defensible answer would be the naive anthropocentric position that consciousness is a property of *Homo sapiens* as a species and is totally lacking in all other animals, but if we define *consciousness* narrowly enough we might legitimately argue that some people possess it while others do not. If we construe consciousness very broadly, however, and use the term to include everything from the rawest sort of awareness or experience to the most sophisticated forms of mentation, then the species-specific view seems absurd.

The Awareness of Animals

No one who has lived in close proximity to, and in communication with, any of our four-footed relatives—whether dogs, cats, or farm animals—can doubt seriously that they experience many things in much the same way we do. The most obvious evidence is the same kind as that from which we infer the presence of consciousness in one another. We share an immense variety of actions and expressions with our fellow mammals, and it is usually obvious when they feel threatened, fearful, angry, or joyfully expectant. Surely there is ample reason to assume that they process sensations, images, feelings, and emotions much as we do. Sifting through the abundant research evidence on animal behavior, we can find little evidence for a sharp qualitative difference between the minds of humans and those of other species. Other animals can learn, remember, and engage in rudimentary reasoning. Chimpanzees can learn to use language much as small children do. They are capable of formulating simple abstractions, asking questions, and denying assertions put to them.

Perhaps only a few thinkers, saturated with the mechanistic outlook confined to some streams of Western thought of recent centuries, would deny conscious experience to animals. But if there is no qualitative gulf between us and other creatures, how can we best characterize the difference that does exist? The simplest assumption would be that other animals possess a consciousness that is less organized and incisive. Carl Sagan (1977) suggests that the waking state of other animals is like the dream state of humans, that they experience vivid sensory and emotional images and have an active intuitive understanding, but that they manifest little rational analysis, ability to concentrate, or sense of individual identity.

This is probably a reasonable commentary for much of animal experience, but it still reflects an anthropocentric bias. It assumes that human consciousness, if not fundamentally different from that of other animals, is at least quantitatively superior. This is surely valid so long as we confine our attention to those mental processes in which we excel, but we grant ourselves an unfair advantage in such a comparison. One reason why our efforts to communicate with dogs and cats often falls short is that these animals are less intelligent as judged by human standards—they do not understand as well as we do in the way in which we understand things. From a canine or feline standpoint, however, human understanding is deficient. They possess a way of perceiving things that will always lie a bit beyond our grasp, and we may never succeed in overcoming our lack.

The problem looms a bit larger when we direct our attention to mammals that have evolved in an aquatic environment. The cetaceans—the dolphins, porpoises, and the larger whales—have brains that rival ours in complexity and size, or size relative to total body mass. They have developed biological capabilities suited to their milieu, and they have some impressive talents that we cannot match. They are adept at sonar navigation, and they can communicate with one another over vast distances in the ocean. Their behavior also poses some riddles we have not yet solved. The humpback whale produces "songs" that may last as long as thirty minutes. We can surmise that a song of this length is not just a sequence of random vocalizations, since the same whale may later reproduce the entire sequence. To the whale the sequence is apparently meaningful, but the meaning is not apparent to us. Perhaps we can learn to decode it. On the other hand, we may not be capable of decoding it. It is possible that the whale possesses a mode of consciousness and a mode of processing information that lie outside the boundaries of our present experience, or even our potential experience. The methods we might employ to decipher an unknown human language may be totally inapplicable, for all human languages rest on a common core of implicit grammatical construction. They reflect a fundamental human mode of processing experience. If the whale song is a language, however, it may not be one in which ideas are strung out in the kind of linear sequence to which all human beings are accustomed. Perhaps impressions that we have to articulate in a linear sequence are grasped by the whale as a whole, and the visual-spatial metaphors that underlie human concepts may be of minor interest to the whale. In one respect whales are unquestionably superior to human beings: they have never attempted to exterminate us. If we do not succeed in rendering them extinct, we can continue to learn from them, and their mental accomplishments may help us transcend our anthropocentrism.

Undoubtedly, we will find that our own capabilities do make us unique in certain respects. There are some advantages to the particular way in which the brain has evolved in humans, especially when this brain exists in combination with an opposable thumb. It may not be clear just what goes on the minds of cetaceans or in the communication that takes place among them, but there is little doubt that no other land animals can come close to us in the development of articulate language and the use of abstract concepts, and we are clearly the supreme makers and users of tools. Jacob Bronowski (1973) suggests that our uniqueness lies in a combination of faculties that enables us to manifest a forward-looking imagination and to function creatively. The diverse and changing products of culture attest to this quality.

The Nature of Our Ancestors

For the purposes of an evolutionary account of human consciousness, it is not really important to decide whether humans possess a consciousness or a mentality that is superior to that of all other animals, but it is important to understand how we differ from our own ancestors. We need to determine how those qualities of consciousness that are distinctly human first arose. Other animals can provide clues, but apes are more helpful than whales, since we do not have to climb nearly so far down the evolutionary tree to locate the point at which our ancestry diverged from theirs. What we would really like to do, of course, is study primeval humans, to observe and attempt communication with people who lived thousands of years ago. Obviously we cannot do this, and we have to content ourselves with an archeological record composed of a few durable artifacts. From these artifacts, unfortunately, we cannot learn directly what went on in the minds of the producers, but we can make some shrewd guesses, guesses often aided by observations of contemporary peoples who create similar products.

Many of our ideas about the evolution of human mind, thought, and consciousness rest directly on a comparison of ourselves with the so-called primitive people living today, and they rest on an assumption that these primitive people are similar in basic ways to our own remote ancestors. The pitfalls in such a comparison have long been obvious to leading anthropologists and other social theorists. Late in the nineteenth century, Herbert Spencer (1898) argued that the so-called primitives of today have actually regressed from a previous state that was higher. Franz Boas (1921) argued that we need to recognize alternative kinds of development and rejected the idea that all the varieties of human culture represent different stages along a single line of evolution. We tend to view the world not only with an ethnocentric bias but with a present-centered bias as well, assuming that our own society is better now than it has ever been in the past and, hence, better than any society of the past. The sensationalist writings of von Däniken (1971) exploit this bias, suggesting that the outstanding architectural and technological feats of past centuries and past millennia could only have been accomplished by visitors from outer space (cf. Story, 1976).

From a biological standpoint, the human species has changed very little in the past few thousand years, and the ancient world had its share of geniuses. There is ample evidence that people in various parts of the world of two or three thousand years ago were capable of accurate and detailed observations of celestial events, that they maintained observatories, and that they developed sophisticated methods for keeping track of dates and seasons for a mixture of practical and ritualistic purposes. People of the past also developed countless technologies that have been lost, and they often manifested a skillful precision with hand tools that we cannot match with the best of modern equipment.

It is not too difficult to appreciate the achievements of an earlier era or earlier civilization when we find evidence of monumental efforts to do things that we also strive to do. It is more difficult to appreciate the achievements of an ancient people when those achievements involve a mode of thinking and consciousness that is quite different from the one our own society cherishes. The eminent Egyptologist R. A. Schwaller de Lubicz (1981) contended that there are two basic forms of intelligence: static and intuitive. The former is favored by our society, and it operates in an analytical and rational manner and requires the objectification of concepts. The latter form of intelligence permits knowledge without objectification and requires a more symbolic form of expression. The intuitive mode enables us to apprehend simultaneities that are incomprehensible from the standpoint of static intelligence, and it provides a basis for understanding facets of reality that modern science, with its emphasis on the analytic and the literal, can only ignore. The intuitive mode underlies the symbolic texts of many ancient cultures, but Schwaller de Lubicz believed that it was cultivated to a high level in ancient Egypt and that the writings and paintings of that culture represent a high point in symbolic expression. For this reason, we misconstrue and oversimplify the content of those productions when we attempt to interpret them in strictly rational terms. If they represent a mode of consciousness and a mode of expression that we have lost, we need to recapture the insights of the great minds of ancient Egypt.

SOME EARLY THRESHOLDS

The ancient Egyptians left an abundance of written records that we may or may not succeed in comprehending. As we move to far earlier times, in an effort to understand primeval stages in human consciousness, we have to work with a very scant record, but some of the facts of early human evolution seem self-evident. Our early ancestors had to make a number of major adjustments to a changing world. They moved from an arboreal environment to a varied terrain. They became increasingly bipedal, freeing their forelimbs for uses other than locomotion. They shifted from a purely vegetarian diet to one that included the meat of many different animals. Drastic climatic changes and migration over long distances required a host of additional adaptations. With every major change in life pattern, natural selection favored those individuals with the larger brains and greater versatility. With every such change, there was probably a shift toward a mode of awareness more distinctly human, but we have little basis for identifying many of the individual psychological steps leading to human consciousness.

The Use of Tools

We know little about the habits of our early hominid ancestors. The fossil record enables us primarily to discern changes in the skull and skeletal structure. At the point where the genus *Homo* finally emerged, some 2.5 million years ago or more, an additional kind of evidence becomes available, for at this point the earliest stone tools appear—alongside the remains of *Homo habilis*. The tools associated with the successors of this creature—*Homo erectus, Homo sapiens neanderthalensis*, and finally modern *Homo sapiens*—show a steady increase in sophistication and variety.

Human intelligence is not required for the use of tools. Apes readily make use of various objects—rocks, sticks, leaves—as an aid in their endeavors, but the tools that they employ are objects that happen to be available at the time they are used. This use of tools was undoubtedly characteristic of all the early hominids. With the emergence of genus *Homo*, we see the apparently deliberate alteration of an object to facilitate its use. This requires a bit more imagination and planning—not a great deal more, since the alteration may be made in preparation for an immediate use. It is an additional step to produce a tool that will be used at a later time. To progress very far into the manufacture of stone tools requires a significant step in consciousness, because it involves a rehearsal in imagination of an event that lies in the future, an event that may involve a scene and a cast of characters that are not present at the moment. Our ancestors probably developed this facility gradually. The earliest meat-eaters in our ancestral line were most likely scavengers who ate the remains of animals that were already dead when found. The use of a tool was confined to picking up a nearby rock or stick to aid them in tearing through the hide of the animal or cracking its bones. The next step would be to strike two stones together to produce a sharper edge. The ultimate achievement in Stone-Age life was to create refined implements that could later be used in the hunt—spears with sharp stone points, spear throwers, and bows and arrows. Such tools could be produced only by people with highly developed imaginations, people capable of foreseeing the hunt well in advance and anticipating their interaction with their chosen prey.

At the beginning of Chapter 1, I noted a couple of biblical motifs that can be understood in terms of stages or facets of emerging human consciousness. One of the most significant motifs in Greek mythology is the deed of Prometheus, who brings fire from the gods to earth for the use of human mortals. Fire has a number of interesting properties that have been a source of fascination for our species for thousands of years. Fire can be used to provide light where there is darkness and to transform materials form one state to another. It offers a way of seeing and a way of creating, and it has served universally as a mythic symbol of creative power and consciousness. In giving us fire, Prometheus has enabled us to claim some of the power of the gods as our own. We can be aware and we can create and no longer be mere pawns of fate. The name *Prometheus* literally means foresight, the ability to look ahead and in imagination to experience events that lie in the future. The tool-making accomplishments of our ancestors provide the archeological evidence of their gradual acquisition of this capacity.

The Capacity for Play

With foresight, we ceased to be totally bound to immediate reality. We could do more than react. With the aid of an image of a situation not yet present, we could prepare for the future. The capacity for play also permits a transcendence of the immediate reality. For the most part, tool-making is guided by very practical aims, but play is not. It provides a release not only from the immediate pressures of the environment but also from the biological demands of the body. While play can become linked in various ways to bodily needs and practical intentions, in its rawest form it does not seem to serve any such purpose. It provides an escape from a present reality through the creation in imagination of a different reality, and this creative process appears to be inherently pleasurable.

Johan Huizinga (1955) contended that play is one of the most distinctive features of the human species and that it serves a key function in the development of civilization and culture, but he also recognized that play is not confined to this one species. Play obviously occurs in many other species, most obviously in the higher mammals. Dogs and cats play, and it is obvious that they make a distinction between the practical reality and the imaginative reality they have created, for in play they operate by a different set of rules. If one fights in play, one may growl and snarl and snap, but one is careful not to bite too hard, since that would most certainly spoil the fun. It is not difficult to find similarities between the play of dogs and cats and that of children, but as we move closer to our own species the resemblance becomes more striking. Chimpanzees have been known to engage spontaneously in rhythmic circular movements that look very much like the playful movement patterns created by small children and the simplest forms of dance found throughout the world.

Joseph Campbell also recognizes the importance of play for humankind, and he suggests that early forms of mythology began to emerge at the point when our species "began to play games of its own invention instead of only those of nature's" (Campbell, 1969, p. 391). The ability to create myth and ritual is basically the ability to create an imaginary or symbolic reality, separate from the immediate practical reality, and to act out or act upon the reality one has created. Thus, myth and ritual have their roots in play, and the various derivatives of these that we know as science, art, and philosophy also do. Play is also necessary for language, for our early ancestors had to play with vocal sounds, just as small children still do, to develop a repertoire of sounds that could convey any meaning beyond that of an immediately provoking stimulus.

Something akin to play has been recognized many times in other terms as an essential aspect of human thought and consciousness. Kurt Goldstein (1963) made a distinction between the concrete and abstract attitudes. He regarded the latter as essential for all the higher mental functions we perform, and he considered its loss to be one of the main consequences of severe brain damage. When we operate via the concrete attitude, our thinking is bound by the properties of the stimuli immediately present. With the abstract attitude, we can act as if there were a different reality; we can deal with possible realities and general categories.

The ability to act-as-if, to pretend, is central to play and to abstract thinking. It is also central to deceit, and Julian Jaynes (1976) suggests that deceit may have had survival value for our ancestors and that it may have contributed to the emergence of consciousness. To be more specific, Jaynes says that it may have served as a source for the creation of what he calls the "analog I." To engage in deception over in extended period of time requires the development of a concept or image of oneself as a person whose actual needs and attitudes differ from those represented by outward behavior.

It is interesting that a talent for deception is one of the characteristics of the trickster figures that appear so pervasively in early mythologies. The basic form of the trickster may be that of a human, as in the case of Hermes in Greek mythology, or an animal, such as a hare or coyote. The trickster is no ordinary mortal, however, for he can change forms with ease and assume either a male or a female identity. Wherever they appear, trickster figures are the most contradictory figures of mythology, for at various times they act like utter fools, they lie and cheat and create disorder, but they are also culture-bringers, and they may function as creator gods. The image of the trickster combines instinctual spontaneity (which may make the trickster appear simple or stupid) with artful deception. Whatever the trickster does, he manifests the kind of awareness that enables him to initiate and create, to do something other than what is habitual, customary, and expected. As a creator god, the trickster marks the advent of an openness to fresh awareness, an openness to possibilities that go beyond the bounds of action that is merely instinctual, reactive, or habitual. It has frequently been observed that the qualities of the trickster often appear in the individual who assumes the role of spiritual guide, guru, or shaman. Such a person may manifest the most profound insight but act at times with the apparent naiveté of a mental defective. Perhaps we could better characterize the naiveté as childlike, for it is childlike simplicity that enables such an individual to see beyond the veil of consensual reality, the reality accepted by conventional thought. The most adept psychotherapists have such a quality, and it enables them to facilitate fresh awareness on the part of others. Perhaps such individuals have played a key role at transition points in the evolution of human consciousness.

Myth

Both tool-making and play, then, reflect a capacity for entertaining a view of reality that differs from the more obvious immediate reality, and both tool-making and play evolve and become more elaborate as human consciousness evolves. The archeological record points to other expressions of the same capacity. From the time of the later Neanderthals we have evidence of deliberate burial—burial sites in which two or more bodies were placed together and sites in which an assortment of flowers was evidently placed in the grave. Death is a recurring event in the animal world, and it is likely that many animals experience something akin to human grief when they lose a mate or an offspring. Every mythology provides ways of dealing with this experience, through an interpretation of death as something more than just the obvious cessation of movement and responsiveness. Burial customs generally reflect an awareness of death as a recurring event in the life of the community and an interpretation of it as a state comparable to sleep, perhaps a prelude to a new kind of existence. Thus, there is reason to believe that the Neanderthals had developed a mythic account of death.

Furthermore, in several mountain sites in Europe there is evidence that Neanderthal people deliberately placed the skulls and long bones of cave bears in arrangements that may have had some symbolic significance. Considering these findings in the light of what is known of later hunting peoples, it is reasonable to surmise that the cave bear, as a principal source of food for the Neanderthals, was revered by them and was the focus of a mythology and set of cult rituals. The art and sculpture produced in a later period of prehistory by the early artists of our species suggest still more elaborate myths and rituals, though we can only guess at the content of these. In many locations, particularly in southwestern Europe, caves have been found to contain the paintings produced by prehistoric people. Animals are the most conspicuous subject matter, and they take many forms, but there is a preponderance of large animals, and these were probably animals hunted by the artists. The paintings were probably used in some sense to prepare hunters for the hunt, but it is unlikely that their use was confined to such practical matters as target practice and the plotting of strategy. If these ancient painters views their prey as preliterate people of the modern era do, we may assume that they experienced the animals with a mixture of reverence, compassion, and identification.

Another subject matter that is particularly prominent in ancient sculpture is the female form. In many parts of Europe, small figurines of the female form have been found. These commonly contain exaggerated breasts, buttocks, and vulvas but lack facial features. Clearly the reproductive role and capacity of the female are highlighted, and these *objets d'art* have been called Venus figurines on the assumption that they express a worship of a mother image or goddess. It is tempting to construe all these paintings and sculptures in terms of the early mythologies known to exist at a much later time, where mother goddesses and animal figures both assumed very important roles. This is a matter of speculation, but it is reasonable to assume that for many thousands of years a major feature of human consciousness has been the experience of mythic images that people have projected onto the world around them.

The development of civilization over the past eight or nine thousand years has involved countless additional changes in the ways in which people have related to one another and to the world as a whole, and these must have involved many concomitant changes in the nature of human consciousness. Early in this period, people of the Near East began to shift to an agricultural mode of living. They began to plant crops, and they began to maintain and breed livestock. Still later, as people gathered in larger communities and the city-state emerged, the various basic early milestones of civilization began to appear: the wheel, the calendar, systems of writing, mathematics, taxation, and ruling and priestly classes. We can characterize many of the changes in human society by saying that people increasingly took an active role in planning their lives and structuring their environment. They were less and less the mere victims and beneficiaries of fate, and the acceptance of the gift of fire from Prometheus was only the first step.

EARLY STAGES OF SELF-AWARENESS

The developments noted so far center about an augmented awareness of reality, the emergency of a consciousness that can embrace both an anticipated future and an imaginary alternative to the more obvious immediate situation. At the same time, the tool-making, play, and myths, as well as the technological and symbolic enterprises that subsequently evolved from these, point to an organism that has acted increasingly in accordance with its augmented awareness. At the core of all the changes we are considering is a gradually changing awareness of self or identity, for self-awareness must change as awareness of the world and one's relationship to it changes. The organism confined to an unreflective expression of bodily needs and reactions to immediate stimuli can have little sense of a separate existence. As many writers have observed, our original experience as infants and as a species must have been one of a mass of impressions as yet uninterpretable in terms of such differentiated components as self and universe, or me and not-me.

Separation and Identification

The experience of individual separateness is largely equivalent to an experience of individual will. The organism that can choose to act in terms of either a practical reality or an imaginary reality and can plan and prepare for an anticipated future must experience some individual will, some awareness of the possibility of acting according to its own wishes instead of according to the dictates of external forces. The experience of separateness and individual will, however, is not a single step that our primeval ancestors took at some point for once and for all. There are many possible degrees of separateness and many possible stages in the experience of an identity. The boundary of the content incorporated into a sense of personal identity can expand gradually, and under some circumstances it may contract. We will recognize certain psychic potentials and contents as lying outside the boundary, and we may relate to these in several ways. We may reject them or disown them and see them as qualities found only in others. We may see them only in others but view them as desirable, as something we cannot personally claim but which complements our identity. We may experience the qualities as part of a whole that includes our experienced identity, a part we can acknowledge and relate to as a constituent of our total being but a part we cannot directly experience in terms of a conscious identity.

It is reasonable to assume that all the primitive hunters from the remote past to the present have moved beyond the most primordial condition of undifferentiated consciousness. They make tools and plan for the hunt, but their experience differs from ours. From what we can observe of them in our own time, they experience themselves as closer to nature, and the animal realm figures prominently in their myth-making. Of course, it is unreasonable to assume that the hunting tribes of the present day do not differ psychologically from the Neanderthals of forty or fifty thousand years ago. We can assume only the persistence of a few elements that are necessarily bound up in the basic hunting lifestyle. Hunters of recent times have generally displayed certain social customs, myths, and rituals that have been broadly labeled totemistic. This term implies a set of customs and beliefs that entail an animal identification. The specific customs and beliefs are subject to much variation, but commonly there is a belief that all members of the tribe can be traced to an animal ancestor. Particular animals or kinds of animals may be viewed as gods or as spiritual protectors of the tribe. An individual of the tribe may be regarded as linked psychically to a specific animal, which may function as a guardian, servant, or alter ego of that individual, so that the fate of the individual is bound up with the fate of the animal. Apart from specific beliefs and customs, primitive hunters generally experience a greater kinship with the natural realm, with plant and animal life, than do people of modern society. They also display an evident compassion for the animals they kill and seem in some way to share in their suffering. In slaying the animal, they may express regret, and in their mythology they may view the slaying as a away of liberating the animal for a new life.

The primitive hunter clearly manifests a strong identification with the animal realm and with certain specific kinds of animals, but this is not the same thing as saying that consciousness is undifferentiated. Certainly the hunter can distinguish between himself and the animal. The totemic identification serves in part to augment the individual identity, and the counterpart in our own society would be an individual's identification with a social group, an institution, or an ethnic group. The totemic identification also expresses a sense of kinship with an animal with whom the hunter's life is closely bound up. The hunter knows full well that in many respects he and the animal share a common fate. The Indians of the plains who saw the great herds of bison slaughtered without compassion by white men knew that the exterminators would, through the destruction of an animal, destroy a people and a way of life.

The concept of *identification* actually embraces a set of

interrelated processes, and these serve several functions in our lives. In the course of growing up, we acquire many of the ingredients of a separate personal identity through identification with other significant individuals and with groups. We can fall short of this achievement, however, if identification is too close or too strong and we fail to realize our separateness from the individual or group with which we identify. Identification may also serve to amplify certain aspects of a personal identity when we identify with a hero, an animal, or a mythic being who represents those aspects in idealized form. Whatever the specific effect, identification always implies a certain elasticity or uncertainty about the location of the ego boundary, the line that separates self from other. It is tempting to assume that if the primordial condition is one in which no ego boundary has yet been formed, the ideal condition is one in which the boundary is sharply defined, but such an assumption is strictly gratuitous. In a way, the sense of personal identity must be considered a convenient illusion. We always live in interdependence with the world and the people around us. Furthermore, our bodies, our actions, and our stream of conscious impressions are subject to forces and processes within that we can never bring fully under conscious control. While it may please me to think, like William Henley, that I am the master of my fate and the captain of my soul, there can be no such thing as a totally independent individual who is fully responsible for the course of his or her life.

To lead a life that is reasonably harmonious and peaceful, we must find a way of relating to forces that are not subject to our conscious will. This requires some accommodation to the people, animals, and forces of nature that surround us and some accommodation to the forces within our own psyches. There are many possible ways of experiencing the intrapsychic forces, but since we are unable to own them as conscious intentions, we tend to perceive them in a projected form, as the intentions of other people, animals, gods, and other mythic beings. The history of consciousness can be described to a great extent in terms of changes in the ego boundary (i.e., changes in the nature and the range of psychic content we are able to acknowledge as our own) and the locus of our projections of content that is considered alien. For the primitive hunter, perhaps only a small range of content is personally owned, while other content is perceived as residing in the community as a whole, in the broader realm of nature, and in certain animals.

The transition to a herding and agricultural economy and to a more complex community does not lead to a fundamental change in the nature of consciousness, but the range of personally owned content may increase, and animal projections may diminish, to be replaced by an assortment of anthropomorphic divinities. In later stages the role and character of the divinities change, and the realm of content seen as under the control of the individual expands. Perhaps the point of balance between what is mine and directly subject to my will and what is other remains uncertain even as it progressively shifts. The God of Moses, who represents the divine other at an early stage of Judaic thought, expressed the issue in an interesting way. When Moses asked God's name, God replied, "I am that I am" (Exodus 3:14). The story of Moses from that moment on is the story of the interplay between the will of God and the will of Moses, but the divine figure actually identified itself as the essence of personal identity, or of subjectively experienced existence. Later generations of Jews and Christians could claim the sense of personal identity as their own only to the extent that the voice of God faded into the recesses of time.

Julian Jaynes and the Breakdown of the Bicameral Mind

Julian Jaynes (1976) has presented a theory of the origin of consciousness that emphasizes the aspect of self-awareness. Unlike most writers, Jaynes contends that consciousness is a very recent acquisition, that it first appeared about 3,000 years ago. To press his case very far, of course, Jaynes must argue that consciousness is not necessary for language, for concepts, for learning, for thinking, for reason, or for the various trappings of civilization that were clearly present well before the year 1000 B.C. Obviously, human awareness and intelligence had advanced quite far by then, and Jaynes's position is defensible only if one defines consciousness in a special way.

Janyes defines consciousness as the "invention of an analog world on the basis of language," and he amplifies the definition by describing six major features of consciousness: spatialization, excerption, the analog "I," the metaphor "me," narratization, and conciliation. In combination these features amount to the creation of the abstract, visual-spatial imaginary world that tends to accompany the development of language, and in particular the cultivation of an image of oneself as an active, willing agent at the center of that world.

According to Jaynes, the stage preceding the emergence of consciousness was not one of undifferentiated awareness, but one he characterizes in terms of the "bicameral mind." He defines this as a condition in which "human nature was split into two parts, an executive part called a god, and a follower part called a man," neither part being conscious (Jaynes, 1976, p. 84). In this condition, there was no conscious will, planning, or initiation of action. Instead, planning and initiative were organized without consciousness and experienced by the individual as a directive issued by a god. Jaynes speculates that the hallucinated voice of the god resulted from stimulation of the temporal lobe of the right cerebral hemisphere, the interaction between god and individual amounting to a kind of "bicameral" interplay between the hemispheres. With the rise of consciousness, the left hemisphere (in most people) assumed a more autocratic role, and the interaction between the hemispheres changed accordingly. Whatever the merits of Jaynes's neurological thesis, the psychological progression that he describes is probably an accurate account of a transition that has occurred among the people of our society. At a time in the distant past, our ancestors experienced more freely the emergence of ideas, impulses, and plans as the will of entities with which they were not personally identified.

Egoic and Pre-egoic Consciousness

There can be little doubt that in modern Western society it is deemed important to think in a realistic and rational way. If we do not expect consciousness to abide constantly by these constraints, we do expect the individual to shift to a realistic and rational mode at once when we engage him or her in conversation. In contrast, consciousness must have flowed in a less controlled and more spontaneous fashion in an earlier era. We see this spontaneous flow in our own dreams, in the creative process, in religious experience, and in much of the waking existence of some schizophrenics. Many individuals among us, however, are threatened by the very possibility of such an uncontrolled flow of impressions and ideas, and they resort to many methods of defending against it and ensuring that their experience remains very organized. Our emphasis on controlled and ordered consciousness is linked to an emphasis on self-consciousness. It is important to maintain control over consciousness because it is important to be a well-defined individual who can be held responsible for his or her actions and thoughts. This is the age of egoic consciousness.

It is more difficult to be certain about the nature of the stage that preceded egoic consciousness. Jaynes believes that the characteristic mode of consciousness in that stage was the hallucinatory dialog. His key evidence for this is that in literary productions from that period—notably the *Iliad* and the book of Amos—we see individuals who lack consciousness in his sense and who act in accordance with directives uttered by gods. Additional evidence is provided by schizophrenics, who have presumably regressed to a more primitive mode of functioning. In the schizophrenic, however, the identification of a specific hallucinatory agent—a god or other specific speaker who addresses the hallucinator—requires a bit of construction on the part of the patient. It is one way in which the schizophrenic introduces order into a disordered flow of experience. The schizophrenic is likely to hear a variety of unidentified voices before arriving at the more stable understanding of events that is afforded by identified voices. In the literary productions of earlier times, the experience of the depicted hero may represent an idealized version, rather than a direct portrayal, of ordinary experience. Achilles, Odysseus, and Hector may be guided by the voices of gods, but it is doubtful that the ordinary individual of ancient Greece experienced most of his or her actions and decisions in that manner. It may have been possible for everyone at times to hear and heed a clear voice of apparently divine origin, but it is another matter to suggest that this was the usual mode of experience.

From the standpoint of contemporary egoic consciousness, the individual who hallucinates is projecting outward a voice coming from within the psyche. From the standpoint of the individual who has not developed an ego in more than a very rudimentary form, there is no clear ego boundary. Ideas arise and perhaps take the form of verbal commentaries and imperatives. Perhaps at an early stage in the evolution of consciousness, there is no clear sense of a particular source for these ideas. As the notions of personal identity, will, and authority begin to take shape, the ideas can be attributed to a specific source, and this may be either a god or spirit without or an ego within. Perhaps personhood and authority are recognized in another before they can be attributed to oneself; this fits the experience of the small child. As René Spitz and other ego psychologists have noted, the infant must first oppose the voice of parental authority and say "no" before any sense of personal will or initiative is possible.

The work of Julian Jaynes contains a valuable analysis of the basic constituents of egoic consciousness. Unlike Jaynes, however,

I do not believe it is useful to confine the definition of the term *consciousness* to qualities associated with the present stage in the evolution of human experience. I think Jaynes has provided a useful account of some of the modes of experience that may be found in earlier stages, but the account is incomplete. There are still more pieces to the puzzle that must be found.

THEORIES OF PRIMITIVE THOUGHT

Over the past hundred years much has been written by anthropologists and psychologists about the nature of primitive thought and perception. Most of the ideas have been drawn from observations of various preliterate peoples, but they have been supplemented in some cases by observations of children and psychotics. To the extent that they provide a valid account of contemporary "primitives," we must at least take them into account in any conjectures about the nature of the human mind in earlier stages of its development.

The Lack of Differentiation

A key idea running through much of the literature is that the primitive lacks a clear differentiation between subject and object, or a clear differentiation between self and world. Lévy-Bruhl (1923) spoke of this in terms of *participation mystique*, or mystical participation. He noted that primitives do have acute experiences of pleasure, pain, and other sensations and recognize these as their own experiences but that they lack a well-defined sense of themselves as subjects. Because the sense of individual personality is only weakly developed, it is not difficult for the primitive to regard himself or herself as being present in more than one place at the same time—to have a soul that is simultaneously present in his or her own body and present in the body of an animal counterpart. Lévy-Bruhl (1966) cites examples of this belief among people in India, Malaysia, Africa, and Europe.

In his views of earlier stages of human consciousness, Carl

Jung was influenced by Lévy-Bruhl, and he makes occasional use in his writings of the concept of *participation mystique*. In the work of Jean Piaget (1929), we find the related concept of egocentrism applied to the thinking of early childhood. Heinz Werner (1948) also notes the lack of a clear polarity between subject and world in both the child and the primitive, and he regards this as an instance of the generally syncretic character of primitive thinking. *Syncretism* (a term used earlier by Piaget) refers to a tendency in thinking and perception to view reality in term of global, undifferentiated schemas, in which many kinds of objects, events, and qualities are seen as belonging together despite a lack of actual relationship among them.

Werner also characterizes primitive thinking as diffuse, indefinite, labile, rigid, and concrete, and these qualities are all regarded as related in some way to syncretism. Most of the characteristics of primitive thought noted by Werner are described in some form by various other writers. Herbert Spencer's earlier description of primitive thinking covers nearly all the same points. Piaget speaks of the emphasis on the concrete in terms of *realism*, while Jung speaks of it in terms of a concretistic quality.

Primitive Logic

According to Werner, primitive thought does not lack logic, but it tends to employ logic of a different kind from that which prevails in the thought of the educated person of Western culture. The primitive view of causality is governed by a tendency to think of events in a diffuse, global manner, rather than in terms of an articulated relationship between a causal condition and its effects. Both the interpretation of natural events (in mythic terms) and the active use of magic (e.g., bringing about the death of an enemy by burning one of his hairs) reflect this global understanding of causality. The most systematized expression of the diffuse and concrete understanding of causality is seen, according to Werner, in the causality-of-fate, an interpretation of all events in a given period in terms of a sense of fatality dominating that period.

It should be noted that Werner is talking about something akin to what Jung calls *synchronicity*, an acausal principle whereby meaningfully related events tend to occur together because they partake of the meaning that characterizes the moment in time in which they occur. While this view may be common among so-called primitives, it is also widespread in Eastern thought. It has been rejected in dominant traditions in Western thought, though it has always been around in some form, and it is apparently being regarded with increasing favor by many modern physicists. More than one physicist has argued that all events are interdependent and that every particle in some sense mirrors the entire universe. It follows that all events of a given moment share a common fate and that an interpretation of events in terms of isolated causal chains is utterly inadequate, but the modern scientist is likely to insist on a discrete and finely articulated description of interrelated events. However "primitive" the interpretive formula may be in this case, science will not settle for the looseness and diffuseness that characterizes its more primitive application.

Another facet of primitive logic noted by Werner and other writers is the simultaneous acceptance of a number of ideas that, to us, appear mutually contradictory. Thus, the primitive may accept the idea that the moon is a man, that the moon is a woman, and also the idea that the moon is an evil spirit. Arieti (1976) has noted that primitives and psychotics have difficulty thinking categorically. The individual starts to think in terms of categories or classes, but these prove unreliable. As a consequence, the primitive is unable to use categories in a consistent way; their use does not respect the Aristotelian law of identity (A is always A) nor the law of contradiction (the rule that the propositions "A is B" and "A is not B" cannot both be true at the same time).

Perhaps it is well to recognize that we may have lost something in moving from the loose thinking of the primitive to the rigidity of thought governed by Aristotelian logic. Arieti acknowledges the value of primitive, or paleologic, thinking for creativity, but surely one reason we need it for this purpose is that so much of Western thinking is constrained by overly rigid categorization. Western thinkers from the classical Greek to the modern, from the profound to the banal, from the original to the trendy, from Aristotle to Werner Erhard, have insisted that a given thing either is or is not, or that a given proposition is either true or not true. Our formal thinking traditionally lacks the subtlety of Buddhist logic, which has traditionally recognized twice as many possibilities: a proposition is either true and not false, false and not true, both true and false, or neither true nor false. There are many things we can never discover if we do not recognize at least this many possibilities. Even in the hard sciences, it has become necessary to recognize that one must sometimes transcend the traditionally recognized logical properties of our models. A modern physicist can recognize that light is both a stream of particles and a wave phenomenon. A physicist of an earlier period would have insisted it could not be both at the same time, since either possibility appears to contradict the other.

Usually when we are concerned with logical propositions and relationships, it is understood that we are dealing with statements composed of signs whose referents are fairly clear and understood in much the same way by everyone. The main thrust of Western thought has been toward increasing insistence on the use of conventional signs of this sort. As many writers have noted, the effect of this trend has been to suppress the free use of symbols, and the symbols to which people in our society once attached great importance have ceased to be meaningful for us. The word *symbol* has been used in more than one way, but I am using it at the moment in the sense in which Jung uses it, to refer to a word or image whose meaning cannot be fully explicated. The symbol may have an obvious literal meaning, but it also points to a meaning that lies beyond our intellectual grasp, a meaning that is not fully conscious and perhaps cannot be brought entirely into consciousness. Scientists may seek to dispense with symbols, but they have always been important in religious discourse. Often the surface meaning of the symbol is paradoxical; it points to properties that are mutually contradictory, but it is understood that the deeper meaning is bound up in the contradiction. In short, the paradox is seen as a key to a deeper meaning that cannot be fathomed by the intellect.

The best-known symbol of this kind in the West is the concept of Christ as understood in mainstream, traditional Christian thought. Jesus as the Christ is a unique god-man figure. Unlike the semi-divine figures of mixed parentage in Greek mythology, he is seen as fully human and therefore not divine, but also fully divine and therefore not human. This is indeed a powerful image, all the more so because it is intellectually incomprehensible. To preserve the power, the leaders of the church began at an early point to brand as heresy any doctrinal deviation that goes either in a unitarian direction (which eliminates the divine side of the paradox) or in the direction chosen by some gnostics (who considered Christ purely divine and denied his human side). The so-called primitive may handle the paradox more comfortably than we do. He may regard the moon as simultaneously man, woman, and evil spirit. He may encounter in the desert a coyote which, though pure animal, engages him for the moment in a profound philosophical dialog. His mythic symbols do not have the same emotional impact on us that they have on him, and we view them as a bit of nonsensical thinking. We need to bear in mind, however, that these mythic symbols represent a mode of thinking and a mode of consciousness that we have recently begun to suppress, and we need to ask whether we have taken a useful step or whether we have lost something of great value (or whether both of these possibilities are at the same time true).

One of the hazards in regarding anything that differs from modern Western thought as being less highly evolved or more primitive is that we end up equating highly evolved consciousness with rationality and view the more symbolic modes as necessarily a bit primitive. It is possible, however, to distinguish degrees or levels of development in the symbolic mode just as it is in rational thinking. Perhaps the true primitive is underdeveloped in either respect. The concrete quality noted by various theorists as a mark of primitive thinking really implies a kind of literal-mindedness. The individual who displays this quality clings to a single egocentric interpretation of each facet of reality. Even though the notion to which he or she clings is paradoxical, the individual is unable to appreciate the symbolic, figurative, or metaphorical implications of the paradox. From the primitive level, thought can develop toward either a greater realization of abstract rationality or a greater realization of the symbolic and imaginative. In the West, we have developed in a one-sidedly rational way. We have allowed our symbols to stagnate and decay, and both the fundamentalist and the intellectual have hastened their demise by literalizing them. We have no greater appreciation of the symbolic than the primitive does, but some of the people we have labeled primitive have actually evolved along this path further than we have.

ANIMISM

Many writers have noted that alongside the concretistic tendency of primitive thought we generally find a contrasting tendency that is most often called animism. *Animism* refers to a tendency to regard physical objects and phenomenon as having the properties of living organisms, or as being endowed with life, consciousness, will, emotions, feeling, sensations, and so forth. Piaget (1929) noted this tendency in small children and regarded it, like realism, as a consequence of the child's egocentrism.

Anthropologists have long noted similar tendencies in the thinking of primitive people. Franz Boas (1921) said that primitives tend to perceive the sky and weather in organic terms and that they view nature generally in an anthropomorphic way. While we strive to understand the world in a rational, intellectual manner, the primitive's impressions are pervasively colored with subjective associations. Similarly, Heinz Werner (1948) notes that in the experience of children and primitives things are colored by moods and other lifelike qualities attributed to them by the perceiver. Werner speaks of this as *physiognomic perception*.

Akin to animism is a tendency, frequently noted by observers of primitives, to regard nature as permeated by a mystic reality, energy, power, soul, spirit, or life principle. There seems to be no adequate way of rendering the idea in English, and yet the idea is recognized independently by people all over the world. The best known name for it, *mana*, comes from Melanesia. In British New Guinea, it is known as *imunu*. To the African Bushman it is *ntum*, while to the Pygmy it is *megbe*. Among the Algonquian, Sioux, Iroquois, and Pawnee tribes respectively it has been called *manito, waken, orenda,* and *tirawa*. While the principle or essence is usually regarded as ubiquitous, it is also commonly viewed as something that can be concentrated in a given person or object to a high degree, with effects that may be either beneficial or harmful.

The Western Outlook

To label as primitive a tendency to attribute lifelike qualities to nature in general or to inanimate objects is equivalent to saying that a mature, civilized outlook requires a distinction between the animate and the inanimate. To the extent that this distinction represents a Western perspective, however, we run the risk of replacing anthropomorphism with ethnocentrism. An animistic outlook was apparent in Greek mythology, but the classical Greek philosophers sought to eliminate it, at least formally, from their own thinking. They struggled with the distinction between living and nonliving matter and were interested in the underlying elements of matter in general. The quest launched by the Greeks led ultimately to the modern sciences of biology and biochemistry, but as these sciences have developed it has become increasingly clear that no sharp line can be drawn between the animate and the inanimate realms of matter. In the main, however, this has not led to a reinstatement of animism, but rather to what might be called *inanimism*. In recent centuries, Western scientists have leaned toward a kind of mechanistic reductionism, toward the view that the properties of living organisms can best be understood through an analysis of their constituents. To the extent that we reduce the principles of biology to those of chemistry and those of chemistry to those of physics, however, we are left with no properties unique to living organisms. Indeed, rather than attributing life to nonliving things, we tend to see animals and people as merely very complicated machines. At times, this tendency has taken the form of denying the qualities of consciousness and feeling to other animals, but continuing to see people as special in some way. This outlook is apparent in some philosophers of the Enlightenment, as well as in modern psychologists who caution against anthropomorphism in the interpretation of animal experiments. George Leonard (1971) believes there is a widespread tendency in our society to view everything as dead, people as well as animals, and that this is linked to a tendency toward an abstracting, "objective" detachment that shows little regard for matter in any form. For those who have adopted this outlook, it becomes relatively easy to take part in modern mass warfare in which we can gloss over subtle distinctions between men, women, children, old people, peasants, and soldiers, confining our interest to the all-important body count of "combatants" that we managed to "waste" in a given day of military effort.

The historical tapestry of Western thought is woven of many threads. There was a mixture of views in classical Greece. For the most part, as the Greeks moved away from animism, they still recognized the kinship of all life forms. This view was denounced in some forms of Christian teaching, which held that only human beings possessed souls. Such a position easily leads to the idea of a qualitative separation between human and other forms of life and between human experience and animal experience. Yet in Christian thought we also find an occasional figure like Saint Francis of Assisi, whose sense of kinship not only with animals but with all parts of nature appears to be profoundly animistic. Saint Francis may represent what is best in Christianity, but as we know all too well, he does not represent what is typical in Christian thought or practice. The animistic view has been suppressed in both Christian and scientific thought, but as a countercurrent it has reappeared many times in the writings of mystics and poets. It certainly appeals to a large segment of our present-day society, and it may well represent the wave of the future. On rational grounds, the notion that mind is confined to certain living organisms is not really any more defensible than the notion that mind is present everywhere. A discernible bit of animism is evident in some of the components of the "Aquarian" spiritual movement of our time—in the ecology movement, in the speculation about the psychic life of plants, and in some of the occult doctrines that have become increasingly popular.

The rejection of animism in the West has been accompanied by an adherence to a monotheism that centers around a personal god. The concept of *mana* is closer to animism and to pantheism, and we view it as primitive. Yet the traditional doctrines of the Orient, whether stated in terms of brahman or tao, are closer to the primitive concept of *mana* than to the central idea of the Judeo-Christian tradition. In recent centuries in the West, ideas that resemble Eastern views have been formulated by such leading philosophers as Leibniz, Bergson, and James, and in this century many people in our society have turned to Eastern philosophy and practices, finding there is something that seems to be missing from Western thought. It is my own suspicion that even in the Christian churches, there is a gradual movement away from a narrowly personalistic theism to a more pantheistic orientation. Perhaps we shall come to regard animism not as something we have successfully outgrown but as something we have not yet adequately realized.

SIMPLER SOCIETIES IN THE MODERN WORLD

The literature on primitive thought shows a fair amount of consistency with respect to the characteristics that are considered primitive. This consistency implies that there is a single dimension along which we can distinguish levels that are uniformly high or low and that the people of any given society might be characterized fairly adequately in terms of a single point on the continuum. The fact that the qualities discussed in the literature are abstracted from observations of many different peoples lends support to the idea that there is just one basic dimension that applies universally.

To gain a clearer sense of the dimensionality of the qualities that separate primitive from advanced thinking or primitive from civilized people, however, we need a clearer picture of the total range of psychological characteristics of the people that have been regarded as representing primitive levels of human consciousness. In relying on the observations of other people, of course, we must be prepared to allow for the inevitable biases that color any effort to gain global impressions of a whole society. The most obvious tendency is to perceive a group of people considered primitive as being primitive in every respect. Indeed, ethnocentrism tends to be accompanied by *theriomorphism*, a tendency to see the people one observes as more animal-like than human. This bias is almost necessary if one is going to justify the maintenance of slavery or harsh colonial exploitation. In the present day, the bias facilitates the conduct of a war. In Vietnam, American soldiers often learned to regard the native inhabitants of that country, regardless of age, sex, or rank, as mere "gooks," and this attitude was consistent with overall military policy. In a classically naive instance of projection, one American general dismissed with a shrug the massive slaughter of Vietnamese civilians by American air power, noting that "those people" do not have much regard for individual human life anyway.

Unfortunately, even a social scientist with more benign intent is capable of similar misperceptions, regarding the presumed primitive as childlike or animal-like in realms of behavior where he or she functions much the way we do ourselves. Certainly some of the early anthropologists made this mistake. Carl Jung, too, was guilty of the error in some of his early writings, when his ideas of primitive people were not yet tempered by any direct contact with them. Thus, in *Psychological Types* he cites a (probably apocryphal) account of a bushman who killed his own son, contending that the love experienced by such primitive people is completely "autoerotic" and amounts to a "tender monkey-love" (Jung, 1971).

Despite the widespread presence of such a bias, accounts of primitive societies contain accounts of many remarkable feats, involving abilities that would be difficult for people in our society to match. Some of these involve telepathic communication. Others involve a high level of intuition or immediate apprehension and rapid interpretation of a complex set of conditions. Some involve a capacity for accurately apprehending and remembering concrete details, a capacity that we have apparently lost in the course of moving to a greater emphasis on the abstract and general. Thus, a preliterate herdsman may be able to recognize individually any member of his flock of several hundred cattle or sheep. He may possess a detailed and intimate knowledge of the appearance and properties of hundreds of different plants growing in his region. In more than one primitive group, it has been found that each member can readily identify the individual footprints of everyone else in the group. The members of a group may have a detailed knowledge of the desert or jungle territory which they inhabit, being able to recognize individual trees, hillocks, clearings, ravines, and so forth, even if the territory covers hundreds of square miles. Through specialization, they may cultivate a highly developed set of skills. Thus, the Polynesian mariners were the world's greatest navigators for centuries before they came into contact with the wonders of modern civilization, and they still merit this reputation. They can navigate over distances of hundreds of miles in the ocean from one small island to another. For this purpose, they use a knowledge of horizon stars to determine latitudes, but they also make use of a "wave compass" (ascertaining the direction of currents from wave patterns), note wind and cloud movements, recognize cloud patterns that tend to be associated with land masses, and derive inferences from the color, temperature, and salinity of the water in which they are traveling.

The Kung Bushmen

Some noteworthy achievements have been noted even among the people who seem most primitive by our standards. Such groups would include the Kung bushmen of the Kalahari Desert, the African Pygmies, the Tasaday of the Philippines, and several other groups living in tropical forests of Southern Asia. In each of these groups we find the basic ingredients of Stone-Age culture: the procurement of food through hunting and gathering, the use of a few simple tools, and a minimum of clothing. Even these traits cease to appear so simple when we examine their expression more closely. The Kung bushmen have shown themselves to be remarkably ingenious at coping with the demands of the Kalahari Desert (cf. van der Post, 1958). In a region of extreme dryness they have developed a knack for "sipping" water from the ground in spots where the sandy soil is damp. They have such an intimate knowledge of the ways of the animals in their region that they seem to know how each one thinks. They show little fear of the lions that share their habitat and will occasionally use lions to kill the prey that they hunt, by driving the prey in the direction of a lion. They commonly manage to locate honey by following small birds that serve as honey-diviners, leading them to hives. They have an intimate knowledge of the plants of their area and are familiar with their potential uses for food, glue, dyes, medicine, and so forth.

According to Laurens van der Post, they have a detailed

knowledge of the hundreds of square miles of desert over which they roam. Though the region looks quite homogeneous to whites who enter it, the bushmen apparently know precisely where they are at any moment in the course of a lengthy hunt and can return to camp with an unerring sense of direction. They have an unusual ability to read the tracks left by animals, birds, insects, and people, so that they can readily identify the print of any specific individual. Seeing the print of an animal, they can tell when the print was made, what species of animal made it, and the age, sex, build, and mood of the animal.

The talents of the bushmen also include noteworthy skills for the manufacture of such practical goods as ropes and weapons. Their artistic gifts are evident in rock paintings that have accumulated in their region over the past 3,000 years. Like other peoples of Africa, they possess a vast spoken literature, rich in folklore. Van der Post (1955) believes that Westerners have much to learn from primitives like the bushmen, who retain their contact with the natural, instinctual realm. The love and care they display for one another stand in sharp contrast to the rather limited "autoerotic" love that Jung suggested was characteristic of primitive people. In *A Mantis Carol* (1975), van der Post focuses on one specific bushman, Hans Taaibosch, who had been uprooted from his people and spent his later years in New York. Van der Post believes that Taaibosch was most clearly distinguished by his capacity for freely loving other people and that the people of our society have lost this capacity for the most part, because they are afraid of love. Perhaps another mark of the intimacy of which the bushmen are capable is their evident ability to maintain telepathic communication with one another no matter where they are. Van der Post (1958) has described an occasion when he accompanied a hunting party that traveled at least fifty miles away from their camp over a period of days. When they returned to camp, it was clear that those who had remained at the camp knew well in advance that the hunters had killed an eland and were bringing it back to the camp with them.

While there may be variation from one society to another in overall level of consciousness, it is interesting that one feature that appears to be universal among human societies is a recognized need for people to seek periodic release from their usual state of consciousness and enter into an altered state that is less rational, less ordered, and less attuned to everyday reality. The means vary, but they frequently include some form of meditation or the use of a psychedelic plant or drug. Sometimes the effect is achieved through rhythmic movement of the sort seen in the trance dance of the bushmen (Campbell, 1983). In the dance, the men of the group circle about a fire through the night as the women clap and chant. Through this practice the dancers endeavor to activate and concentrate *ntum*, or spiritual power, which can be used for healing purposes. After a long period of dancing the dancers enter into a trance. In doing so, the younger men usually fall down in a comatose condition, or state of "half death." The older men have learned how to gain and maintain more control over the force of *ntum* and may manifest unusual powers in a trance state, being able, for example, to pick burning brands from the fire and rub them over their bodies. Some of the inner experiences reported by the bushman dancers bear a striking similarity to accounts that turn up in other cultures. For example, they speak of the *ntum* as rising up the spinal column, much as the *kundalini* is said to rise in the accounts of yogis in India. They speak also of spiritual journeys in a trance state that are very similar to journeys reported by shamans of other cultures.

Shamanism

Shamanic practices are of particular importance for our subject because they represent a way of deliberately altering and regulating consciousness that is both very widespread culturally and very ancient. While there are many elements in the procedures and associated myths that are specific to particular cultural settings, these overlie features that are so universal that one cannot help suspecting they are rooted in the very nature of human consciousness. The term *shaman* apparently comes from the language of the Tungus people of Siberia (Harner, 1980). It was first applied by anthropologists to the medicine men found in that society, but it was obvious that in essential features these differed little from comparable individuals found in neighboring societies. Indeed, allowing for a bit more variation, we can find men or women playing basically the same kind of role in societies throughout the world. For this reason, the term has come to be applied to all individuals of non-Western societies that have been known in the past by such terms as witch, witch-doctor, medicine man, sorcerer, wizard, magician, and seer. Whatever the cultural setting, the shaman is essentially an individual who has developed an ability to enter an altered state of consciousness at will, and who uses this ability to cure the illnesses of others, to find solutions for tribal problems, to gain power, or to acquire knowledge from the hidden reality he or she is able to enter through a change in consciousness.

There is much evidence to suggest that shamanism predates recorded history by thousands of years (Halifax, 1982). It appears to have originated in the paleolithic period in hunting societies, and it is always associated with animal motifs that link it to the world of the hunt. Campbell (1983) notes that many of the features of the paleolithic cave paintings found in Europe strongly imply shamanic practices. He suggests, in fact, that thousands of years ago some of the shamanic practices of hunting societies spread from the Eurasian continent south through Africa and, to the east, across Beringland and down through the Americas. We do find a ritual use of ecstatic experiences among people ranging from the bushmen in the southern part of Africa to the tribes of Tierra del Fuego at the southern tip of South America. There can be little doubt that practices associated with bear cults spread through northern Europe and Siberia into the Americas. It is less clear that all shamanic practices point to early diffusion from a single point of origin. Even if this is the case, diffusion alone cannot explain the fact that shamanic practices are so widespread and have persisted so long. It is clear that these practices have struck a resounding chord in the human psyche wherever they have appeared, and there may well be something in our nature that made their appearance almost inevitable.

It is not only the animal symbolism of shamanism that ties it to hunting societies. As Campbell (1969) notes, shamanism entails a certain emphasis on individualism, for the shaman seeks a very solitary kind of experience that may set him or her apart from the rest of the group. The individualistic principle becomes important in the world of the hunt in a way in which it was not important in earlier gathering societies and is not important in subsequent agricultural societies. In some hunting societies (e.g., among some North American Indians) the individualistic theme that figures prominently in the initiation of the shaman spread into the puberty rites for all youths, who may be expected to undertake individual vision quests to attain manhood. On the other hand, shamanism is not confined to hunting societies. Once it has appeared, it may persist in many essential features through the development of agriculture and the advent of the city-state. This would indicate that it serves a need that goes well beyond the world of the hunt. As the society evolves, the mythic symbolism associated with shamanism changes, and the roles of the shaman may evolve as well. It would be a mistake to assume that shamanism represents just one stage either in the evolution of human society or in the evolution of human consciousness.

The Beliefs of Shamanistic Societies

Despite cultural variation in details, there are certain mythic belief elements that tend to accompany shamanism throughout the world. The shaman is recognized as having something more than an ordinary human identity. Commonly the shaman is identified with an animal of importance to the group. The animal is usually a large, untamed source of food and clothing. Along with this animal identity, the shaman may have other kinds of animals as assistants. The shaman may also be regarded as having an interspecies identity—between that of humans and that of gods—and is often thought to be capable of transformation at will into various forms that correspond to the nonhuman facets of his or her identity. Such an individual is obviously uniquely qualified to serve as a channel for the transmission of knowledge or power from the natural or spiritual realm to the ordinary human realm.

In the view of shamanistic societies there is a life energy or spiritual power underlying everything that we see in the world (the pervasive essence I noted earlier in the section on animism), and the basic talent of the shaman can be understood in terms of an ability to concentrate and channel that energy and an ability to cope effectively with it when confronted with beings using it in a destructive way. As we might expect, this view tends to be accompanied by an animistic view of nature in general. Trees, plants, rocks, and bodies of water, as well as people and animals, are seen as having personal identities.

Of special importance are the realms that lie beyond the ordinary, observable reality of people and nature. Nevill Drury (1982) and Joan Halifax (1982) both note that people in shamanistic societies commonly think in terms of a universe composed of three levels, or worlds, and often view these as linked by a world, or cosmic, tree. Michael Harner (1980) notes also that certain kinds of spirits are encountered universally in the journeys of the shaman, and that a mandala composed of concentric circles is also found in many societies to represent the realm to which the shaman travels in a trance. Actually, all of this mythic symbolism is quite universal and hardly confined to shamanistic societies. In the three-world scheme, the ordinary world is the middle realm. Outside this, there is an upper spiritual realm and a lower spiritual realm, often associated with death. This earth-heaven-hell scheme is familiar to us from its expression in both Judeo-Christian and Greek mythology. The shaman is believed capable of traveling to the spiritual realms, either in the sky or deep in the earth. Such journeys also figure in the mythology and literature of the Western world, but in shamanistic societies they are viewed as a common occurrence. The symbolism of the tree, whose roots extend deep down into the earth and whose branches reach up toward heaven, is also universal, and its spiritual significance is evident in the cross of Christianity and the Bodhi tree under which Gautama sat when he achieved enlightenment.

The Practices and Lives of Shamans

The journey of the shaman, of course, is an inward journey that usually entails a well-defined procedure of induction. The procedure may involve dancing, solitary retreat, psychedelic drugs, or a repetitive drumbeat. Sleep deprivation, fasting, suspended breathing, and many of the procedures associated with Eastern meditative practice may be employed. By these and other means the shaman enters a special state of consciousness, or trance, in which he or she can experience a journey to another realm or communicate with beings who dwell outside ordinary reality. In contrast to the schizophrenic, or even the usual spiritual medium, the shaman has great control over the trance state, can freely explore whatever realms are opened through the state, and can retain a complete memory of the experience. Commonly as a result of long practice, the shaman may be able to enter and leave the trance at any time without resorting to a special procedure.

The original introduction of the shaman to the spiritual realms often involves an initiation that is far more dramatic in form and content than the journeys subsequently taken. Initiation may occur in early adolescence, but it is possible at any later point in life. To become a shaman, the individual may be subjected to isolation, prolonged fasting, and near-death from exposure to heat or freezing temperatures. Initiation may come about through dreams or through visions brought on by extreme physical deprivations. It may involve a psychological crisis that has all the earmarks of a profound psychosis. It may involve physical illness, often quite serious and possibly lasting for as long as a year. The shamans themselves may describe their initiation in terms of death and subsequent reawakening, and sometimes in terms of being devoured, dismembered, or mutilated by a demon or animal. Some initiation practices involve painful mutilations of the body, but this theme often appears in a mythic form, with the tortures imposed by spirits of various kinds. In general, the initiation tends to be seen in terms of a solitary suffering that prepares the individual for a life that demands more independence and courage than are needed by an ordinary member of the community. The initiation may occur only once, but often the shaman is said to go through such a process periodically, progressing at various points in life to deeper levels of spiritual realization.

The shaman is usually seen as a unique member of the group. The role is not one that everyone is capable of assuming. A special sensitivity evident in childhood or adolescence may mark a particular individual as a likely candidate for the life of a shaman, but the initial trial, crisis, or initiation will determine whether the essential gifts and endurance are really present. Initiation into the role may involve a period of great physical and psychological instability, but it is recognized that in a true shaman unusual strengths will result. The individual who proves worthy to be a shaman may emerge with a high level of stability and may well appear to be the most competent member of the group in a variety of ways. Often highly intelligent and knowledgeable, the shaman usually remains psychologically grounded by taking part in all the usual social and economic pursuits of the community.

The sophistication of the shaman extends to the nature of the mythic symbolism bound up in the shamanic role. More deeply than other community members, the shaman recognizes the mythic symbols for what they are and is adept at thinking in images. The deeper the experience of the shaman, the more he or she realizes that the account of the inward journey in mythic terms is only a way of rendering it somewhat intelligible to others, and that the deeper reality actually experienced cannot be described in words. With this realization, the shaman may resort to various tricks and fabrications to impress, intimidate, or mislead nosy anthropologists, as well as the simpler or more boorish members of his or her own community. The healing practices of the shaman may also involve a few tricks, such as pretending to draw stones, bugs, and various other objects from the bodies of ailing individuals. Undoubtedly, as placebos, these tricks are often quite helpful.

Many observers of shamanic practices are convinced that some shamans have developed very unusual psychic abilities. They not only develop extensive contact with an inner realm that remains unconscious for most people, but they may manifest telepathic, clairvoyant, or precognitive abilities to a high degree. The basic experience sought by the shaman is clearly of the mystical kind, and it has been suggested that it represents on a primitive level the same sort of experience sought by mystics of the more highly evolved societies of Eastern and Western culture. We may ask, however, by what right we would label a form of mysticism as primitive merely by virtue of its occurrence in a society that is relatively simple. Surely the fact that people in the surrounding community hunt bears or plant corn with the aid of a digging stick, rather than operating computers or engaging in abstruse philosophical debates, tells us nothing about the nature of the mystical experience itself. David Paladin, who had surveyed the shamanic practices and traditions of many societies, once told me that shamans in general are seeking an experience of unity, or mystical transcendence, an experience devoid of specific image content that cannot be described in ordinary language. To the extent that this is true, the shaman seems little different from the yogi of Hindu culture. In the course of a lifetime, the shaman may move toward a profound mystical experience through successive approximations, and the depth of spiritual realization is likely to vary from one shaman to another, as well as from one shamanistic society to another. Whatever the societal context, the mystic moves toward an experience that is truly universal. The specific practices and myths of the particular society are relevant insofar as they encourage or discourage the spiritual quest and color the early experiences once the quest has begun, but ultimately the mystic transcends the specific culture, and it may not matter too much in what cultural setting the whole process began.

Communication with Animals

The psychological talents that impress us when we encounter them in preliterate and pretechnological societies are not confined to the gifts of shamans. One of the talents commonly noted in people who remain closer to nature is an apparent ability to communicate with other species in ways that seem mysterious to us. We are accustomed to thinking of other species as either qualitatively different from us or as simply so inferior intellectually that only limited communication is possible. Since we assume that "real thinking" and "real communication" must of necessity involve the kind of rational, linear processing for which our languages are so well suited, most of our scientific efforts to explore the possibilities of inter-species communication between humans and other creatures have entailed some attempt to see whether we can teach them to communicate the way we do. Under these conditions the anthropoid apes achieve modest success, provided we extend them the courtesy of allowing them to speak manually rather than vocally.

In the literature of our own society there have been many anecdotal, and therefore less rigorously scientific, accounts of highly successful efforts to communicate with animals (e.g., Boone, 1954). The interesting thing about these is that very often the nonpsychologists responsible for the efforts have taken it for granted that other species do not communicate in the same way we do and that, if one wants to do something more than mere animal training, it is necessary to stop spouting words, perhaps even stop thinking in words. With this precondition, one may achieve a direct telepathic communication not only with other people but with other species as well.

Lyall Watson (1979) cites a couple of apparent instances of this in simpler societies. The first is an account by Arthur Grimble of an incident on the northernmost atoll of the Gilbert Islands. Grimble joined the villagers on a day arranged weeks in advance. At the appointed time, the porpoise-caller of the village lay on the beach summoning the porpoises "in a dream." In the late afternoon, as thousands of people stood waiting, there was a cry announcing the arrival of their friends from the sea. Then an immense shoal or porpoises, streaming in from the water, began to crawl up onto the beach, as the villagers greeted them with soft clapping and soothing words, embracing them now and then to help ease them over the ridges of sand.

In the second instance Watson describes an experience of his own. While staying for a while in a fishing village on an Indonesian Island, he came to know a man called the *djuru*, a man known for his ability to locate and identify fish underwater, even in the dark, just by immersing his head and listening. While living there, Watson had an opportunity to observe many large green marine turtles come to the island, but he hoped at some time to see a specimen of the largest variety of sea turtle, the rare leatherback *Dermochelys coriacea*. He mentioned his desire to the *djuru*, who promised to show him one. In fact, the *djuru* said, "I will dream one for you." About a month later, the *djuru* informed Watson that his wish would be fulfilled later that day. In the afternoon the two of them went to a secluded corner inside the reef, where the *djuru* crouched at the water's edge waving his hands and fingers through the water for about twenty minutes. Then the great shape of the leatherback came gliding toward them through the water. Four or five times, the great turtle swam and gently rolled over past the two men. Then she beached and moved toward the *djuru*, who held one hand out of the water toward her. Thereupon she raised her head, nibbled at his fingers, turned, and swam back through the gateway of the lagoon and into the open sea. If we take such accounts seriously, we may heave a sigh while entertaining the thought that a loss of this kind of contact with nature is the price we have paid for building an advanced civilization. If we are willing to forego this bit of self-indulgence, it may occur to us that our own ancestors probably lacked such talents. In all likelihood, these dreamers of the Pacific represent an alternative, rather than a prelude, to the kind of civilization in which we live.

4

The Psychic Development of the Western World

Now that we have considered the prehistory of consciousness and the developments apparent in some simpler societies, it is time to consider the development of consciousness in people of the more complex civilizations of the East and West. This is not an easy task, for in both parts of the world we are dealing with extremely heterogeneous cultures, and within any one society at any one time we find much variation, with different groups of people thinking and experiencing the world in markedly different ways. Furthermore, the East-West distinction itself is an arbitrary one, with a boundary that can be drawn in various ways to separate two cultural regions that have never been completely isolated from each other. At all known times in history and on back through the stretches of prehistoric time, there has been movement across boundaries. Ideas have been transmitted from East to West and from West to East, often undergoing a succession of reinterpretations as they were absorbed by different peoples. If I draw a distinction now between East and West, it is only for the sake of convenience. In some sense, there is undoubtedly an underlying unity and consistency to human culture and perhaps to the psychic evolution of humanity, but it is easy to be dazzled and confused by all the fluctuation and multiformity that we see on the surface, and we need to simplify the chore of sifting through this multiverse.

To discern major transitions in the consciousness of a people, we must shift through a great mass of historical facts and identify those that afford useful clues. The changing modes in the arts, in mythology and religion, and in philosophy and science are of greater interest than the usual political history. We must still determine, however, when a change in aesthetic or intellectual fashion represents a fundamental change in experience. In general, there are three kinds of evidence that would point to an augmented or transformed consciousness. The first would be evidence of a new mode of awareness—perhaps a kind of perceptiveness not previously manifest, a fresh mode of understanding, a psychic facility, a way of relating to symbols, or something in the realm of rational judgment. A second would be evidence of a change in the way in which people view themselves—a change in the kind or range of content by which they define themselves, perhaps a corresponding change in the experience of will, choice, and responsibility. The third would be evidence of change in the experience of the "other," a change in the qualities not recognized as part of ourselves but attributed to other people, gods, idealized images, animals, and nature. Within the realm of the other, there may be changes with respect to the division between those characteristics viewed as strictly alien and those viewed as our own unrealized potential.

Changes in Mythic Images

Many of the important shifts in views of self and other are reflected in the progression of mythic images over time. An idea often expressed by writers steeped in the Judeo-Christian tradition is that there is a natural movement from polytheism to monotheism, the latter representing the highest development of religion, but the advocates of this position overgeneralize from a simplistic reading of their own history. We have seen that the so-called primitive may view the world as inhabited by a host of spirits but maintain at the same time a notion of a unitary underlying energy or life force that pervades everything. A simultaneous appreciation of the divine in unitary and multiple forms is not confined to primitive people, and at any one point in the history of a people there may be factors that will tend to promote either the single grand image or a multiplicity of images. Factors leading in both directions were present from the earliest stage at which mythic images began to take an anthropomorphic form. At times people have attached greater significance to one central figure; at other times the host has been accorded greater attention.

Perhaps a more reliable indicator of a shift in consciousness is a change in the nature of the god. A progression often seen is from a god who is remote, or transcendent, of a nature far removed from that of ordinary mortals, to a being closer to the human realm. In Christianity, the transcendent god becomes a god incarnate. In other cultures, the figure that is originally remote is converted in the course of successive generations of myth-tellers to a human hero, perhaps passing through a semidivine existence along the way. Several intermediate steps are possible. The god who is relatively indifferent to the human realm may become a champion of humankind, initiating human consciousness, through a gift of fire or the equivalent. Later the divine champion is replaced by a semidivine hero, who may be mortal or immortal and who lives a human existence but performs superhuman deeds. In a later retelling this figure becomes just an exceptional mortal, and ultimately an ordinary mortal whose fate it is to perform a great deed.

In this progression, the qualities and deeds may become trivialized, and new mythic images may assume the importance that this one once had. To the extent that the qualities and deeds of the god remain unaltered in the course of humanization, the progression points to an expansion of consciousness, an increasing recognition that the power once attributed to the gods lies within the range of human potentials. In Jungian terms, this would mean that a greater portion of the total self has been incorporated into the ego. This kind of progression tends to be accompanied by a change in the experience of causality and fate. At an early stage, events are regarded as governed largely by the gods, by fate, or by unknown forces that may be benevolent, malevolent, or indifferent to human needs. At a later point, more events may be seen as under human control, but it is the group, the society with all its traditions and customs, that has power. Further evolution of the individual ego is required for an experience of clear separation between the individual and society. Then individual will and choice, which were once experienced only in the minor decision of the moment, become a significant factor in the direction of one's life as a whole.

There may also be change in the way in which the image of the divine is interpreted. The image may be taken quite literally and regarded as an accurate representation of the divine. The alternative is to recognize the image as a symbol or metaphor, which points to a realm that cannot be fully grasped or directly represented in a simpler way. In most societies, popular religion tends to be more literalistic than the religion of the intellectual or spiritual elite. On the whole, the Judaic and Christian traditions of the West tend toward greater literalism than do most religious traditions of the Orient. In modern times, literalism is equally apparent in the Christian fundamentalist and in the scientifically oriented atheist, whose position presupposes a theistic god that is first construed literally and then denied. Among the serious scholars of the Hindu and Buddhist traditions, this has never been an issue, for literalism has always been viewed as a bit absurd, an error that tempts only the unsophisticated person. As a Zen Buddhist once remarked, "There is a Buddha for those who do not know what he really is; there is no Buddha for those who do know what he is."

A somewhat different issue concerns the ultimate nature of the divine or the nature of its ultimate realization. Here we have the various positions embraced by such theological concepts as transcendence and immanence. Deists, theists, atheists, and Eastern mystics would all have somewhat different views on the question of how our conception of the divine shifts as we become more enlightened or aware, and some of these views are evident in treatments of the evolution of consciousness.

THE GREEK LEGACY

Most of the important developments in Western civilization over the past two thousand years have roots in the advanced cultures that ranged around the Eastern end of the Mediterranean Ocean in early times. The contributions of Greek and Hebrew culture are of particular importance, but contributions emanating from ancient Egypt, Iran, and Mesopotamia also had a significant influence on Western cultural development in general. The ancient culture that we now recognize as Greek represents in itself a blend of influences. We know that many gods and goddesses figured in the thinking of the Greeks prior to the emergence of the major philosophical thinkers of that country, but the pantheon depicted in the early writings of Homer (who was probably two or more people) and Hesiod represents only one period in the consolidation and evolution of that system.

Greek Mythology

From all available evidence, it appears that at one time the dominant mythic figure in Greece and in most or all of the neighboring cultures was the mother goddess. She was known by a different name in each culture, but there is little doubt that this basic idea arose in many settings at an early stage in mythic thinking. As the Hellenic people moved into Greece and extended their influence over a broader region, they assimilated many of the figures of local mythologies into their own system. A number of the female deities that we now recognize as a part of the Greek pantheon originated as local variants of the Great Mother, their character and rank having been altered as they were absorbed into a larger system. This description certainly applies to Gaea, Hera, and Demeter, but these are merely the most obvious cases. Over time, the mother goddess, by whatever name, was accorded reduced attention, and a more patriarchal pantheon emerged. The pairing of Gaea and Uranus as the goddess and god of a creation myth may have been an early step in this direction. Eventually, Zeus emerged as the supreme figure in the pantheon, with Hera, who had once been the all-important Great Mother, playing the role of a faithful and subordinate, though sometimes resentful, wife.

The shift from matriarchy to patriarchy, which can be seen as well in many other mythologies, has sometimes been interpreted as a reflection of a corresponding shift in the structure of human societies, but this seems unlikely. A mythology centering around the Great Mother does not really presuppose a society governed by women. It is more likely that the shift reflects a change in the conscious orientation of the people those minds furnish and maintain the myths. The mother goddess creates by letting nature take its course and by being at the heart of nature. She gestates, gives birth, lactates, and nourishes at a bountiful breast. The patriarchal god creates by acting upon nature. As infants we all move from the matriarchal to the patriarchal realm as we abandon a state of close union with the mother and enter a world of power interplay, where our efforts are either encouraged or opposed by controlling adults. The change appears to us to be determined by the dictates of the gods who rule our household, but these gods are simply responding to the fact that we have begun to explore, manipulate, and interact with the environment more extensively.

In a similar fashion, our ancestors, Greek and otherwise, shifted their attention from the mother goddess to the dominant figures of a patriarchal pantheon as they ceased to experience the world in terms of a total dependence on the uncertain bounty of nature. The patriarchy expresses the experience of a people who have begun to think in terms of a more active manipulation of a world in which their efforts may be abetted or foiled by the gods of nature. This constitutes a step toward an experience of active will, but it is only a small step if will is attributed to the gods but still not regarded as something the individual can claim as a personal attribute. In Greek mythology the emergence of Prometheus, a figure who ultimately overshadowed Zeus in importance, represents a further development. Though still a god, a Titan, himself, Prometheus fosters the consciousness of people. By bringing fire from the heavens to earth, he provides for us the power to creatively transform, to bring light into regions of darkness, and thus to know, to foresee, and to act in a deliberate and planful way in the world. This deed sets the stage for the human hero to assume a more active role in myth and legend and to pursue various projects and adventures, with or without the assistance of the gods. Homer's *Odyssey* is the story of a human hero seeking to establish his own identity. In the process, he is harried by Poseidon and aided by Athena, but his ultimate success is a product of his own awareness and willful action. The *Odyssey* and the later works of such classical writers as Sophocles probably reflect a very late stage in the mythic thought of Greece.

The Cults

The gods do not die an easy death. There is a tendency for the god to be replaced in myth by a human figure as consciousness expands, and the story of the human hero serves as a prototypal guide for individual human development. We tend to reinvoke the god, however, when we are confronted with a mystery or a crisis that we cannot penetrate and resolve with the power of conscious rationality. The human hero may be deified and cease to serve primarily as a model for our own action and growth. An example of this process late in the era of Greek mythology was the emergence of the Orphic cult. It is possible that the stories of Orpheus originated with an historical individual who, like Jesus and King Arthur, was mythicized after his death. In any case, we know of him through stories in which he appears as the supreme poet and musician of ancient Greece. Though unusually gifted, he was mortal—though of semidivine ancestry, according to some accounts of his life. In the best-known story of Orpheus, he lost his beloved wife, Euridyce, to the underworld and barely failed to retrieve her from that region. In utter despair he sat on the bank of a stream, where Thracian maidens, attracted by his beautiful singing, sought his attention in return. He repulsed their advances, however, and they tore him limb from limb.

The Orphic cult apparently grew out of an existing Dionysian cult in the fifth or sixth century B.C., and the god Dionysus played a prominent role in the thinking of the Orphics. He symbolized an imperishable spiritual element in humankind, and a doctrine of reincarnation, very similar to that found in Hinduism, evolved from his myth. According to legend, Orpheus was the founder of the cult, but there is more than an accidental parallel between the myths of Orpheus and Dionysus, and Orpheus himself can be viewed as a human double for the god. Like Orpheus and like Osiris in Egyptian mythology, Dionysus was torn to bits at one point and, like Osiris, he was subsequently reassembled. I have never read that Orpheus was successfully reassembled, but we are told that his head and lyre continued to produce music after he was ripped to shreds—hardly a feat of which many can boast. Not much is known about the ritual practices within the Orphic cult, but there is reason to believe that they included the ritual eating of flesh, which was regarded as the flesh of the dead god and symbolized the power of renewal. Many of the mythic elements that appeared in early Christianity undoubtedly had their roots in Orphism.

During the same period in Greece there was also a cult devoted to Kore and Demeter. The story of Kore, or Persephone, resembles that of Euridyce in that she too was lost to the god of the underworld, but she was ultimately returned to her grieving mother, Demeter. The recurrent disappearance and return of Kore is most readily understood symbolically in terms of a seasonal cycle, and the ritual practices associated with the story related primarily to the planting and harvesting of crops. It is possible to read a deeper meaning into the story, however, that connects it, like the stories of Orpheus and Dionysus, to the seasonal cycle of human life and the mystery of death.

Orphism appeared at about the same time that science and philosophy were born in the Western world. Like Greek philosophy as a whole and like the writings of the Brahmin priests of India, it represents a major step in the evolution of mythology, a movement away from the pure mythic image to a philosophical interpretation of the image. Greek philosophy on the whole, however, is rational and orderly, or in Nietzsche's terms, it is Apollonian. Orphism was not a rational cult, but rather a mystical one, whose adherents sought the kind of understanding made possible by a relinquishment of rationality. It is Dionysian rather than Apollonian. This element is not altogether lacking in Greek philosophy, however, for some of its most monumental figures, notably Pythagoras, had a mystical side that reflected an Orphic influence. To the extent that Greek philosophy stressed rationality, movements like the Orphic cult continued to arise and flourish in later centuries as a compensation for this intellectual emphasis.

Philosophy and Science

Western science and philosophy may be said to have begun in the sixth century B.C. with the work of Thales, who sought material answers to basic questions about the universe. Over a span of two or three hundred years, Thales was followed in the relatively small population of Greece by some of the greatest thinkers the world has yet known: Anaximander, Anaximenes,

Pythagoras, Xenophanes, Heraclitus, Parmenides, Empedocles, Anaxagoras, Zeno, Melissus, Democritus, Protagoras, Socrates, Plato, Aristotle, and others. These philosophers saw in the earlier myths an attempt to explain natural phenomena in a figurative way, and they sought a translation of mythic images into abstract principles and, to some extent, into concrete mechanisms. Broadly speaking, all the major developments of Western science and philosophy are anticipated in the work of classical Greek philosophers. All the basic questions about life and the universe are asked, and all of the most fundamental concepts and modes of explanation are employed to answer them. It is doubtful that any modern thinker, operating with only the limited information available to these philosophers, could improve significantly on their work.

The psychological climate of Greece appears to have been uniquely suited for the emergency of science and philosophy (see Russell, 1959). This development represents not just the beginning of a new set of ideas but the transition to a new mode of consciousness that started in one class of people and gradually spread to an ever larger population. Thales had asked about the ultimate nature of things and concluded that water was the one fundamental substance. This may seem naive to us, from the perspective of the twentieth century, but it reflects the sophisticated observation that water is essential for life and that it can be observed to pass through solid, liquid, and gaseous states. Both the question and answer reflect a new way of looking at things. To ask such a question is to assume that it is possible for people to identify underlying ingredients and unifying principles in terms of which they can make sense of things, animals, people, and the rest of the universe, and by which they can systematically describe all processes and relationships. The implications of this outlook are vast. If ideas are not just something to be handed on from one generation to the next and accepted on faith, if we regard ourselves as able to discover or invent ideas, to manipulate them logically and arrive at all sorts of novel combinations, and to test them against fresh experiences and observations, then what is to stop us from claiming all the wisdom of the gods as our own? Greek philosophy provided a totally new way of looking at the universe and at ourselves. On the one hand, it offered ways of describing people in terms of an early, materialistic, natural science (using such concepts as the four humors). On the other hand, it expressed a new confidence in the human will, in the capacity of people to understand and to take charge of themselves and their world.

Abstract principles, subject to gradual modification, lead to more precise explanation and understanding, but unlike the mythic images they replace, they cannot provide an emotional experience of connectedness to the sacred, to the great mystery of the universe. In Greece a counterbalance to the rise of science and philosophy was provided by the persistence of mystical cults, by oracles, by a widespread popular belief in demons, and by a growing interest in astrology. Greek philosophy itself, however, was not an atheistic enterprise. To be sure, the gods and goddesses of the pantheon tended to be translated into abstract concepts, but the colorful crew on Mount Olympus had already ceased to provide an adequate foundation for the religious needs of that time. In the writings of philosophers from Xenophanes through Aristotle, we find expression of a monotheism more universal than anything then current in Judaism. Like many writers of the Orient, Antisthenes argued that the deity cannot be adequately comprehended through an image, since his nature is unlike that of anything else.

There is always a danger that a god that is too highly abstracted and tied neither to image nor to vital experience will vanish into a maze of theological dogma. The mythic image, on the other hand, has a natural emotional power but poses the risk of literalistic absurdity. In the West, the interplay of image and concept has been with us for well over two thousand years.

Richard W. Coan

THE HEBRAIC LEGACY

The onset of the Christian era introduced the germ of a new phase of human consciousness in the Western world, but for almost two thousand years, the nature of this germ has remained a subject of debate. However we decide to characterize the novel element in Christianity, we must regard much of this movement as a blend of earlier traditions. Christianity is an outgrowth of Judaism, but it contains a considerable admixture of Greek, or Greco-Roman, thought, along with borrowings from some of the surrounding cultures. To gain a clearer picture of what Christianity represented at its inception, we must consider the Judaic, or Hebraic, tradition that preceded it.

The Hebrew Bible, or Old Testament, reflects stages in the development of Judaism extending over a span of about one thousand years. Some of the earliest of the books point to myths and traditions held in common by Jews and other Semitic peoples of the ancient world. The Bible contains a record of a gradually changing conception of God, bearing several names in the original Hebrew and manifesting qualities that may be traceable to the myths of different, though neighboring, tribal peoples. One of the names, *Elohim*, is plural. Though commonly rendered as *God* in English, it may have been understood originally as referring to a group, or perhaps a host, of divine beings. As a singular being, God was first understood as the god of a particular people, and the idea of a universal deity was a subsequent development. Even in his fully evolved form, the God of the Hebrew Bible remains a complex and somewhat contradictory figure, acting both as a loving, compassionate father and as a harsh, remote being who demands absolute obedience. This ambiguity underscores a moral dilemma long regarded in Judaic tradition as the lot of the human individual. Judaism assumed that humans were created as free agents and given the ability to choose between good and evil. Even in the creation myth described in Genesis, Adam and

Eve are depicted as willing agents capable of acting in opposition to God.

Abraham

Later figures in the Bible may be assumed to represent stages in psychic development corresponding to the periods in which their stories were recorded. The fist major figure of the Bible who may be deemed a historical figure is Abraham, who may have lived in the sixteenth, seventeenth, or eighteenth century B.C. and who is generally regarded as the founder or father of the Hebrew nation. The story of Abraham is commonly taken as an illustration of the nature of religious faith, for Abraham is given directions by God, and he follows them. Late in life, he is told by God that his aging wife will bear a son, Isaac. When Isaac is still a small child, Abraham is instructed by God to slay his beloved son and to present him as a burnt offering. Though the order is withdrawn before it is fully executed, Abraham shows his willingness to obey.

In one of the most elaborate philosophical treatments of the story, Kierkegaard (1954) portrayed Abraham as a representative of the highest stage of development, the religious stage. In this stage, according to Kierkegaard, the individual can rise above personal desires and external ethical systems and follow the inner voice of the divine wherever it leads (see Kierkegaard, 1941, 1944). By contemporary standards, a man who acted as Abraham did might be deemed psychotic, but his basic mode of functioning may not have been so uncommon in an earlier period. It was undoubtedly more common in Abraham's time for people to hear and heed an inner voice. By the standards of his time, he would not have been viewed as mentally deranged simply because he had an unusual sensitivity, a greater than usual capacity for tuning in to the inner voice. I think we must also say, however, that if this sensitivity constitutes an extensive awareness of a certain kind, it also represents a lack of conscious development in another respect. From the biblical account, we are left with the impression that Abraham had only a limited sense of his own will. Faced with major decisions, he did not exercise great conscious judgment, carefully weighing alternatives and assessing their respective merits. Instead the major decisions were dictated by the inner voice. Abraham recognized the possibility of choosing either to obey the voice or to disobey it, and he is credited with obeying it. Over three thousand years ago, a man who proceeded in this way could serve as an inspiration for a nation of people, and his life could serve as a model for new ethical codes, but in most parts of contemporary Western society we would expect a bit more than this. To balance the ledger a bit, however, let us be honest enough to recognize that Abraham may have possessed a greater sensitivity to parts of his psyche than most of us and that most of us are much more inclined than he was to conform to the herd in which we find ourselves.

Moses

Abraham was open to messages from the depths of the psyche that lie beyond the reach of organized consciousness. We see this kind of sensitivity in the shamans of various cultures, and we see it in a succession of major prophets who appeared over several centuries following Abraham and furnished the revelations that underlie a growing body of Judaic doctrine. Each of these men claimed to have heard the voice of God and believed himself summoned to preach and to disseminate new ideas. Thus, they all represent the same mode of consciousness shown in Abraham. Among Jews, Moses is generally regarded as the greatest of the prophets, the prophet who established the most intimate dialog with God, as well as the man who led his people out of Egypt and into the Promised Land.

While a number of dialogs are reported in the Bible, there are two key moments of revelation in the life of Moses that are of particular importance. The first occurred when a voice called to Moses from a burning bush and told him that he was to lead his people out of Egypt. The speaker identified himself as "the God of thy father, the God of Abraham, the God of Isaac, and the God of Jacob" (Exodus 3:6). Later, Moses asked God his name and received a reply that is translated in the King James version of the Bible as "I am that I am" (Exodus 3:14). It may also be construed as "I am who I am," "I am what I am," or "I am what I will be." The first of these identifying statements is ostensibly designed to clarify the situation for Moses, to make it clear who is speaking to him. On the deeper level, however, the statement served to underscore Moses's ethnic identity, to express the realization that the God of his father was at the same time the God of Abraham, Isaac, and Jacob. According to Jewish tradition, Moses was of Hebrew birth but grew up in the royal Egyptian court. Freud (1939) speculated that Moses was, in fact, of Egyptian ancestry. Whatever his true lineage may have been, and despite the unique circumstances of his childhood, all the recorded events of his adult life would seem to indicate that he came away from this encounter with a very close identification with the Hebrew people and a sense that it was his destiny to lead them.

The second identifying statement uttered by the voice from the burning bush is concerned with an identity that goes beyond mere ethnic bounds. In saying that he is that he is, or that he is who he is, the voice is claiming personal identity or self-aware being as his very essence. Moses has only a partial sense of his own identity. He experiences a group identity, but it is not one he learned in the course of his early development. As an adult, he does not arrive at this identity through conscious realization and decision. The identity is imparted by the voice of a divine other, and, like Abraham, Moses depends on that voice to guide him through a series of heroic decisions and actions. Like many of the great political and military leaders of history, Moses had a sense of identity that remained closely bound up with a particular ethnic or national group. The sense of a unique individual identity lay beyond his grasp and could only be experienced as the possession of a divine other, a guiding voice whose source lay outside his own consciousness. Of course, it is impossible to know what transformations occurred in the telling of this story between the lifetime of a man called Moses and the point at which the story was recorded and included in the book of Exodus, but I assume the interpretation I have just offered is consistent with the mode of experience common to people of that general period.

The second major moment of revelation in the life of Moses came much later, after Moses had led the Hebrews out of Egypt. In the course of their wandering, they came to Mount Sinai (or Horeb), and Moses felt a call to climb the mountain. He spent forty days and nights there alone or, as he experienced it, in communion with God. Moses is said to have received from God, during this solitary journey, an elaborate moral and social code. This code centers around the ten commandments, but includes a great number of additional rules pertaining to religious practices, sexuality, property rights, and various aspects of human interaction. In setting forth this code before his people, Moses assumed the role of the moral conscience and supreme judge of his people. Though he experienced all the rules as the dictates of God, he remained in the unique position of being God's spokesman, for no other individual who has assumed a significant place in history has ever claimed to be the vessel for transmitting such an elaborate moral code.

The code consists in part of reasonable rules for impartial justice, but some of it is calculated to ensure unswerving loyalty to a jealous monotheistic Lord, who made it clear that he would not tolerate the worship of any divine competitor. The fact that these two aims are somewhat incompatible underscores Moses's unique role as an interpreter and executor of the will of God. Though the ten commandments contain a basic proscription against killing, there are specific references to various kinds of people who are to be put to death either by the hand of God or by the community. On various occasions, Moses ordered the slaughter of three thousand of his people deemed guilty of idol worship (Exodus 32: 27-28), various neighboring peoples with different beliefs and practices, those found making sacrifices to other gods, and a man who was observed gathering sticks on the sabbath (Numbers 15: 32-36).

Much of this must be understood in terms of a particular stage in the social and psychic evolution of the Hebrew people. The God of Moses may have been a blend of several more specific gods worshiped at an earlier time, but Moses felt a call to solidify the ethnic identity of his people and to champion a specific single godhead as the guiding symbol of that identity. People who continued to worship other Semitic deities, such as Moloch, had to be stoned, so that they might not interfere with this divine mission. While Judaism moved in later centuries toward a much more equitable morality, it remained ethnically biased under Moses. Even the early prescription for neighborly love reflects this limitation: "Thou shalt not avenge, nor bear any grudge against the children of thy people, but thou shalt love thy neighbor as thyself" (Leviticus 19:18). In this context, *neighbor* must be understood as another member of one's own group or nation, not an outsider. Let us bear in mind that Moses lived over a thousand years prior to the Christian era—perhaps around the thirteenth century B.C. At that time, Judiasm had not evolved a general concept of a human being, an individual equally worthy of justice and love, whatever his or her race, ethnic background, and belief system. But then, such a concept did not exist in any other culture at that time. Indeed, it is doubtful that any language at that time contained a word that referred unambiguously to people in general. The closest thing to such a word would have been the word that was usually applied to the members of one's own tribe or community. Those outside this group were less likely to be viewed or treated as strictly human.

Richard W. Coan

CHRISTIANITY

The Life of Jesus

While Moses was a monumental figure in the history of Western religion, there is a later individual whose life opens into a far deeper mystery. Though he came to be known as Jesus of Nazareth and as Christ, his original name was presumably Yeshua ben Yoseph (or possibly ben Miriam), or some variant of this. The stories of his birth indicate that he was born during the time of Herod the Great, during a year in which the Romans were conducting a census, and perhaps at a time when some unusual celestial event was noted—most likely between 7 and 4 B.C. Little is known of his life before the age of about 30, though the gospels included in the New Testament refer to an incident that occurred when he was twelve. In all likelihood, he received an education in a school associated with the local synagogue, and he probably learned the carpenter's trade under the guidance of his adoptive father, Joseph. He began a ministry at about the age of thirty and was executed after he had preached for only a few years. During this career, he traveled over a very small part of the Near East, and he left behind no writings. Yet by virtue of the effect that he had on his listeners and the growing influence he continued to have after his death, this man has come to have a greater impact on Western civilization than any other single individual of any time.

It is not known what specific training Jesus may have had prior to the onset of his ministry, but it is conceivable that he spent some time in one of the devout sects of that day, perhaps in a community of the Essenes. His ministry began with an initiation comparable to that of many shamans and of the Judaic prophets who preceded him. When being baptised in the Jordan by his cousin John, Jesus reputedly saw a vision of heaven and heard a voice saying, "Thou art my beloved Son; with thee I am well pleased" (Mark 1:10-11). He then underwent a forty-day fast in isolation on a mountain. After this, he proceeded to preach, telling people that the kingdom of God was at hand.

Jesus was apparently regarded by his followers, or at least by many of them, as the son of God and as the messiah for whom the great masses of Jewish people at that time were hoping. *Messiah* literally means the "anointed one" and is equivalent to the Greek derivative *Christ*. It is clear that many Jews looked for the appearance of a divinely chosen leader who would led them to a better way of life. It is also clear that, while Jesus fit the expectations of some of them, he failed to fit the expectations of those who looked for a bold military and political leader who could defy the Roman government. There is little doubt that he was a very unusual man. He was highly intelligent. He was able to communicate very effectively through the use of parables, and when challenged with rational argument, he proved quite adept at responding in kind. He evidently had extraordinary psychic abilities. He often displayed a foreknowledge of events and an awareness of the thoughts and lives of the people he encountered, and he was able to heal people with various kinds of afflictions.

Jesus preached an ethical code that represents a step beyond anything found in the Judaic writings of earlier periods. The most fundamental ingredient is the prescription of universal love and nonviolence. The teachings of Jesus express concern for the poor and the sick and praise for peacemakers. One of his basic commandments is to "love thy neighbor as thyself" (Matthew 22:39). Unlike Moses, in speaking of a neighbor, Jesus was not referring to a fellow male of one's own tribe, but a fellow human wherever encountered. The meaning is underscored by the parable of the good Samaritan, which expressed the virtue of acting as a "neighbor" to anyone in need (Luke 10:30-37). The departure from earlier doctrine is even clearer in the advice to respond to anger with love and to violence with gentleness. Thus, Jesus commands "that ye resist not evil: but whosoever shall smite thee on thy right cheek, turn to him the other also" (Matthew 5:39). The position is stated still more strongly in the commandment to "love your enemies, bless them that curse you, do good to them that hate you, and pray for them which despitefully use you, and persecute you" (Matthew 5:44).

Here and there in the gospels one finds statements that stand in very sharp contrast to these, but that is presumably an indication that they cannot be taken literally. For example, there is the statement, "Think not that I am come to send peace on earth: I came not to send peace, but a sword. For I am come to set a man at variance with his father, and the daughter against her mother, and the daughter-in-law against her mother-in-law. And a man's foes shall be they of his own household" (Matthew 10:34-36). At another point, he stated, "If any man come to me, and hate not his father, and mother, and wife, and children, and brethren, and sisters, yea, and his own life also, he cannot be my disciple" (Luke 14:26). For dramatic effect, Jesus spoke in terms of violence and hatred, but he was basically enjoining his listeners to rebel, to break with tradition, and to abandon false loyalties. It is also possible to construe the message in part as a prescription for giving up attachments that stand in the way of spiritual realization. At various times, Jesus cautioned against attachment to material wealth and social status, and he recommended a childlike humility. For many of his followers, the spiritual path he advocated required a total break from the individual's prior pattern of living.

Jesus's advocacy of universal love was accompanied by a recognition that we are hindered from a realization of this love by our tendency to look for faults in others and to project onto other people those qualities we do not want to admit in ourselves. He said, "Judge not, that ye be not judged. For with what judgment ye judge, ye shall be judged: and with what measure ye mete, it shall be measured to you again. And why beholdest thou the mote that is in thy brother's eye, but considerest not the beam that is in thine own eye?" (Matthew 7:1-3). When asked to pass judgment on an adulteress, he said, "He that is without sin among you, let him first cast a stone at her" (John 8:7). In the treatment of both sinners and enemies, the views of Jesus represent a sharp departure from the Mosaic code. He knew that we create our enemies by projection and that to love an enemy is to dissolve the projection.

In moving from the Mosaic prescriptions for sin, Jesus abandons the idea of automatic punishment, advocates forgiveness, and stresses the differences between outward action and inner awareness and intention. The last point is evident in a story that appears in one of the early manuscripts of the Gospel of Luke: Seeing a man working on the sabbath, Jesus says to him, "Friend, if you know what you are doing, you are blessed; but if you do not know, you are accursed as a breaker of the Law" (Jones, 1966, p. 101). According to this story, the highest form of piety and faith is not something that can be reduced to a mechanical observance of rules and ritual.

Jesus was a man of unusual wisdom and compassion, but he was not a perfect being. While he said "judge not," he occasionally judged. He had his own shadow side, and it was projected most obviously onto the Pharisees. He and his closest followers may, in fact, have been Pharisees, but he nonetheless saw that sect as embodying a resistance to his teachings. He characterized Pharisees as greedy, lacking in compassion, and hypocritical. He felt that they insisted on the careful observance of rituals and utterance of traditional dogma while neglecting the experiential side of religion. According to the gospel descriptions, he railed at times against the "Pharisees, scribes, and hypocrites" and treated them with a bit of arrogance of his own.

Many people find great significance in the life of Jesus without agreeing as to the nature of his significance. His life is open to a variety of interpretations. Perhaps the simplest view is that he advocated a new way of life governed by universal love and acceptance and an expansion of self-awareness that entails an abandonment of projection. In playing such a role, he could be said to have heralded a new stage in the evolution of human consciousness, a stage in which we move toward a goal defined in terms of relatedness, or an elimination of the barriers that separate us from one another. Obviously we have still not mastered the lesson he taught, and we have moved only a short distance into this stage. The so-called Christian world remains, as ever, fraught with curious contradictions. Many wars have been fought and countless heathens have been slaughtered on behalf of the Christian God and the Prince of Peace.

Other ideas regarding Jesus's special significance concern his status as a representative of God or as a divine figure himself. It appears from biblical accounts that he sought to fulfill earlier messianic prophecies, thereby establishing himself as an individual of very special status, quite possibly the Messiah. A messiah, of course, is simply an individual anointed or specially chosen by God for an important task. Earlier Jewish kings had been considered messiahs in this sense. There was a widespread belief at the time that Jesus appeared, however, that the Messiah to come would not simply be a descendant of the house of David who would become a king and throw off the Roman yoke, but that he would usher in a new age, a millennium of peace, and that he would rule over a kingdom of God on earth. According to some accounts, Jesus not only claimed to be the Messiah, or the Christ, he claimed to be the son of God. He further stated, "I and my Father are one," and said, "The Father is in me, and I in him" (John 10:30 and 38).

Jesus does not make such claims in any quotation offered in the gospels of Matthew and Mark, and the proper interpretation is open to question. The expression "son of God" appears in Hebrew in a few places in the Old Testament, where it is meant in the sense of a special psychological relationship to God. A more literal rendering is supported in the gospels of Matthew and Luke by a story in which Jesus is conceived in the womb of a virgin mother by action of the Holy Spirit. We must view this myth in the light of both Hebrew and Greek traditions. Other figures in the Bible—notably Isaac, Samson, and John the Baptist—are also the products of miraculous conceptions arranged by divine intervention in women who could not otherwise conceive. In many mythologies, great heroes are viewed as having a divine set of parents as well as a mortal, human set. Many of the great heroes of Greek mythology were said to be semidivine, most of them being born of women who were impregnated by gods, and this idea was applied in popular thought to prominent political and intellectual figures of the classical period. The essential difference between the action of the Hebrew god and that of Zeus is that the former was less capricious; he was interested in producing a son, rather than in securing his own pleasure.

Today a literal interpretation of such a phrase as "son of God" can only be dismissed as naive, and if Jesus's use of the phrase is accurately reported, it would be unreasonable to assume that he was so naive as to have meant it literally. He knew how it might be understood by his listeners, but from all accounts, his understanding was far deeper than theirs. Three kinds of individuals known through history have claimed to be living gods or sons of gods. Some are psychotics afflicted with megalomania. Some are charlatans seeking fame and fortune, and two or three of these have come from the exotic East in recent years to prey on the spiritually callow population of the land of opportunity. The third group are people of greater spiritual realization who understand this language in a symbolic sense. To say that one is God incarnate or the living expression of God is to say that one has transcended his or her own individual ego and has come to recognize a true nature that is broader, deeper, and more universal. In Jungian terms, this means the realization of the self. In Hindu terms, it would be the realization that one's true nature is the atman (or individual soul or self) and that there is no difference between atman and brahman (the universal soul). In Eastern thought, to realize one's true nature is to realize that one is an expression of universal consciousness and that separate individuality is an illusion. The self in Jungian theory remains an individual entity, but it is collective or universal in character and is the source of the image of God. From a mystical perspective that has found expression in all parts of the world, we are all potentially gods incarnate, in the sense that a full realization of our true nature amounts to a realization of our godhood, our divine nature, our ultimate inseparability from the total universe or universal ground of consciousness. In claiming to be the son of God, Jesus was professing an awareness of his own divine status but at the same time pointing to the divine within every individual. In playing this role, he served as both prototype and herald for a stage of consciousness characterized by movement toward a goal of ego transcendence.

Competing Christian Sects

Jesus was understood in various ways by his listeners, and after his death he continued to be interpreted in a variety of ways by his would-be followers. The gospels were largely written during the century following his death and continued to undergo alteration over a couple of additional centuries. There were competing sects and doctrines in early Christianity, and the disputes among these were settled at least superficially only when an organized church gained the support of the Roman emperor Constantine and charges of heresy directed toward dissident factions could be backed up with legal and military authority. The four gospels incorporated into the New Testament are not the only ones written following the crucifixion. They are the four approved by the early organized church. These four present a view that is not entirely unitary, but the variation is not serious. We know of some of the others as a result of recent discoveries of buried manuscripts. There was a time when one could be executed for merely possessing a copy of one of the gnostic gospels, and it is fortunate that a few devout monks saw fit to place some of their manuscripts in earthen jars and bury them or hide them in caves, instead of burning them up. Perhaps there are others still waiting to be discovered, and perhaps there are many more of which no trace exists. The written record of early Christianity is not simply incomplete, but biased as well, since material was selectively destroyed or retained.

We know of a number of early gospels written by gnostics (see Nag Hammadi Library, 1977, and Pagels, 1979). There were gnostics in the Greco-Roman world before the time of Jesus, and for the most part their traditional roots lay outside Judaism. Those who embraced some of the teachings of Jesus did not see him as the Messiah, because they were not looking for the kind of national leader of whom so many Jews had dreamed. To be a gnostic meant to attach primary value to direct, personal experience of the divine realm, and this experience took precedence over any tradition. Many of the gnostics regarded Jesus as a divine being who only appeared to be human. To the extent that his very appearance was illusory, the crucifixion could not be considered an occasion involving human suffering, but in combination with the resurrection, it could be viewed as an occasion demonstrating the imperishability of the divine self, or Christ. The gnostics tended to embrace a universal mystical position that is surprisingly consistent with many of the ideas of Eastern thought. Thus, they tended to see the ultimate ground and source of being as a god beyond any god of imagery, an essence embracing both the masculine and the feminine that cannot be captured in any one specific image. From this perspective the jealous god of the Old Testament is not the ultimate being, but a lesser being, jealous because he is insecure and insecure because he is dimly aware that he is not really the ultimate authority that he claims to be. While Jesus as God incarnate is seen in terms of a human image, the image is an illusion that serves only to provide people with a link to the ultimate being that resides beyond the image. In much of gnostic thought, God is seen as identical with the ultimate nature of the individual self. Hence, to know oneself fully is to know God.

In gnostic writings, the kingdom of God is understood as a transformed consciousness, that is, as a full realization of the self and, hence, of God. Interpretations either in terms of an afterworld or in terms of a new social order in the world of people are rejected. Thus, according to the Gospel of Thomas, when Jesus was asked by his disciples, "When will the Kingdom come?" he replied, "It will not come by expectation; they will not say: 'See, here,' or: 'See, there.' But the Kingdom of the Father is spread over the earth and men do not see it" (*Gospel according to Thomas*, 1959, pp. 55-57). Thus, the kingdom (like enlightenment in Buddhist thought) is already here; we have only to realize it. The idea that entering the kingdom is equivalent to seeing beyond the consensual world of appearances, separations, and differences is brought out in an earlier passage in the same work. There Jesus says, "When you make the two one, and when you make the inner as the outer and the outer as the inner and the above as the below, and when you make the male and the female into a single one, so that the male will not be male and the female not be female, when you make eyes in the place of an eye, and a hand in the place of a hand, and a foot in the place of a foot, and an image in the place of an image, then shall you enter the Kingdom" (*Gospel according to Thomas*, 1959, pp. 17-19).

There is much in the four gospels of the New Testament to suggest that Jesus had a high regard for women and for the feminine element in human experience. He seems to have been quite androgynous, an individual able to give ample expression to both the masculine and feminine components of his own nature, and in the realm of social interaction he was quite egalitarian. The feminine element is highlighted even more in the writings of the gnostics. Thus, there are descriptions of God as both Father and Mother, and there are references to Sophia, a goddess of wisdom, as the mother of the masculine god. In stories of Jesus and his disciples, Mary Magdalene plays a prominent role. She is treated not simply as a disciple, but as the leading disciple and the closest confidante of the master.

The Ministry of Paul

The gnostics were suppressed in due time, but their outlook was one that seems destined to be resurrected over and over again in all parts of the world. It is a wonder that Christianity itself did not disappear, for as a minor Jewish sect whose novel views were met with general rejection by the elders of the synagogue, it must have seemed destined for oblivion. This might have been its fate if it had not been for a man known as Paul, or Saul, of Tarsus. Paul was of Jewish ancestry and religion, but he was also a Roman citizen, and he had a thorough command of Greek. As a well-educated man with a mixed cultural background and a great natural zeal, he was better equipped to spread the Christian word than any of the disciples of Jesus. So far as we know, he never actually saw Jesus, though he was born about twenty years before the crucifixion. He was a Pharisee with an ample command of Judaic doctrine, and he initially regarded Christianity as a heretical movement that needed to be stamped out. He preached against it and took part in persecutions. In the course of this effort, he set out one day on the road toward Damascus. Along the way, he fell to the ground and saw a blinding light. Then he heard the voice of Jesus calling him to a new mission in life, and the man who arrived in Damascus was no longer the man who had set forth toward that city.

After this conversion experience, Paul preached over a wide territory, spreading the message to the gentiles, and he saw the message as a universal one. While he had come to accept Jesus as the Messiah, this Messiah was not for him merely a leader of the Jews. His god was a god for all people, and the Christ Jesus was the one mediator between God and humankind. The fact that Paul's experience of the image and voice of Christ was untempered by any direct contact with the man from Nazareth known as Jesus had several interesting consequences. It meant that he had a deep faith resting on his own religious experience. As a teacher, he was not repeating the words heard from the mouth of a living master; rather, he was speaking from his own inner experience. Clearly he felt that the Christ he had never encountered in the flesh now spoke within him and through him. In that respect, his experience was much like that of the earlier Hebrew prophets. Perhaps he came closer than they to experiencing the divinity not as a divine other but as the true essence of his own being: "I am crucified with Christ: nevertheless I live; yet not I, but Christ liveth in me" (Galatians 2:20). At the same time, he regarded the Christ, the true self, as a universal ground, the self of all people: "There is neither Jew nor Greek, there is neither bond nor free, there is neither male nor female: for ye are all one in Christ Jesus" (Galatians 3:28).

Paul had a major role in shaping early Christian doctrine, and he could be considered the first theologian of Christianity, but his views undoubtedly departed in some particulars from those of Jesus. In some respects, his thinking was fairly radical, but in other respects he retreated to a position that was more conservative than that of Jesus. There are passages in his writing that suggest a more rigid abhorrence of sin, and his ideas regarding women were certainly less egalitarian, for he believed it was the man, not the woman, who was made in God's image. The proper role for women was to be modest in attire and to learn in silent submission from men.

Early Developments in Theology

Paul did not develop a very systematic theology, and basic doctrinal disputes continued to erupt in the early church. Some of the most basic ones were formally resolved in church councils convened by emperors during the fourth and fifth centuries. At the first of these, the Nicene creed was adopted. This states essentially that the Father and the Son are of one substance and co-eternal. A council of the fifth century adopted a trinitarian doctrine in which Jesus Christ is declared to be one person in whom reside two natures, the human and the divine, permanently united though unconfused and unmixed. In the course of the councils, competing views regarded as overemphasizing either the divine side or the human side of Christ were condemned. Since the decisions of the councils were backed by the full authority and might of the Roman empire, the church became doctrinally unified within the empire, and subsequent schisms tended to follow geographical lines. Only the congregations outside the boundary of the empire were free to adopt positions condemned by the councils.

Christianity began with the intense personal experiences of a few people who defied an established orthodoxy, but in time a Christian orthodoxy was established. In the course of this development, many of the ethical precepts that originally guided the faith would seem to have been lost. From a religion of love there arose a church interested in the exercise of absolute power. Perhaps there is an inevitable movement in the evolution of any religion from the fresh insight of the prophet and mystic to the abstract doctrine of the theologian who seeks to capture the essence of the insight in words. The disputes of the fourth and fifth centuries may have been heated, but they appear to have centered around very abstract concepts. They could be conducted only by people no longer able to distinguish between the underlying message and the verbal medium through which it is expressed. They waged a war of words, and at each council, the reigning emperor, in the interest of solidifying his own political power, sat by waiting to see which faction had the most votes.

Perhaps I over-simplify, for the clerics at these councils were shaping a system of symbols that has served as a source of guidance for millions of people in the centuries that followed their work. I believe, however, that the basic messages that Jesus of Nazareth brought to the world had little to do with the church councils of the fourth and fifth centuries. Despite the councils, despite the greed and corruption that have often appeared in the church, and despite the violence often committed in the name of Jesus Christ, the messages have continued. Even if we can quibble over how best to articulate them verbally, they have been rediscovered, relived, and exemplified by a number of figures throughout the history of Christianity. An obvious example is Francis of Assisi, who lived in the twelfth and thirteenth centuries. In our own time, we see the message in the lives of people like Mother Teresa and Thomas Merton. If we think of the role of Jesus in Western psychic evolution as initiating a period of greater movement toward the realization of universal love and ego transcendence, it is possible that a gradual unfolding has taken place over the past two thousand years and that developments within the organized church are actually only incidental to the unfolding within the broader culture. It is also possible that in the further progression of this unfolding the church will continue to play a diminishing role and that we will cease to think of it in traditionally religious, let alone Christian, terms.

THE MIDDLE AGES

We owe the terms *Middle Ages* and *Dark Ages* to intellectuals of the fifteenth and sixteenth centuries who saw their own time as a period of rebirth or "renaissance," a renewal of the intellectual and artistic spirit of antiquity. From their perspective, little of significance had happened in the realm of art, poetry, or thought since the decline of the Roman empire. Ever since the Renaissance, people have tended to cling to the simplistic view that for a period of over a thousand years following the decline and fall of the Roman empire, Europe lapsed into a psychic slump in which everyone was too bound up with superstitious beliefs and practices to be capable of thinking great thoughts or doing anything creative. We see a contemporary expression of this view in the writings of Jacob Bronowski (1970). Bronowski regarded the Middle Ages as a period of contemplative civilization, where significant works such as tapestries and cathedrals were produced anonymously by craftsmen rather than by artists. He believed that great art and science require the recognition of the creative individual and that the Middle Ages, as an anonymous period, was a time in which such activity could not flourish.

Bronowski's supposed facts are open to question. It is not all that clear that the production of poetry, art, sculpture, and architecture, great or otherwise, was characterized by greater anonymity in the Middle Ages than it had been in ancient and classical Greece. Noteworthy art and literature did appear during the Middle Ages, but since nearly all the literate people resided within the church, there was some restriction on the modes and lines of inquiry that were encouraged. Philosophical treatises tended to deal primarily with theological issues. Nonetheless, there was some secular literature, and we shall never know how much of it, for lack of reproduction, has been lost without a trace. In the late Middle Ages, at least two monumental literary figures appeared—Dante Alighieri and Geoffrey Chaucer—and a secular romantic literature began to flourish.

The Medieval Church

In the latter half of the Middle Ages, we see a period of great intellectual productivity within the church. Thomas Aquinas introduced a rational strain of philosophy based on the work of Aristotle into Roman Catholic thought, and he has been the single most influential religious philosopher within the Roman church ever since. It takes very narrow vision, however, to see this as the high point of that age, for much else was going on. Paying particular note to the art of that period, Robert Nisbet remarks that "we have come to know well that the High Middle Ages must be ranked among the very greatest ages in world history so far as intellectual and cultural achievement is concerned. This holds for science and technology quite as much as for art and humanistic scholarship" (Nisbet, 1980, p. 77). This was a period of tremendous mechanical inventiveness, sufficient to constitute an early industrial revolution. Terry Reynolds (1984) says that European industry really began with the inventive use of water power in the eighth or ninth century. Noteworthy scientific work was done by Roger Bacon and others. The kind of rigorous, systematic work that we look for in modern science did not exist then, but we do not find it in classical Greece or in the Renaissance either.

To call the Middle Ages "dark" bespeaks an unreasonable bias, but what does it represent in the evolution of Western consciousness? Certainly there is nothing very obvious in the realm of religion or social progress that signifies a fresh kind of awareness. If we look for signs that the sense of universal love was spreading to more people, we can readily point to the example of Francis of Assisi, who brought fresh life into the church and served as a living example of unbounded love for people and nature that has inspired millions over the centuries. Yet the age of Francis of Assisi was also an age of violence for a large part of Europe. There were bloody crusades. People were arrested and tortured on suspicion of minor crimes. There were brutal public executions, and the crowds enjoyed them. The handicapped and underprivileged were subjected to a mixture of pity and mocking humiliation, and the religion that sometimes inspired joy also inspired a fear of the horrors of Hell.

In many respects, popular religion differed little from the sort practiced earlier, in the Greco-Roman period, though some of the images had been replaced. Few people could experience God in quite the way that Jesus, Paul, and the earlier prophets had. Most people regarded God as a remote figure to whom they could not comfortably relate, and the more Jesus was deified by the church, the more remote he became for most people. The saints of history, however, were often experienced as figures who had become familiar through stories and paintings, and people tended to address their prayers to these figures. A cult of guardian angels, which served a similar function but may have reflected an unmet spiritual need, arose toward the end of the Middle Ages. Earlier in Greece and Rome the common people often worshipped household or tutelary deities, regarding the grand figures of the pantheon as standing too far beyond their reach. There may be elements in the human psyche that tend to lead toward the unitary conception of a monotheism, but there are also elements that lead in the opposite direction. Christian monotheism has reverted at many times to a thinly disguised polytheism, and the worship of saints and angels in the Middle Ages is such an instance.

The Discovery of the Individual

The best evidence of an expansion of consciousness lies not within the organized church or in the sphere of popular religion, but in the secular realm. In the high and late Middle Ages there was a widespread interest in self-knowledge, which took many forms and dealt with aspects of individual being and interpersonal relationships about which writers in earlier times had shown little interest or awareness. According to Colin Morris (1972), in fact, the discovery of the individual was the most important cultural development during the period from 1050 to 1200 A.D. We are accustomed to thinking of classical Greece and the Renaissance in terms of an individualism lacking in the Middle Ages, but those periods favored a kind of individualism that assigns great value to the realization and expression of artistic and intellectual potential. The highly creative individual was admired, and uniqueness and independence were respected, but knowing oneself as an individual involves many things besides discovering whether one is able to produce a great painting or poem. It may entail a lengthy inner journey that discloses a host of feelings and images but does not culminate in a specific artistic or intellectual product.

Morris notes that some of the characteristics we commonly attribute to the Renaissance, such as a revival of interest in the Greco-Roman classics, were present in two earlier periods, the Carolingian period and the twelfth century. The Renaissance of the fifteenth century was actually the third Renaissance, one dominated by cultural developments in Italy. The Renaissance of the twelfth century was dominated by France. The evidence cited by Morris for an associated focus on the individual in the twelfth century is primarily literary. The literature expressed a common interest in self-knowledge and an interest in psychological issues, such as feelings and the nature of motivation. There was also a concern with relationships between individuals, either in the form of friendship or of love. Many autobiographies were published, and here we have a genre essentially unknown in classical times, the first major work of this kind being the sixth-century *Confessions* of Saint Augustine. In art, the concern with the individual was expressed in the production of portraits. Morris argues that Christianity, as well as classical Greek culture, contributed to the Western concern with individuality. In the religious writings of the twelfth century, there is a strong emphasis on the relationship of the specific individual being to God.

The quest for self-knowledge takes many forms, and one of the forms that is not treated in Morris's book is revealed by the alchemical literature of the Middle Ages. Alchemy is a curious mixture of art, science, esoteric philosophy, and ritual that originated well before the Christian era. We do not know for certain where and when it originated, but it existed long ago in countries as widely separated as Egypt and China. It was introduced into Europe in the latter half of the Middle Ages and attracted interest in many parts of that continent. We are accustomed to thinking of alchemy as a primitive endeavor to transmute base metals to gold, an endeavor that, although vain, led to the science of chemistry. While the transmutation of metals may have been the primary aim of some alchemists, we know from their writings that for many other alchemists the various operations performed with alembics, beakers, and flasks were understand more as a symbolic ritual through which the alchemist could experience an inner transformation. It is evident, furthermore, that some of these people experienced profound effects, on occasion an ecstasy that can readily be compared with many experiences of religious conversion. As we now understand it, we could say that they experienced a realization or contact with the larger self underlying the more limited ego with which one normally identifies. Of course, this is also what the religious prophets of earlier periods had done, but let us note some important differences. The language in which the experience was described and interpreted was no longer that of traditional Judeo-Christian concepts, and the alchemist attempted to set the stage for the experience, in order to gain greater understanding of the psychic process involved and to achieve some control over it. He wanted to find the key to the realization of selfhood, rather than waiting to be caught by surprise on the road to Damascus.

It is possible that some of the obscure language of the alchemists was designed to disguise their work, to make an unorthodox spiritual pursuit appear to be nothing more than a technological enterprise. The kind of inner journey they undertook was shared by a few people within the church, but these were not the dominant theologians, like Albertus Magnus and Thomas Aquinas, or the men in positions of greatest ecclesiastical power. They were mystics like Meister Eckhart, who would speak of the birth of Christ as an event that every individual could experience within the depths of his or her own soul. This may have been what Jesus and Paul actually had in mind, but it expressed a doctrine of immanence regarded as heretical by some of his more powerful contemporaries.

New Myths

This was also an age in which a new mythology, expressed in poetry, songs, and stories, began to flourish in Europe, and it spoke to a far larger audience than the writings of the alchemists and mystics. It was a secular mythology in which the gods and goddesses were replaced by kings, queens, knights, beautiful maidens, wizards, and sorceresses. It encompassed the tale of

King Arthur and the knights of the round table, a host of romantic tales, and endless variations on the quest for the holy grail.

The grail quest is one of the most enduring themes of the late Middle Ages. The original nature of the grail itself is obscure, and it has usually been identified as a chalice, bowl, or dish used at the Last Supper. While symbols of that event—the vessels used for communion—exist in every church, it is the task of the grail hero to find the one true vessel, and only the knight of genuine purity or innocence is capable of seeing it. In Arthurian legends, the hero is usually Parsifal (or Perceval, Parzival, etc.) or Galahad, but the quest also appears in stories independent of Arthurian lore. The various attributes of Parsifal illustrate the general pattern. Parsifal has been described as a simple, unsophisticated fellow who grew up in a forest retreat in the company of his widowed mother. Lacking in worldly wisdom, he possessed a purity founded on his own untainted nature. The name *Parsifal* may actually mean "innocent fool," although several other suggested translations are equally plausible. In the stories of the grail quest, we clearly have a new kind of hero. It is no longer a hero who stands above all other men because he is half god by birth and possesses superhuman strength, but a hero who rises to great heights because he possesses in pure form the natural instincts and spirituality common to all people. We now have a mythology that glorifies the natural qualities of the human individual and focuses on an inner quest for the realization of a supreme spiritual goal, for which the guiding voice comes from the individual's own uncorrupted nature. Joseph Campbell speaks of this as a "mythology of the self-moving self-responsible individual" and says that it is the earliest definition of the secular mythology that is now the guiding spiritual force of the European West (Campbell, 1968, pp. 564-65). This kind of individualism was not really evident in earlier times, but it persisted into later centuries and is certainly evident in the experience of people in our society today.

Romantic love is a second major theme that is central to the emerging mythology of the late Middle Ages. It was expressed at that time in the tales of Tristram and Isolde, Lancelot and Guinevere, and many other pairs of lovers. We can find a trace of this form of love in earlier tales of Orpheus and Euridyce and of Amor and Psyche, but it assumed an importance in the late Middle Ages that it had never had before. It is a form of love to which the theologians and the Greek philosophers had given little heed. It was neither the unselfish caring of *agape* or *caritas* nor the pure sensuality or pleasure seeking of *eros* or lust. The growing emphasis on romantic love has important implications for the changing relationships between the sexes and for shifts in the way in which people related to the masculine and feminine. We might characterize its essence as the glorification or idealization of an individual human other, and this may be experienced with a passionate intensity that for many people since the Middle Ages has certainly exceeded anything felt in the realm of religious ecstasy. As an experience of the masculine and feminine, we might view romantic love as an intermediate level of development, for the contrasexual quality (the masculine for the woman, the feminine for the man) is appreciated, or even viewed as incredibly valuable, but is recognized primarily in a projected form, rather than within. A more comprehensive realization of self might embrace romantic love but would not stop at that level of experience.

When we examine the characteristic forms of the medieval romance, we can see another way in which this theme blends with the rest of the emerging mythology. The love that is discovered by all the great lovers of the medieval tales is an illicit love, a love that cannot be sanctified by the church because it violates the bonds of matrimony, or a love that defies the bounds of custom and family alliance. The lovers fail in love despite all the contrary forces in the surrounding society, having found all the necessary justification within. Romantic love, like the grail quest, is an enterprise guided by the inner voice of the individual's own personal experience, a voice that says, "That wonderful being was somehow meant for me; I care not who says otherwise."

THE RENAISSANCE AND BEYOND

The Renaissance carried this stress on the individual further in one respect: it was marked by increasing opposition to established authority and a decreasing reliance on the church as the ultimate arbiter in matters of thought, morality, and aesthetic taste. The new emphasis on a return to the humane studies of the past and on the powers of the individual thinker and creator stimulated imaginative production in the arts and gave a great boost to science. In contrast to the late Middle Ages, there may have been less encouragement to pursue inner spiritual growth, but there was much more encouragement to explore the world without. The church did not relinquish its authority willingly. Giordano Bruno was burned at the stake in 1600 for supporting the views of Copernicus, and Galileo was threatened still later with a comparable fate.

Exploration, nonetheless, occurred. The European view of the world underwent drastic changes as sailors returned from distant lands to announce their discoveries. In the late Middle Ages, a few people like Roger Bacon and William of Ockham had foreshadowed the scientific spirit that began to emerge on a large scale in the Renaissance. Copernicus, writing in the early sixteenth century, is generally credited with presenting a theory that revolutionized Western thought, the heliocentric view of the universe. The idea was not new, for Aristarchus and perhaps others had held a similar view back in classical Greece, but Copernicus marks the beginning of a major challenge to the authority of the church, with its reliance on a literally interpreted Bible, and the beginning of a major shift in the outlook of the Western world as a whole. Copernicus himself did a masterful job of reconciling the heliocentric view with all known facts and showing that it is less cumbersome than the geocentric view of Ptolemy. With the later revisions, observations, and theory introduced by such men as Galileo, Kepler, and Newton, it was inevitable that people in general would abandon the idea that God had created for us a home right in the very center of the universe.

As people began to realize that their place in the universe was not as special as they had supposed, they developed a compensating faith in the power of the human mind to unravel the mysteries of the universe. The allegiance that had been accorded the church has tended gradually to be replaced by a faith in the power of science. This has meant, of course, that the basic orientation of the scientist has been regarded as the best mode of psychological functioning. The dominant Western outlook since the Renaissance has been rationalistic, empiricist, materialistic, mechanistic, and analytical. This has meant a tendency to suppress modes of functioning that are more mystical, more intuitive, or more holistic.

This basic thrust was less apparent in the thinkers of the Renaissance than it was later in the eighteenth century, the age of the Enlightenment, when an emphasis on reason and the independent human intellect dominated both philosophy and political thought. The independent advocates of Reason played a prominent role in both the French and American Revolutions. After the French Revolution, which spelled the end of the established monarchy, the Goddess of Reason was enthroned in a public ceremony. Her throne was soon usurped by Napoleon Bonaparte, but in Western culture as a whole people had begun to question the divine right of kings and the wisdom of hereditary rule. They had come to see governments as human inventions that should serve the needs of the people under their rule and to believe that ordinary people had a right to a voice in governmental affairs.

The Reformation

Another outgrowth of the forces that shaped the Renaissance

was the Reformation, which took place well before the great revolutions. It was led by Martin Luther in Germany, who was followed by Huldreich Zwingli in the German part of Switzerland, then by Guillaume Farel and John Calvin in Geneva. Not long afterward, Henry VIII declared the Church of England independent of papal authority. In general, the reformers felt there was too much corruption within the Roman church, and they challenged the absolute authority of the papal government on doctrinal issues. In England, the change was essentially political: Henry VIII felt that he, not the papal government, should rule his church. Luther, Zwingli, and Calvin introduced various reforms in doctrine and worship, arguing that many of the positions of the Roman church represented a misinterpretation of scripture.

Of the three great reformers, Martin Luther was probably the most brilliant, the most irrepressible, and the one most deeply inspired by his own religious experience. Dispensing with some of the accumulated practices and dogma of the church, he advocated a childlike trust in God and Christ and sought a return to the experience of the early Christians. Perhaps he succeeded personally in achieving such a return, but it is unlikely that he went as far as Jesus or Paul in realizing the self, or the divine ground of his own being. In contrast, Calvin's experience of God was much more harrowing, while Zwingli's approach to religion was basically rational and intellectual. On the whole, the reformers were no more tolerant of free thought than the men of power in Rome. Luther, for example, attacked Copernicus for perverted ideas that ran counter to sacred scriptures. The Reformation, however, was part of a general loosening of intellectual controls, and once people accepted the notion that the Pope was not the absolute authority, they saw no need to assign that role to Luther, Zwingli, or Calvin. For this reason, with or without church sanctions, science his flourished better in the Protestant countries of Northern Europe than it has in the Catholic countries to the south.

The reformers dispensed with much of the ritual and

symbolism of the church and attacked the veneration of saints, seeing the pure faith in terms of a more radical monotheism. Whether this is an improvement is a matter of opinion. The individual who grows up in the Roman Catholic Church grows up in a world of rich symbols to which he or she can relate most of the important and powerful experiences that occur in the course of a lifetime The individual who grows up in a mainstream Protestant church becomes familiar with a few basic rituals, but the primary role of the church is to offer a set of beliefs that tend to be experienced as intellectual puzzles because they have lost much of their impact as symbols. They have ceased to provide us with any sense of deep meaning as we pass through the major crises of life or when we get in touch with the great mysteries that defy human understanding. The Roman church has always tended to cling to outmoded symbols, resisting the natural evolution of imagery that occurs in any religion, while the Protestant churches have indulged in a radical pruning of images. Either way, the church has played its part in a general deterioration of symbols and a loss of a sense of meaning that has occurred in Western culture in the past few centuries.

Trends in Recent Centuries

If we examine the developments that have occurred in science, religion, and other realms of Western thought since the Renaissance, it is possible to discern a fairly consistent pattern of trends that encompass much of what has happened. One trend has been an increasing emphasis on individuality, individual separateness, or individual selfhood. While we have never managed to eliminate pressures for conformity, which at times are overwhelming, Western culture is unique in the degree to which it has adopted the idea that the goal of life is the full realization of the individual's own specific potentials, tastes, and style of life. A second trend is an increasing emphasis on rational and analytical modes of thinking as the key to arriving at truth and settling all important questions and disputes. Both of these trends have been characterized in terms of an emphasis on a set of values that may be deemed masculine, patriarchal, or Apollonian.

Closely related to the stress on rationality is a pronounced literalism, an insistence on an interpretation of concepts in terms of specific concrete referents, or an insistence on communication in terms of signs rather than symbols. In part, this trend is a function of the growing role of science and scientific method in Western thought, but it is not a recent innovation. We see it in the fourteenth century in the views of William of Ockham with respect to both scientific and religious issues, but the roots are still more ancient. Within the realm of religious thought, a certain emphasis on literalism is peculiar to the Judeo-Christian tradition, where there has long been an insistence on the historic reality of myths. In an earlier era, this did not present a problem. An insistence on the literal truth of the stories in Genesis did not interfere with the symbolic function of these myths. They helped to give people a sense of their roots and their place in the universe. The fundamentalist who now insists on the literal validity of the story of Adam and Eve in the Garden of Eden is merely working in concert with his atheistic opponent to bring about the final demise of the myth, since he is preaching a message that every educated person recognizes as an intellectual absurdity. In a subtle way the church has tended to combine forces with science in the destruction of traditional religion. Of course, there has always been a quiet, unbroken stream of mystics, flowing from Jesus and Paul to moderns like Thomas Merton, who find religious values in their own experience, who find their own ways of relating to traditional symbols, and who are not fooled by the nonsense often uttered in the pulpit. They, too, are a vital part of this culture, and they may or may not represent the wave of the future, but they have certainly not been the dominant influence in recent centuries.

Several influences have combined in recent centuries to

undermine our traditional symbols and myths. Nietzsche's proclamation of a century ago that "God is dead" is a valid summary of the experience of the great mass of people. At the same time, our overemphasis on rational, analytical thinking has served to undermine our sense of the symbolic. It is difficult for us to live with any symbol for long, because we tend to analyze and deaden our symbols in our frantic search for literal meanings. The needs expressed through symbols remain, and we tend to symbolize in a rather casual, promiscuous fashion, looking for our gods in the stars of sports and entertainment that happen to be on the screen before us at the moment.

Closely akin to the loss of meaning that goes with the decline of symbols is a sense of alienation. This concept has been used in various ways by various people since Karl Marx introduced it in the nineteenth century, but all the usages have to do with a loss of a sense of meaningful relationship, whether to other people, to society, to our work, to traditional moral values, or to various parts of our selves. To the extent that traditional symbols serve as a vehicle for conveying traditional values, for showing the individual his connection with the group or society, and for guiding the individual through the stages and crises of life, a loss of symbols necessarily implies various forms of alienation. The rise of science and the changing influences of the church and religion have played a role in the development of an increasing sense of alienation in Western people, but there are many other factors that may be even more significant, such as the growth of industrialization and the accelerated rate of change in the modern world.

I am not speaking of a uniform culture, nor of a uniform progression over the past five hundred years. The dominant trends have recurrently evoked counter-movements, eruptions of mysticism, romanticism, and fantasy. In contrast to other cultures, however, the Western world has apparently specialized in rationality and in a sense of separate individuality, and this emphasis has been particularly evident in the past few centuries. It is difficult to say whether this represents a mode of consciousness in which people of our culture as a mass have manifested progress over, say, the past two and a half millennia. If we confine our attention to the few people in whom rational consciousness is most highly cultivated, it is certainly not obvious that there has been a great change over this time span. In classical Greece, there were a number of individuals of genius in whom clear rational-analytical thinking was developed to a high degree. There is little reason to suppose, from any evidence available, that any mathematician of recent or modern times manifests this mode of consciousness to a higher degree than Euclid or Pythagoras, or that any modern philosopher has developed it to a higher degree than Plato or Aristotle. Perhaps there has been more obvious progress in scientific thought than in mathematics or philosophy, but this is simply a reflection of the cumulative nature of science. The development that is represented by the shifts in viewpoint from, say, Ptolemy to Copernicus to Newton to Einstein has nothing to do with an increasing level of analytical consciousness. It is simply a function of an accumulation of information and a few changes in the models, presuppositions, and methods of science.

Our thinking has been influenced by many technological and social developments. Over the past two and a half millennia, we have moved from the work of the individual scribe through various systems of printing to modern systems of rapid reproduction and information storage and retrieval. The power of the human brain has been augmented by the various capacities of the library and the electronic computer. We have not only accumulated facts and ideas; we have learned to do it more and more efficiently. Developments in science and technology have to some extent fed on each other, and the fruits of science and technology have become available to larger and larger portions of the population.

The spread of education has been part of the change. Through most of the time span we are talking about, literacy was confined to a small segment of the population. Now we take for granted the fairly recent idea that everyone has a right to an education that extends beyond the mere essentials of literacy and the idea that everyone has a right to virtually all the information available in print. This obviously means that the ideas once shared by an elite can be shared by a far greater proportion of the population. The educational system we have developed over the past few centuries is designed primarily to enhance rational and analytical thinking, and the people most adept at this mode of functioning are the ones who succeed in it. For the most part, the system tends to discourage intuition and extrasensory capacities. It teaches us to tune out our feelings and to pretend they are different from what they are. It usually operates in such a way as to discourage originality or creativity. To the extent that it works the way it is apparently intended to work, it has fostered the development of a high level of rational consciousness in more and more people, and this may well be the principal way in which consciousness has evolved for people in general in Western society during historic times.

THE CONTEMPORARY SITUATION

It is always difficult to read trends while they are occurring, and most readings prove after the fact to be incorrect. There is always a temptation, however, to proclaim with the dramatic flourish of the typical commencement speaker that we stand at a crossroad, or at the brink of a new era in human consciousness. After all, this is not merely the first day of the rest of our lives; it is the very beginning of what remains in the life of the entire universe. So long as we stand at this point, we can imagine that what lies ahead in the future will be much different from what we know has existed in the past, but since we always stand at this point, we can always imagine. The vision changes a bit, depending on the dominant concern at the time. Charles Reich's *The Greening of America* (1970) reflects the concerns of 1970, while Marilyn

Ferguson's *Aquarian Conspiracy* (1980) reflects the concerns of 1980. Both books capture some of the undercurrents of our time and attempt an extrapolation into the future. Perhaps I can do little better than this. I, too, think I can discern some trends, but I have little faith in my ability to forecast the future.

I think there are many signs that more and more people are questioning our overemphasis on rationality and patriarchal values. One obvious reason is that our investment in rationality has fostered the rapid development of a technological capacity that has wrought a curious mixture of benefits and hazards. Many people have come to feel that all the benefits are not sufficient to outweigh the hazards posed by the nuclear arms race and by our increasing pollution of the streams, oceans, and atmosphere of the planet. There are increasing concerns with the rather lopsided thrust of our educational system, and complaints that it not only tends to stifle creativity and intuition but also fails to allow for a wide range of natural modes of perceiving and processing information. I think, too, that there is an increasing awareness of needs we cannot satisfy with sheer rationality. We have attempted to replace religion with science, or to make science our religion, and we are finally beginning to realize that not everything we want to achieve in consciousness can be achieved by the kind of rational understanding that is central to science. As Viktor Frankl put it: "What is demanded of man is not, as some existential philosophies teach, to endure the meaninglessness of life; but rather to bear his incapacity to grasp its unconditional meaningfulness in rational terms" (Frankl, 1963, pp. 187-88).

There seems to be more and more recognition of a need to develop potentials that we have neglected, a realization that we need to develop our intuition and imagination and our awareness of feelings. We need to cultivate a host of qualities traditionally viewed in terms of "feminine" values, and we need to find new ways of relating to one another, to people in other parts of the world, and to the earth itself. I think there is also increasing recognition of the parts of ourselves that we have tended to deny vehemently and to project outward. This is evident in shifts in attitudes toward international affairs. In an earlier age, most people might have assumed that their own group (their tribe, community, city-state, or country) was inherently right and virtuous and therefore justified in attacking and conquering any other group. Today, a young man who is asked to put on a uniform and fight for his country is much more inclined to question the motives and wisdom of government leaders. It has become more obvious to many people that we tend to create our enemies by projection and that the existence of nuclear weapons has made it very risky for everyone to keep doing that. The basic alternative is to recognize that each of us has a potential for evil and violence. Once we have fully recognized this and dealt with it, we no longer need an enemy. Jesus of Nazareth said as much; yet the message has been particularly hard for Christians to digest. In deifying Jesus, Christianity has tended to portray him in terms of an image of perfect love and virtue. Growing up in a Christian church, one learns to identify with this image, with the result that Christianity fosters a repression of evil. The evil we deny in ourselves can be seen only in the other person. For centuries, Christianity has promoted the very trap that its founder sought to eliminate. If more and more of us are becoming aware of the trap, perhaps we can do something about it.

Theodore Roszak (1975) suggests that much of the searching that is going on now amounts to a genuine spiritual or religious quest, and he speaks of its varied manifestations in terms of the "Aquarian frontier." If Joseph Campbell is correct in arguing that the grail quest is the guiding myth of our time, then the Aquarian frontier is just the cutting edge of a movement that has been developing in our culture for several centuries. Perhaps the quest for full self-knowledge has become more urgent than it ever was in the past, and perhaps it has just now become the dominant motif in the ever-changing flow of Western consciousness.

It is worth noting that just as our attitudes toward science have been changing, science itself has been undergoing a great deal of change. Th is is particularly apparent in physics, where some fundamental revolutions have occurred within this century. Throughout science in general, there has been an increased awareness that our theories are basically constructions or inventions, rather than discoveries, that there is no ultimate truth to be found in science, and that in a sense we actually construct the reality with which we deal in science. There is an increased awareness that the notion of the detached observer, long viewed as an ideal in scientific research, is a misleading fiction; we cannot observe without being involved, and we cannot observe without influencing what we observe. At the same time, the simple assumptions of mechanism and causality that underlay nineteenth-century science have been abandoned in modern physics. They have given way to a recognition that all events are interdependent, and a number of physicists have argued that in some way each tiny bit of the universe reflects the character of the totality at any given moment. A number of writers have suggested that the outlook of modern Western physics has moved closer and closer to that of Eastern mysticism (see Capra, 1975).

5

The Psychic Development of the Orient

To discern fundamental changes in consciousness in the Orient, as in the West, we must sift through a mass of historical information and search for pertinent bits of information. To complicate matters, we are dealing here with several distinguishable civilizations, and there is tremendous variation from one region to another. In both East and West, the information yielded by literary productions reveals more about the literate segment of the population than it does about the rest of the population. The early Brahmin priests of India, like the priests of the Roman church in the Middle Ages, were a small minority.

The literate minority has usually tended to be psychically more advanced that the rest of the population, both in terms of overall intelligence and in terms of range and kinds of awareness. Within the ranks of the unpublished masses, however, we may find modes of awareness and thinking that are not represented in the elite stratum, modes that ultimately find literary expression long after their expression in popular discourse has become commonplace. Various developments in Indian and Chinese thought, like the romantic literature of the late Middle Ages in the West, represent an eruption from an underground stream that had long been flowing but gone unnoticed.

It is important to remember that the total experience of people within a culture is always far richer than the experience reflected in the writings of any select group. Whatever differences we discern between East and West, each culture contains in some form the elements we see as more pronounced in the other culture. As I have suggested before (Coan, 1977), the same polarities (e.g., rational vs. mystical) that operate in religious and philosophical thought in the West can be found as well in the East, where their dynamic interplay yields much the same effects.

Differences Between East and West

It is possible, nonetheless, to discern some difference in psychological emphasis between East and West, and many terms have been offered to capture this. Western thought tends to be rational, linear, analytical, discriminative, and objective, while Eastern thought tends to be more holistic, intuitive, and mystical. An emphasis on analysis and discrimination tends to be accompanied by an emphasis on precision, on a precise fit between sign and referent. For this reason, Western thought tends to be more literalistic than Eastern thought. In the West, while the scientist espouses a form of positivism, the religious individual may insist that his image of the godhead is a correct representation of the one true god. His Oriental counterpart is more likely to regard his image as a symbol that points to an underlying reality that cannot be captured fully or directly in any word or image.

An emphasis on analysis and discrimination is conducive to a view of the world as composed of discrete entities. The application of this view to people leads naturally to an emphasis on the separateness and individuality of each person. In Western mythology this outlook is manifested in the idea that people were created by a god or gods as separate beings with free individual will. The two major sources of Western traditions agree on this, but Campbell (1976) notes a significant difference in ways of dealing with human separateness. The religions that arose in the Levant emphasize the mutual dependence of God and human but view God as the creative factor and the human individual as inevitably subordinate. Hence, they stress the importance of aligning individual will with divine will to permit a harmonious relationship. Greek culture, on the other hand, produced the image of the superhuman hero who claims his own right to creativity and independence, the Prometheus who continues to shout his defiance of Zeus no matter what torments are dealt forth by the most powerful of gods.

Both versions of the basic Western myth are tragic in the sense that the burden of separate existence represents a loss of a prior security and entails all the agonies of individual consciousness. Adam and Eve, like Prometheus, must learn to endure their pain, for there is no way to avoid it. The traditions of the Orient, however, all regard the pain as avoidable, since they see separate individuality as either a total illusion or a temporary and partial reality. They stress the possibility of overcoming the duality we have created in viewing ourselves as separate and in maintaining attachments that perpetuate the sense of separateness. From an Oriental perspective, the underlying reality is an unbroken whole. If there is a divine or spiritual realm, it is immanent in all things and ultimately indistinguishable from the realm of human existence, and it is only through ignorance that we think otherwise. Campbell suggests that within Eastern thought, as in Western, two major paths can be distinguished. The traditional path of India is world-negating, and the ultimate release from the pain of experienced separateness is seen as a release from the repetitive cycle of terrestrial incarnations. The traditional paths of China and Japan, on the other hand, are more world-affirming, for the way to surmount the pain of a dualistic existence is seen as an acceptance of the flow of nature and an abandonment of efforts to interfere with it and control it.

EARLY STAGES IN INDIAN THOUGHT

The continent of Asia contains several distinct civilizations, and each of these in turn is a product of a mixture of cultural influences. A number of peoples have inhabited or invaded the subcontinent of India over the centuries, and the history of Indian thought reflects an interplay of traditions that have different roots. We do not know when people first entered the region of India, but we know that there was a mixture of peoples there prior to the influx of Aryans that began around 1500 B.C. A number of distinct languages are spoken in India, and those spoken in the southern portion of the country are predominantly of the Dravidian language family. These are the modern forms of languages that have been spoken in that country for thousands of years. The Indo-Aryan languages, derived from the tongues of the invaders who began arriving around 1500 B.C., predominate in the northern parts of the country. Archeological evidence also points to mythic motifs present in early times that run counter to the myths of the Aryans but were ultimately integrated with Aryan beliefs at a later period. In particular, there is evidence of early worship of a mother-goddess and perhaps of the ultimate godhead as a feminine figure.

Early Writings

It is a common practice to identify Hinduism with India and to equate its origin with the writing of the Vedas. These are still regarded by Hindus as sacred scriptures. They are the work of the Aryan invaders, and they were produced over a period of several centuries, probably during the period from about 1500 B.C. to about 1000 B.C. The Vedas include a mixture of hymns, prayers, and various prose and verse formulas. Their content is not altogether unitary, for they reflect the religious mixture of the various invader groups. They contain references to a variety of deities, nearly all male, but in some of the later writings there is evidence that the writers entertained a concept of a divine ground from which the gods themselves arose.

During the period from about 800 B.C. to about 300 B.C., the foundations for modern Hinduism were laid in three bodies of writings produced by priests of the brahmin caste: the brahmanas, the aranyakas, and the upanishads. These works were intended by their authors to provide a systematic interpretation and application of the ideas contained in the vedas, but they advance from interpretation to philosophical speculation that goes well beyond the Vedas. The sequence of ancient literature in India thus reflects a movement from an age dominated by early myths to an age of more systematic philosophical thought. This parallels the transitions evident in pre-Christian Greece, as well as those seen within the Judeo-Christian tradition as we turn from the earliest books of the Old Testament to the later books and then to the Talmud and the New Testament.

The progression from the Vedas to the Upanishads cannot be understood, however, as just a refinement of the thinking within one stream of thought. Certainly the gods are accorded progressively less importance as we move through the Brahmanic writings, but there are other changes in outlook, and radically new ideas are introduced. The Brahmanas initiate a shift from the life-loving tone of the Vedas toward a world-negating philosophy. A doctrine of transmigration is first expressed in these writings. In all subsequent Hindu thought this doctrine centers around the concepts of samsara, karma, and moksha. *Samsara* refers to the seemingly endless cycle of death and rebirth through which the individual soul passes. *Karma* refers to the effects of one's deeds in a given lifetime that are carried into the next lifetime and determine the quality of the rebirth. *Moksha* refers to release from the samaric cycle and, hence, a release from the miseries of an earthly existence. As Campbell (1976) notes, there are ideas in the Upanishads that clearly represent a departure from the mythology of the Vedas, and they probably represent an assimilation of ideas from the non-Aryan cultures of India. The

Upanishads contain a legend of a great goddess, and such figures are certainly important in later periods in India. In this body of writings, we also find the first elaborate treatment of atman, of the identity of atman and brahman, and of certain ideas basic to yogic practices.

Various Spiritual Paths

During the period in which the Brahmins produced their major works, there were competing sects and sages who preached somewhat different messages, and many of these had non-Aryan roots in pre-Vedic times. Many of them engaged in ascetic practices and sought some kind of gnosis. The Jains, who practiced an extreme asceticism and embraced a world-negating philosophy were part of this stream. Their best known advocate was Mahavira, who lived in the fifth century B.C., but Jainism had been present in India centuries before Mahavira, and it survives today as a minor religious movement distinct from Hinduism. Gautama, the founder of Buddhism, was also strongly influenced by the ascetic sages, though he ultimately chose a path as distinct from theirs as it was from that of the Brahmin priests.

The practices that have come to be known collectively as yoga also have their origins in early shamanic pursuits of pre-Vedic times, but at about the time the Upanishads were written they came to be seen as closely linked to the philosophy of the Brahmins and an integral feature of Hinduism. In terms of the philosophy that began to emerge with the Upanishads, yoga was seen essentially as the means for achieving an experience of unity or identity with the brahman. It is not clear whether yogic practices were regarded as having quite this aim during the earlier centuries in which they were employed. There is little doubt, however, that they were used to bring about a transformation of consciousness and an awareness somewhat different from that of ordinary experience.

Hinduism has long been a heterogeneous enterprise. Though

there are some threads of commonality running through it, it embraces a great number of sects and several systems of philosophy. Perhaps the most important system of thought, or darshana, is Vedanta, which may be viewed as an elaboration of the ideas of brahman, atman, and maya as treated in the Upanishads. These concepts are subjected to somewhat different treatment by different schools and expositors of Vedanta, but the central doctrine is that our true nature is brahman, the impersonal subjective aspect of all being. The world as we ordinarily perceive it, including ourselves as individual beings within it, is understood to be maya, or illusion. In moving beyond our customary but false experience of individual identity, we come to realize the atman, our true soul or essence. Beyond this lies the realization that atman is brahman, that the individual soul we have discovered is in fact the universal essence.

BUDDHISM

The Life and Teachings of Gautama

Gautama supposedly lived from 563 to 483 B.C., but the earliest known account of his life was written a few centuries later, and it is difficult to distinguish the factual details of his life from the mythological overlay. Whatever the specific facts may be, there is little doubt that he undertook a quest for a deeper understanding of life and, toward that end, became familiar with all the major paths toward salvation or enlightenment recognized by his contemporaries. According to tradition, he finally achieved enlightenment while meditating under a *bo* tree, or tree of wisdom. In view of its subsequent consequences for the thinking and experience of countless millions of people, the moment at which this occurred may be the most important moment in the entire history of human consciousness. Gautama emerged from his meditation with all the basic essentials of his teachings, and he devoted the remainder of his long life to their propagation.

At the core of his system are the Four Noble Truths and the Noble Eightfold Path. The first of the Four Noble Truths is that all life is characterized by suffering (i.e., *dukkha*, which may also be construed as frustration, imperfection, unsatisfactoriness, grief, anxiety, illness, etc.). The second truth is that suffering arises from craving or desire. Desire, or more specifically, egoistic desire, is in turn a consequence of ignorance, and ignorance is at the root of ordinary consciousness and of our ordinary ways of perceiving the world and ourselves as separate entities within the world. Gautama recognized that we might speak of the self as a sense of personal identity, but he rejected the idea of a permanent, fixed personal self or soul. He noted that the self that we experience (or construct) is a product of the "five skandhas," that is, a product of such factors as sensations, emotions, perceptions leading to memory, and consciousness. Since these factors are constantly changing, the sense of identity that they yield cannot represent a fixed underlying essence. The third truth is that a cessation of suffering is possible and that this entails the cessation of desire. The fourth truth is that the way to this cessation is provided by the Noble Eightfold Path.

The Eightfold Path includes eight steps leading to wisdom, moral virtue, and concentration. The steps specify the nature of right understanding, intention or aspiration, speech, action, livelihood, effort, mindfulness, and concentration. The steps are interrelated, and they form the basis of an ethical code called the Middle Way. The Middle Way is also expressed in lists of precepts that cover much of the same ground. The term *Middle Way* implies a middle course between the extremes of asceticism and sensual or emotional indulgence. The steps and precepts indicate specific ways of avoiding harm to others. The underlying idea is actually the avoidance of attachments and emotional involvements that serve to accentuate and perpetuate a sense of personal egoic identity.

Gautama's position is an outgrowth of Hindu tradition, but it is also a reaction against the expressions of that tradition that were dominant at the time. Gautama changed the interpretation of some basic Hindu concepts such as karma and nirvana, and he rejected others. He rejected the Brahmanic doctrine that atman is brahman, for he regarded both of these concepts as meaningless. He rejected the presumed authority of the Brahmins, seeing their contributions as largely empty abstractions, and had little regard in general for the caste system (wherein the Brahmins enjoyed the highest status). He introduced a deeper understanding of the nature of consciousness and its various contents. His psychological understanding was deeper than that of his Greek contemporaries—Pythagoras, Xenophanes, and Parmenides—as well as their successors in classical Greece. One might well argue that it exceeded anything yet produced by Western psychology in modern times. His insights center around a notion—that suffering is the inevitable price of consciousness—that has been expressed in countless forms in the West, from Greek and Hebrew mythology to Carl Jung and contemporary existentialism, but Gautama's treatment of this idea remains one of the most profound elaborations of it.

Like Jesus of Nazareth, Gautama, who came to be known as the Buddha, the awakened one, manifested a level of understanding far greater than that of other people of his time. Like Jesus, he exemplified a mode of consciousness available as a potential to everyone but he was often seen more as a god than as an exemplar, and his basic message was subjected to a variety of transformations by would-be followers. There is little doubt that he became an object of worship among some early Buddhists, and both Buddha and other presumed buddhas or bodhisattvas are worshipped today in some Buddhist sects. This practice, however, runs counter to the basic doctrines of Gautama, who regarded full enlightenment, or realization of one's inherent buddhahood, as possible for everyone. From the standpoint of more astute Buddhists, the worship of a Buddha interferes with the achievement of enlightenment, because the inner potential is viewed as existing only without, in an idealized other being.

Richard W. Coan

The Subsequent Development of Buddhism

For a few centuries Buddhism flourished in India. Many communities of Buddhist monks were established, and their members generally followed the precepts of Gautama rather closely. The ethical code of Gautama was inevitably subjected to much philosophical elaboration, and disagreements arose. Within the first three centuries, at least eighteen or twenty different schools of thought developed. During the first century A.D., a new movement that came to be known as Mahayana Buddhism began, and splits subsequently occurred within this movement. The divisions within Hinayana Buddhism (the early eighteen or so schools) and within the Mahayana movement centered largely around metaphysical issues. Some Buddhists held that only present events are real, while others contended that past and future events are equally real. There were also questions regarding the reality of the self, the external world, and consciousness, with resulting positions that might be roughly characterized as pluralistic realism, nihilism, and subjective idealism. Having dispensed with the metaphysical scaffolding of the Brahmins, Gautama might not have regarded all these rational systems as useful extensions of his basic doctrines.

Obviously the development of Buddhism in India involved more than just a series of intellectual disputes. The growth of Mahayana Buddhism brought some significant changes in ideals and practices, even though this movement was rooted in the work of Gautama. The Mahayana Buddhists stressed the concept of the *bodhisattva*, the enlightened individual who delays entry into the bliss of nirvana in order to aid other people on their path to spiritual salvation. Earlier Buddhists had stressed the ideal of the *arhat*, the enlightened individual who has transcended ignorance and earthly attachments, and in Hinayana Buddhism this ideal had come to be interpreted primarily in terms of wisdom. In stressing the ideal of the bodhisattva, the Mahayana Buddhists were assigning equal weight to compassion. In many respects the Mahayana Buddhists offered a system with a more universal appeal, one that provided for a wider sector of society. In doing so, they provided some of the seeds that facilitated the spread of Buddhism to other climes. Nonetheless, during the first thousand years of the Christian era, as Buddhism spread to most of the other countries of Asia, it underwent a steady decline in its country of origin. For the past thousand years, it has had few adherents in Indian and has not played a significant role in the culture of that country. Some of the developments in Hinduism during this period, however, may be viewed as a result of an earlier Buddhist influence.

LATER DEVELOPMENTS IN HINDUISM

Gautama lived during the period when the major Brahmanic writings were produced, and there were further developments within Hinduism during the growth and subsequent decline of Buddhism in India. Some of these developments are even further removed from the doctrines of the Brahmins than Buddhism was, and this fact illustrates the arbitrary elasticity of the word *Hinduism*. Though Buddhism may be considered an outgrowth of Hinduism, perhaps it is convenient to consider it a separate system in the light of its ultimate geographic separation from India. For reasons that are equally casual, we no longer regard Christianity as a form of Judaism, but we view Roman Catholicism, Eastern Orthodoxy, the teachings of the Coptic church, and Protestantism in all its varieties as forms of a single Christian religion.

The work of the Brahmins was continued in the development of six systems of thought, or darshanas, the most important being Vedanta. Yoga is considered another of the darshanas, one that has yielded a vast array of meditative and psychological practices. There is little doubt that Westerners have much to learn from both of these systems. The methods of yoga are designed to serve a number of purposes in addition to the gnostic experience of brahman-identity. For centuries, yogis have achieved a level of bodily control that Westerners, using such techniques as hypnosis, autogenics, and biofeedback, have only begun in recent years to duplicate.

In popular Hinduism a few major deities continue to play a prominent role. The great goddess important in pre-Vedic times remains important in the experience of most Indians and tends to be equated with such figures as Parvati, Kali and Durga. The tales of Krishna depicted in the great epic poem the *Mahabharata*, continue to arouse popular interest. The *Bhagavata Purana* of the tenth century A.D. portrays Krishna as the lover of the Gopis, the wives of a whole community of cowherds, and strikes a highly sensual note that stands as a striking counterpoint to the ascetic restraint and introverted yogic practices that are more prominent in Hinduism. The gods of greatest importance in popular Hinduism, however, are Vishnu and Shiva (though Krishna is considered one of the incarnations of Vishnu), and there are a number of sects devoted to the worship of each of these gods. From the standpoint of the Upanishads and of Vedanta philosophy, the ultimate divine ground is the impersonal brahman, and our true nature is indistinguishable from it. Worship of the brahman makes no sense: rather the aim is *gnosis*, a realization of brahman-identity. To the devotees of Vishnu and Shiva, *bhakti*, loving devotion to a deity, may assume more importance than gnosis as a way to salvation. This is particularly true within the Vaishnava bhakti movement of southern India, which rests on a theology in which the supreme soul, personified as Vishnu, is viewed as a loving, personal god.

Some of the developments in Hinduism over the past thousand years have occurred as a result of contact with other cultures. A Moslem invasion of 1000 A.D. brought Hindus into contact with Islamic ideas. Since the sixteenth century, Indians have been exposed to Christian influences. British colonial practices brought India into contact with another side of Western culture and provoked various forms of nationalism, including the militancy of Bal Gangadhar Tilak and the ahimsa of Mohandas Gandhi. All the significant developments in Hindu thought in a modern era reflect cultural blends of one kind or another. We may note three major figures who have exerted considerable influence on modern Hindu thought: Ramakrishna Paramahamsa, Mohandas Gandhi (who became known as Mahatma Gandhi), and Aurobindo Ghose (who became known as Sri Aurobindo). Ramakrishna and his most prominent disciple, Vivekananda, saw all religions as equally valid and regarded the theological content of a religion as less important than its expression in life and society. The monks who follow their teachings lead lives devoted to chastity, poverty, and an active expression of love of others. Gandhi was a shy and bookish youth who, in his mature years, traveled widely, lived simply, and became the greatest social leader in the twentieth century. Inspired by Western writers as well as Eastern systems of thought he stressed the concept of *ahimsa*, or nonviolence. This concept tends to imply an underlying attitude of love toward all creatures, and Erik Erikson (1969) suggests that for Gandhi it implied a deep respect for the essence of inherent truth in every individual. Of the major figures in modern Hinduism I noted above, Aurobindo was probably the most profound scholar. Having received a classical British education in his childhood and youth, he developed a system, which we shall consider further in the next chapter, that combined the modern evolutionary thought of Western science with traditional doctrines of Hindu philosophy.

Basic Trends in Hinduism

From this brief account of the history of Indian thought it is evident that at least within the creative stratum of that society, consciousness has evolved along a path somewhat different from the one we see in the West. To be sure, there are common ingredients. We find an early shift from mythic projection to a philosophical translation in which the gods are taken less literally and given a psychological interpretation. Greek philosophy, however, provided the foundation on which Western science was ultimately built. The work of the Brahmins contained many of the same ingredients, but it did not lead to the same result. In Greek philosophy, the rational element outweighed the mystical. In Brahmanic philosophy, the mystical element outweighed the rational, and transcendence of egoic identity was stressed from an early point.

Despite various popular departures from this theme, the emphasis on transcendence as a goal has been a persisting feature of Hinduism, as well as such diverging philosophies as Buddhism. As a result, Indians have tended to neglect what I called the modes of efficiency and creativity as developmental goals, and the kind of science and art we know in the West has not flourished in India. On the other hand, the emphasis on transcendence and the cultivation of yogic disciplines as a means to its realization have enabled countless Indians over the centuries to acquire an awareness of various states of consciousness and their contents. Many of them have achieved a bodily awareness that permits greater voluntary control over physiological processes than most Western biologists, perhaps until very recently, have considered possible. In many Indians, we also encounter a level of intuitive and extrasensory perceptiveness that is extremely rare among people of Western societies.

Forms of awareness associated with the mode of relatedness have followed an irregular course in both India and the West, and in both settings there are curious contradictions. Perhaps a sense of tribal identity is common at an early stage in any culture and precedes a sense of distinct personal identity. In the West, the teachings of Jesus of Nazareth mark a crucial point of transition, since they indicate the possibility of abandoning the projections that separate us from the enemy and the outsider as well the tribal neighbor, and the implication is that we can move on to a love for all people, seeing in each one just a different expression of the same human elements that we find in ourselves. In the West, we have often perverted this teaching, even to the extent of using it as an excuse for violence. We have often ignored it, placing more emphasis on our individualistic traditions. We have continued to struggle with it, however, and it may well be that the importance of the teaching has been realized by an increasing number of people.

In early Hinduism such an idea is not evident. The traditional path of Brahmanic philosophy stresses withdrawal from other people for the sake of individual enlightenment (to be sure, an enlightenment wherein individuality is transcended). In popular Hinduism, something akin to Christian love has been expressed as bhakti, but this implies love of a deity first of all and secondarily love of other creatures for the divine essence that lies within each one. In Buddhism, the traditional emphasis is non-harming for the sake of non-attachment, but this too can shade into active compassion for others. Active compassion and love for all people seem to be elements that have become more conspicuous in both Hindu and Buddhist thought in recent times. In India, however, the caste system has stood for many centuries as a symbol of the failure of that country to move very far as a total society in this direction. The caste system originated long ago in the subjugation by the invading Aryans of the darker-skinned Dravidians, and it was reinforced by a rationalization in terms of the Brahmanic concepts of samsara and karma. It is significant that many modern leaders have advocated the elimination of caste distinctions.

CHINESE THOUGHT

Early Stages

It is difficult to gain a clear picture of the early history of China, since many legends were projected into the past by historians of later periods. We do know something of early religious beliefs and practices, however, from writings that have survived. We know that various nature deities were worshipped and that there were fertility rites and cults. During the Chou dynasty, which lasted from 1027 B.C. to 771 B.C., the highest deity was the Supreme Ancestor and was equated with Heaven (T'ien). This figure was regarded as being in control of the seasons and the cycle of death and renewal and capable of ensuring the fertility of people, animals, and crops. The *Book of Songs*, a collection of poetry from this period, contains hymns addressed to the gods and to the royal ancestors. The stress on reverence for royal ancestors, with accompanying references to various features of feudal society, reveals some of the characteristic flavor of that time. Other writings reveal something of the shamanic religious practices of that period.

The sixth century B.C. marks a time of transition, because it is the beginning of an age of great philosophers. In China as in Greece and India, there was a shift, at least within one stratum of the society, from mythic projection to philosophical speculation, and while the gods may have survived in popular belief and practice, the philosophers generally dispensed with them. From the sixth century B.C. to the third century B.C., there were numerous philosophers, with as many different points of view, formulating ideas and debating with one another. We recognize two major streams of thought, often loosely called religions, in which the most significant figures appeared during this age. One is Confucianism and the other Taoism, but each of these can be considered a tradition with much more ancient roots in the misty past. We usually think of the philosophical formulation and elaboration of these two systems as beginning with K'ung Fu-tzu (Confucius) in the case of Confucianism and Chuang Tzu and Lao Tzu in the case of Taoism. Joseph Campbell (1976), however, notes that, while K'ung Fu-tzu may have been a dominant figure in his tradition, it is impossible now to determine which, if any, of the writings ascribed to him were actually written by him. He further suggests that Lao Tzu, the supposed author of the *Tao Te Ching*, is a "complete mirage."

Whatever the nature and writings of these two men, there

is no doubt that Confucianism and Taoism are two of the three major traditions in Chinese thought. The third is Buddhism, which was introduced at a later time from India. As Buddhism developed in China, it was strongly influenced by the two native traditions and became more distinctly Chinese. In turn Taoist and Confucian thought were influenced by Buddhism. There is a certain quality to Chinese thought from early to modern times that distinguishes it from Indian thought. Where Indian thought stresses union with the absolute through withdrawal from the external material and consensual world, Chinese thought stresses harmony, both among people and between people and the whole of nature. This theme is present in the very early writings, it is evident in different ways in both Taoism and Confucianism, and it is central to the Chinese version of Buddhism.

Confucianism

K'ung Fu-tzu was a contemporary of Gautama, but it is quite unlikely that either man knew of the other. He was followed by numerous Confucian and Neo-Confucian philosophers who built on his work, or on the classic writings commonly ascribed to him. The two leading successors in the early age of philosophers were Meng Tzu (Mencius) and Hsün Tzu. These three dealt with many of the issues embraced by classical Greek philosophy, but they differed a bit from one another. Hsün Tzu was the most realistic of the three, Kung Fu-tzu and Meng Tzu being more idealistic, and it has been suggested that the three form a succession that parallels that of Socrates, Plato, and Aristotle.

Like the Brahmins who wrote the Brahmanas and Upanishads, K'ung Fu-tzu saw his task as the transmission and interpretation of ideas of an earlier age (the Chou dynasty). Like the Brahmins, he used the documents of the earlier age as a springboard for the development of a system of values and practices that was not really evident in the earlier material. Confucian philosophers in general emphasize reason and oppose superstition and supernatural forms of religion. They focus primarily on human social life and expound principles that they view as central to social harmony. While Christianity has traditionally emphasized altruistic love of fellow humans (in Latin, *caritas*; in Greek, *agape*) as the key, Confucianism stresses such concepts as *jen* and *li*, which have no exact equivalents in English.

Jen refers to the basic attitude toward others that promotes harmony, and we may render it approximately in English as benevolence, unselfishness, deference, and loyalty. *Li* implies a general sense of courtesy and agreeable conduct, which includes proper manners, appropriate dress, and observance of ritual. K'ung Fu-tzu devoted particular attention to the expression of jen and li within five specific kinds of relationship: between ruler and subject, between father and son, between an older and a younger brother, between husband and wife, and between two friends. In each case, benevolence was deemed essential for the older or more dominant individual, while respect and loyalty were considered essential for the younger or more subservient individual. Much that K'ung Fu-tzu considered a natural and fundamental order is bound to strike a modern Westerner as the conventional order of another era and culture.

One other quality stressed by K'ung Fu-tzu is sincerity, or *ch'eng*. The individual who manifests this can permit the full development or unfolding of his or her own inborn nature and also foster such development in others. Perhaps *sincerity* is as good a translation of *ch'eng* as any, but these ideas are strongly reminiscent of Carl Rogers's (1961) concept of congruence, as well as the concept of self-actualization as elaborated by Kurt Goldstein and Abraham Maslow (1970).

Taoism

Many voices spoke in China during the early age of philosophers. In addition to the Confucians with their concern for the family and the social system, there were many schools of quietists or mystics, who sought instead an inner completeness through various methods of contemplation or meditation. The most prominent of these schools was Taoism. Like K'ung Fu-tzu, the great champions of this movement, Chuang Tzu and Lao Tzu (assuming there was such a person), saw themselves as following a tradition that was already ancient. The traditional founder of Taoism was the great Yellow Emperor, Huang Ti, who supposedly lived 5,000 years before Chuang Tzu and Lao Tzu, but Huang Ti can best be deemed a purely mythic figure. As James Legge notes, no writings prior to those of Lao Tzu and Chuang Tzu survive, and Chuang Tzu's own account of earlier phases of Taoism must be regarded as a fictitious account (Legge, 1972, pp. 1-4). In all likelihood, the ideas of the Taoist philosophers are based not so much on earlier documents as they are on magical and shamanic practices that arose in a much earlier period and continued into the age of the philosophical writings. No doubt these practices had a strong appeal for those philosophers who felt they could best deal with a troubled society by withdrawing into the wilderness, observing nature, meditating, and seeking gnosis. Confucianism, on the other hand, would have appealed to those philosophers who believed they could promote a better society by preaching an ethical code designed to correct the ills of the existing society.

The most basic concept of Taoism is the concept of the *tao*. A literal translation might be something like "the way" or "the path," but in Taoist writings it refers to the way or course of nature or of the universe. The nature of the tao itself, however, is beyond the reach of the intellect, and it cannot be specified. We can characterize it only in terms of what it is not. It is nameless, limitless, void, beyond all dualities. To the extent that we think we have understood it and can describe it, we have failed to understand, for "the tao that can be spoken is not the tao." Lao Tzu speaks of the tao as the "mother of all things" (Tao Teh King, 1962, pp. 45-124). He makes rare use of the term *ti*, which might be translated as *god*, but it seems fairly clear that for the

Taoist philosophers the impersonal principle of the tao essentially replaced any theistic concepts for explanatory purposes.

From a Taoist standpoint, the aim of existence is to attain and maintain harmony with the tao, and the basic means of doing this is expressed in the concept of *wu-wei*. This may be approximately rendered as *inaction*, but the basic idea, in Taoist usage of the term, is acceptance of the flow of nature and refraining from action that runs counter to it. Joseph Needham (1956) notes that the term was also used by Buddhists, Legalists, and some Confucians with different shades of meaning.

Taoists also sought wisdom, but it was a wisdom that comes with living in harmony with nature, an intuitive or gnostic kind of wisdom, rather than one that depends on knowledge or the acquisition of facts. Indeed, it was held that the acquisition of the kind of knowledge that scholars prize can stand as a barrier to the attainment of great wisdom (Blofeld, 1978). Despite this mystical orientation, Needham (1956) believes that the outlook of the early Taoists was more favorable for the development of science than was that of the Confucians The Confucians were a bit like the rational theologians who refused to look through Galileo's telescope (for if what they saw agreed with Aristotle, the telescope was superfluous, while anything they saw that did not agree could not be true). The Taoists were more open to observation and less trustful of established authority. Being less aristocratic, they were also much more inclined to work with their hands and thus get involved in manual operations and experimentation that might yield a practical knowledge of objects and materials. Needham notes that, despite their empiricism, the Taoists never developed a systematic theoretical account of nature, comparable to what we find in the work of Aristotle in the West, but then that was never their interest or intention.

We have now seen a number of ways in which the Taoists differed from their Confucian contemporaries. The Taoist orientation was introverted; the Confucian was more extraverted. The "Confucians favored a harmonious feudal society. The

Taoists tended to withdraw from society and favored a more primitive and cooperative kind of social system, perhaps matriarchal in character. Needham suggests that the Taoists were both mystical and empiricist. We might say, in Jungian terms, that the Taoists stressed the irrational functions (sensation and intuition), while the Confucians stressed the rational functions (thinking and feeling). The mystical, intuitive side of Taoism is more evident in the early literature, and it leads to an interesting difference between the two schools in their views of language. The Confucians stress the importance of assigning the correct labels to things, people, and relationships, while the Taoists stress the verbal inexpressibility of their central concept, and they seek a wisdom that cannot generally be captured in words. Furthermore, the *Tao Te Ching* suggests that whatever can be clearly expressed is trivial at best and can mislead us into thinking we have captured an important truth, for "words that are strictly true appear to be paradoxical" (Tao Teh King, 1962, p. 120). As a final point, we may note that the Taoist writings emphasize an orientation that is expressed in such words as *feminine, yielding,* and *receptive.* The *Tao Te Ching* speaks of the victory of the soft and weak and of the female overcoming the male. All of these words and phrases are expressions of wu-wei. The Confucian attitude is more masculine in the sense that it is oriented more toward the establishment of social order and the maintenance of status hierarchies in society.

Other Early Schools and Concepts

As I noted, there were many different schools of thought in the age of philosophers, and we have considered the two most influential ones, but it is important to recognize the diversity of thought in that period. As in Greece, there were philosophers who took a particular interest in logic, and there were philosophers, such as Tsou Yen, who were interested in the development of naturalistic science. Tsou Yen made extensive use of a five-element scheme comparable to the earth-air-fire-water system of the Greeks. As in the Greek system, the Chinese elements (earth, wood, metal, fire and water) acquired an overlay of symbolic connotations and were put to many uses. There were also the Mohists (followers of Mo Tzu), who favored utilitarian social policies, condemned aggressive warfare, and advocated universal love as a practical basis for promoting the common good. In contrast, there were also the Legalists, who favored a strong authoritarian government and glorified war.

The concepts of *yang* and *yin*, like the system of five elements, were used extensively in early Chinese thought as a basis for interpretation of all sorts of diverse matters, and they have continued to play a role in the many centuries since the age of philosophers. The roots of these concepts are obscure, and they were undoubtedly used long before anyone thought of the five elements. These concepts have gained a certain popularity of late in our society, and we tend to think of them as equivalent to masculinity and femininity. Perhaps they originally meant something like the light and the dark, or light and shade. Richard Wilhelm (1967) says, in fact, that *yang* and *yin* meant specifically, "banners waving in the sun" and "the cloudy" or "the overcast." Early in Chinese thought, however, they began to embrace a wide array of paired meanings: masculine and feminine, light and dark, hard and soft, warm and cold, dry and wet, good and evil, upper and lower, joy and sorrow, life and death, love and hate, active and passive, positive and negative, steadfast and changeable, agreeing and opposing, heaven and earth, white and black, great and small, reward and punishment, man and woman, father and son, advancing and retreating, odd number and even number, and so forth. They thus came to constitute a sort of ultimate duality in terms of which just about anything could be interpreted. It is characteristic of Chinese thought in general that these two basic principles should be regarded as complementary. Problems arise when either is emphasized to the exclusion of the other. Harmony in every realm of events requires a proper balance of the yang and the yin. Westerners, traditionally less oriented toward harmony, are accustomed to asking which of two ultimate principles is better than the other. We see this tendency carried to an extreme in much Christian thought, where the ultimate dichotomy is good versus evil, and the good is definitely preferred. We acknowledge the good, while we repress the evil within and project it outward. This leads to both intrapersonal and interpersonal difficulties that are more easily avoided in the Orient.

Another facet of Chinese thought is evident in one of the best known expressions of the yin-yang doctrine, namely the classical book of divination, the *I Ching*. The core of this book is a system of 64 hexagrams, each consisting of a particular combination of six broken and/or unbroken lines. Originally a collection of linear signs used as oracles, the system attracted the attention of a number of philosophers, and an elaborate system of interpretations and commentaries developed over a period of centuries. The traditional method for using the *I Ching* is to settle on a question to be answered, then follow a standard procedure (involving either the tossing of coins or successive divisions of a set of yarrow stalks) designed to yield a specific hexagram at random. The interpretations and commentaries that accompany the hexagrams are of an abstract, symbolic character, and the remarkable thing about the *I Ching* is that it is always possible to construe the content that one obtains in response to a question as an answer that is meaningful in terms of the issues embodied in the question. It is very tempting for a Western psychologist to explain this fact by saying that the book is simply an ingenious system of verbal projective stimuli, so ingenious that it does not really matter what hexagram our coin tosses or stalk sortings yield. We will interpret the message we receive in such a way that it makes sense and constitutes sound advice. If this is all there is to it, the *I Ching* is still useful, since the mental procedure occasioned by its use often facilitates an awareness of matters we have overlooked or tended to avoid seeing.

The traditional use of the *I Ching* in China, of course, assumes that the random procedure can lead to a specific correct answer. There are a number of ways this could be rationalized in Chinese thought. Carl Jung (1967) has offered an interpretation in terms of synchronicity that is probably consistent with a large body of Chinese thought. While the principle of causality has long been important in Western thought, Chinese thought traditionally attaches more importance to chance, tends to regard all events as interdependent, and views the events of any given time as bearing the imprint of the moment.

In this early period, in which so many different schools of philosophical thought appeared, all of the major strands that seem important in traditional Chinese thought are evident. Alongside the early philosophical schools there were popular religious practices and beliefs surviving from earlier times. Apparently the ordinary people continued to feel a need for shamans, sorcerers, magicians, and a belief in gods, personalized spirits, divine ancestors, and some sort of heaven. Neither Confucianism nor Taoism met these needs, and the popular beliefs have persisted to the present day. Evidently a systematic account of popular Chinese religion has never been written, and it is likely that popular beliefs vary considerably from one community to another. In general, they have not been codified in a way that would enable them to become well-known outside a given community, and the Western habit of proselytizing and spreading the domain of a given belief system is a bit foreign to Chinese culture. There was one abortive attempt to achieve a kind of unity of popular religions at the beginning of the Ch'in dynasty in the third century B.C. Inspired by Legalism and seeking to solidify his own power, the emperor visited shrines throughout China, seeking to establish himself as the supreme sovereign over both the people and the many gods of the land.

Subsequent Development

Confucianism has persisted through the centuries as a rationalistic and essentially nontheistic philosophy. It has undergone some fluctuations in influence but has remained the guiding system of thought for the educated elite. It has undergone elaboration in the hands of many scholars, but it has remained largely unaffected by the popular religion. Both because it is less rational in character and because its advocates have never represented such a distinct social stratum, Taoism has undergone much more change over the centuries. A Taoist church was in existence as early as the second century A.D., and the religion of this church was a far cry from the mysticism of the fourth and third centuries B.C. It was a religion of salvation, in which the devotees were offered a number of possible routes to paradise, including piety, confession, atonement, charity, abstinence, and service in the religious community. In its popular forms, Taoism embraced a host of deities, and it adopted a variety of practices from earlier popular religion. Taoist priests made use of magic charms, and they engaged in a variety of shamanic practices, entering trances and seeking communication with spirit entities.

The more advanced Taoists engaged in alchemical pursuits and developed a variety of yogic techniques. The latter included breathing exercises, certain dietary and sexual practices, and meditation. One of their aims was the achievement of immortality. It is not clear to what extent this was meant to be taken literally in its early use, but some of the yogic practices of the Taoists were undoubtedly designed to preserve youthful vigor and prolong life. In recent centuries, *immortality* among Taoists has come to mean much the same thing as *enlightenment* in Hinduism. Perhaps Taoist thought in recent centuries reflects the influences of Buddhism and possibly other streams of Indian thought. Whatever the source of ideas, Taoists obviously recognize that the body is destined to die and decay, but they speak of immortality as a merging with the limitless source of all being, or a realization that one's true nature is the undifferentiated tao. John Blofeld (1978) has described some of the Taoist immortals he has met. They were not men of great formal learning or sophistication, but they manifested unusual serenity, joy, and intuitive depth. Blofeld adds an observation that is best left in his own words:

> There is a dramatic means of identifying those rare beings who have reached the very highest attainment. During a conversation with such a being on some serious subject, an opportunity may occur to look, without making one's intention obvious, straight into his eyes, or, in special circumstances, he may himself choose to confer a revelation (as, on one unforgettable occasion, happened to me). In either case, it is as though for an ecstatic moment a curtain has been twitched aside, revealing unimaginable immensities; for the space of a single flash of thought, one shares the vastness of a sage's inner vision! The bliss is indescribable, but not to be endured for more than a fraction of a second, its intensity being too great to be borne by ordinary mortals. Either he, knowing what is occurring, will lower his eyes, or one must tear away one's own. The fruit of such a momentous encounter is of inestimable worth, for never again will one's conviction of the reality of the supreme apotheosis waver (Blofeld, 1978, pp. 186-87).

Buddhism in China

There was a Buddhist influence in China by the middle of the first century A.D. at the latest, but Buddhists may have first entered the country many years before that. Buddhism was widely regarded as a form of Taoism, perhaps because the Buddhists and Taoists engaged in many similar practices, such as meditation, yogic disciplines, fasting, and abstinence. In principle, there were fundamental differences between Buddhism, which denied the existence of the individual personality, or at least its permanent existence, and Taoism, which was concerned at that time with the perpetuation of the individual personality. Over time, much mutual accommodation occurred. Taoists were influenced by Buddhism, and Buddhism was modified as a result of contact with Taoism and various form of popular Chinese religion. Both Hinayana and Mahayana forms of Buddhism were introduced to China, but only the Mahayana survived there. Within the first four or five centuries of the Christian era, at least ten distinct schools of Buddhism developed, and several of these were purely Chinese derivatives of basic Buddhist philosophy.

One of the Chinese schools was Ch'an Buddhism, which held that one can achieve a realization of his or her buddha nature through sudden enlightenment. While the Ch'an school held that the buddha nature was the only ultimate reality, another mystical sect, the Chen-yen, had a more elaborate system of beliefs, and its adherents practiced a form of meditation in which they identified with the various deities of the tantric pantheon (Parrinder, 1981). Two other schools which enjoyed greater popularity over the centuries than either of these two mystical schools are the T'ien-t'ai school and the Pure Land school.

The T'ien-t'ai school makes some use of meditation but treats it as no more important than ritual, moral discipline, or study of the scriptures. This school has produced many scholars and a systematic philosophical treatment of basic Buddhist ontological concepts. An idea running through much of their philosophy is the interpenetration of all modes of being. Thus the realm of temporary reality (the realm of appearances, or reality as we ordinarily recognize it) is inseparable from the realm of noumenon or void (the ultimate nature of things beneath appearances and beyond all the dualities in terms of which we describe things in words). Furthermore, everything in a sense involves everything else, and whatever is manifest in one being is in the nature of all other beings. Hence, even the most depraved individual has a buddha nature and is inherently good, while the Buddha, however good, is at the same time evil. However complex this doctrine may seem, it is rather democratic in the sense that it leads to the view that all beings are qualified by their inherent nature to become Buddha and that the one broad path of Mahayana Buddhism is suitable for everyone as an avenue to enlightenment or salvation.

The Pure Land school has enjoyed still greater popularity since it first appeared in China in the fourth century A.D. It is based on an idea, which originated in India but diverges considerably from the theses of Gautama, that certain buddhas created special buddhalands into which one may be reincarnated as a step toward the achievement of nirvana. Of particular interest is the Pure Land created by the buddha Amitabha somewhere in the west. Whereas other schools teach the importance of achieving enlightenment through procedures that require much personal effort, this school holds that one may be assured of rebirth in the Pure Land if one has sufficient faith in Amitabha and makes a regular practice of repeating his name. Indeed, upon death one can expect to be greeted personally by Amitabha in the Pure Land. Here and in some other popular forms of Buddhism, we see buddhas and bodhisattvas elevated to the status of gods and worshipped by admirers who prefer to rely on the power of the idealized figure rather than depending on their own power.

For several centuries after its transplantation from India to China, Buddhism flourished and underwent creative development. In the ninth century A.D., it was subjected to brutal suppression during the reign of the emperor Wu-tsung, who favored the Taoists over the Buddhists and saw Buddhism as a foreign importation that created various problems in Chinese life. Most of the creative growth in Buddhist thought after this time occurred in other countries of Asia. In China, Buddhism, like Taoism, survived as a popular religion, while its more profound teachings and practices were confined to small communities that exerted little influence on the cultural life of the country as a whole. As a popular religion, Buddhism has remained a significant feature of Chinese life through the twentieth century. During the early years of the Communist regime, starting in 1949, there were efforts to suppress all forms of popular religion. Since they conflicted with the more materialistic outlook of Karl Marx and Mao Tse-tung, they were viewed as "counter-revolutionary." The government has adopted an attitude of greater tolerance, however, since the death of Mao in 1976. It is difficult for outsiders to gain a clear picture of the changes that have actually taken place in the thinking and consciousness of the mass of Chinese people during the second half of this century. Undoubtedly any ideology or system of thought that receives wide attention has a certain impact on the conscious experience of many people. Over the past two or three centuries, the Chinese have had increasing contact with Western ideas. Christian missionaries have been present, but Christianity itself has had only a minor influence. It seems likely that Communist ideology will have a far greater influence.

In reviewing the history of Chinese thought, we have seen that in many respects it differs from both that of the West and that of India. It shares with both India and Greece an early movement from a period dominated by deities and a concern with one's relationship to them to an age in which philosophy flourished. The philosophy of China was more like that of Greece than was the work of the Brahmins, for there was a proliferation of schools representing a range of views comparable to that of the Greek schools. Both mystical and rational orientations were represented within the Chinese schools. Certain features of

Chinese thought apparent in the age of philosophers, however, point to a persisting difference from Western thought. Instead of the Greek stress on the cultivation of the individual and the notion of heroic achievement, we see an emphasis on inner harmony and a harmonious relationship to nature and the rest of society. In place of a growing Western concern with causality, we see an acceptance of a natural order that the human intellect cannot readily penetrate and that appears to be governed by chance. These features all point to a more holistic style of consciousness, one that is less concerned with defining a simple order in the world and more open to the interrelatedness and interpenetration of all phenomena. The characteristic style of consciousness in China is traditionally more extraverted on the whole than that of India, but it is similar to that of India in being more conducive to a broad, intuitive grasp of reality and less conducive to a precise, well articulated focus on a limited portion of reality than is Western thought.

The early trends evident in Taoism and Confucianism were augmented by a Buddhist influence that began somewhere near the beginning of the Christian era. While Buddhism could not survive in China without being extensively modified to conform to the main thrust of Chinese thought, it undoubtedly stimulated some development within the mystical stream of Chinese thought by introducing a great repertoire of meditative practices and introducing the idea of ego-transcendence. If this ideal was not altogether new, it was at least more adequately formulated than anything similar to be found in earlier Taoist writings. Mahayana Buddhism in China also provided a movement within which people could experience new modes of relating to one another, a movement in which the idea of compassion played a greater role than it had in the two major traditions already present in China. As in the case of India, we can infer trends over past centuries only in terms of what appears in the writings of a rather select stratum of Chinese society, but we have to assume that the ripples we see on the surface of the stream bear some relationship to the flow of the great body of water beneath them. The dominant emphases and trends we have seen in Chinese thought differ from those of Western thought in many respects, and it is reasonable to infer a somewhat different evolutionary progression with respect to consciousness in that culture.

JAPAN

Japanese culture presents another contrast with the West. Despite some major historical links to China, it also differs in important respects from that country. In comparison with India and China, it is a young country, since the extensive literary and philosophical development that occurred in pre-Christian times in those other countries did not occur in Japan. We do know that the Mongoloid people we now know as Japanese invaded that land from the mainland and from the islands to the south, and that they were preceded by the Caucasian Ainus, who are now confined to the northern islands. The details of the early history are not known with certainty, however, for the earliest historical accounts surviving in written form date from the eighth century A.D., and a bit of mythicizing is evident in them. One of these accounts, while important as a Shinto document, cannot be taken as a literal history, since it is designed to show the divine origin of the imperial family. Other early documents point more plausibly to shamanic practices in early periods and suggest that women functioned as shamans and mediums and, in that capacity, may have served as rulers.

One of the distinguishing features of Japanese society that is quite apparent in the modern industrial era but has certainly been present for many centuries is a social order in which each individual seems to identify closely with his or her role and accepts the responsibility for helping to make the whole system operate smoothly. There is probably no other country or society with a population comparable to that of Japan in which one would find so little internal conflict. The kind of social harmony that the Confucians tried to promote in China has long existed to a higher degree in Japan, and it is unlikely that the Confucian influence there had much to do with it. Joseph Campbell (1976) also notes a number of emotional qualities that he considers distinctly Japanese. For one thing, the people of Japan tend to be more emotional than rational. In Jungian terms, this may mean that they rely more on the feeling function and, perhaps, the sensation function than on the thinking function. For this reason, they tend to be affected strongly by the atmosphere of the environment and are inclined to take far greater care in arranging their environments so that they feel right. This pervasive aesthetic concern is evident in such unique customs as the Japanese tea ceremony. Campbell points out also that the Japanese maintain a sense of wonder and a delight in the numinous that has disappeared among people in most other advanced civilizations. (Hence, the Japanese, like the Bushmen, are capable of making us aware of how dead we have become under the weight of our own civilization.)

Major Religions in Japan

The native religion of the Japanese is Shinto. Shinto has two main branches, State Shinto and Sectarian Shinto. All Japanese citizens are assumed in principle to be members of the national, or state, branch, regardless of whatever other beliefs they may hold. State Shinto is concerned with rites and ceremonies that serve to enhance national sentiment and promote veneration of the emperor as a symbol of the state. Sectarian Shinto embraces thirteen recognized sects and numerous subsects, which vary somewhat in guiding ideas and ceremonial practices.

The Japanese speak of the focus of their sentiments in terms of *kami*, which is often translated as "god" or "gods." Westerners find the concept confusing, however, because it seems at times to be applied to the spirits of various ancestors, historical or mythological, to the spirits of certain deceased emperors, to certain national heroes, and then to a vast assortment of spirits in nature that cannot be specifically identified. They may then complain that Shinto seems to involve a very primitive form of pantheism, without a well-defined theology, philosophy, or ethical system. Indeed, the essence of Shinto does not lie in any verbally formulated system. This does not mean that it is primitive, however; it simply means that, if we are to consider it a religion, it is one quite foreign to the Western conception. If it is a religion, it is a religion of feelings, rather than ideology. The rituals, the ceremonies, and the dances of shinto are designed to evoke various feelings in the observer and the participant: a sense of awe at the wonders of the universe and the state, a sense of connection with the mysteries of nature, an aesthetic participation in the movement of the dance and in the physical environment. The kami may or may not be precisely defined, for they are not primarily something to be thought about but something to be felt. As a means of expressing and evoking feelings, the rituals of Shinto are among the most highly evolved in the world. In this respect at least, Shinto may be more advanced than any Western religion.

Both Confucianism and Buddhism were introduced to Japan well over a thousand years ago and have had some influence on Japanese culture. Confucian writings were probably first brought in during the fifth century A.D., and the ideas of K'ung Fu-tzu subsequently provided the foundation for competing schools of Confucian thought. These schools developed different social philosophies, some favoring the preservation of a fixed social hierarchy and some favoring a more egalitarian society. In Japan, the Confucian schools have probably exerted their greatest influence on the political and educational institutions.

Buddhism has had a far deeper influence as a religion or way of life. It was first introduced in the sixth century A.D., when the emperor was given a packet of Buddhist scriptures by a Korean King. The teachings of all the ten schools of Chinese Buddhism were subsequently introduced, but the schools that embodied the most distinctly Chinese forms of Mahayana Buddhism had the greatest impact, and the leading Japanese schools were derived from these. Just as Buddhism acquired a Chinese flavor in China, it has developed a Japanese flavor in Japan, and it could be argued that each of the Japanese schools of the present day has evolved beyond its Chinese parent stock.

The Pure Land school developed into four sects in Japan, and together these constitute the most popular form of Buddhism in that country and the doctrines of this form of Buddhism remain relatively simple and undemanding for the adherent. Amitabha, known in Japan as Amida, remains an object of worship. From the teachings of the T'ien-t'ai school there arose in Japan the school of Nichiren, who preached a rather extreme nationalism. The Chen-yen school of China gave rise to the Shingon school of Japan. From the teachings of the Ch'an school were derived the doctrines of Zen Buddhism, which is represented by two major schools, the Rinzai school and the Soto school.

Zen Buddhism has less popular appeal than Pure Land Buddhism because it offers a more demanding and solitary path to enlightenment. Zen monks may spend many years in monasteries, leading frugal and disciplined lives, in a quest for sudden enlightenment. In principle, enlightenment is assumed, as in the Ch'an view, to come in an instant, but in practice it is recognized that there may be many instants of sudden insight along the path to full enlightenment. Two basic practices are employed by Zen Buddhists as means for achieving or facilitating enlightenment. One is meditation, which is stressed by the Soto school. The other is the *koan*, which is employed primarily by the Rinzai school. The koan is a kind of nonsense puzzle or riddle, an apparently rational problem that has no rational solution, which the monk or student of Zen is asked to solve. There are hundreds of koans employed in Zen monastaries, and they take a variety of forms, but they have in common the aim of provoking insight, an insight which comes usually at the moment when the student abandons all efforts to achieve a rational solution.

Zen Buddhism has attracted considerable attention in this country over the past twenty or thirty years, and a sizable literature has appeared in English (e.g., Watts, 1957, and Suzuki, 1974). The most distinctive features of Zen, of course, reflect their earlier roots in Ch'an Buddhism, which in turn may be viewed as a blend of Indian Buddhism with Taoism. One important feature is an emphasis on naturalness and spontaneity, which involves the idea of wu-wei. Another feature is an emphasis on recognizing the illusion of the ego, or the illusory nature of the personal concept with which we identify. A full realization of the illusion is achieved in the experience of enlightenment, or *satori*. In satori, we achieve an intuitive apprehension of the world, in which we see everything free of the structure imposed by our dualistic mental habits.

Joseph Campbell offers an interesting capsule characterization of the differences between Indian, Chinese, and Japanese Buddhism: "The Indian Buddhist was disillusioned in the universe, the Chinese in society, the Japanese—not at all" (Campbell, 1976, p. 489). The Indian Buddhist found life in the world around him dissatisfying and tended to see withdrawal in some form as a solution. To the extent that the samsaric doctrine was incorporated into Indian Buddhism, the ultimate solution was seen as a withdrawal from earthly existence. The Chinese Buddhist, like the Taoist, might have been comfortable withdrawing into nature to avoid the ills of society. The Japanese Buddhist is more interested in being at peace with the world as it is. The difference is evident even in a subtle feature of meditational practice. The Indian Buddhist or yogi meditates with eyes closed, as if to block out the world of material maya for the sake of achieving ego-transcendence or an experience of unity with universal spirit. The Zen Buddhist meditates with eyes open and focused at a point on the floor. Meditating in this way, one more readily experiences a sense of union with the surrounding world. In either case, dualities dissolve, but the universes with which the two meditators experience a sense of unity are not quite the same universe. The Indian mystic develops an unusual comprehension of an inner realm but often appears to be cut off from the physical and social environment. The Japanese mystic more often appears to possess a heightened awareness of everything that goes on in his or her vicinity. Indeed, the life styles, customs, carefully nurtured surroundings, and art associated with Zen Buddhism reflect much the same sensitive feeling response to the environment that characterizes Shinto practices.

The Nature of Japanese Culture

For a mixture of geographic, cultural, and political reasons, Japan has been relatively insulated from foreign influence during most of its history. Europeans first reached Japan in the middle of the sixteenth century, but a significant Western influence has developed only since 1854, when Admiral Matthew Perry of the American Navy sailed into a Japanese harbor, and demanded an end to Japan's commercial isolation. The Japanese resumed trade with many other nations, soon saw the importance of industrialization, and proceeded at a rapid pace to convert their country to a modern industrial nation. Few Americans prior to World War II realized how well they had succeeded, since the Japanese shipped their finer exports to other parts of the world. For the Americans, whom they viewed as consumers of junk, they cranked out the gimcracks that seemed to impress our profit-minded merchants.

Japan lost the war, of course, but Japanese industry has recovered fully from it, and in each field of production it enters it appears to operate with an efficiency that American industry cannot match. There are probably several reasons for this, most of them a function of basic cultural differences. The Japanese worker is more likely to be concerned with the quality of the product on which he or she is working. Furthermore, within every company, one finds the kind of social cohesiveness that is characteristic of the society as a whole. Workers and managers together have a kind of esprit de corps and want the system to function smoothly. The worker identifies with the company to a much greater extent than does his or her American counterpart, and management policies and economic benefits serve to enhance this tendency. On the whole, the Japanese manager probably takes a greater interest in the product and less interest in personal profit than does his American counterpart. Company executives in Japan, on the average, do not receive annual incomes so far beyond those of their workers as do American executives. Oddly enough, an American statistician by the name of W. Edwards Deming played an important role in the early postwar years in fostering the success of Japanese industry (Halberstam, 1984). At that time, Japan was in a difficult economic plight. An industrial nation with a very limited territory and a large population like Japan must import raw materials and export products to survive, and the Japanese were having difficulty competing in the world marketplace. A group of Japanese engineers asked Deming to give a series of lectures on statistical quality control. He said he would do so only if their company heads also showed up. To his surprise a large group of industrial executives assembled to hear his lectures. They listened very carefully, followed his advice, turned out products of very high quality with increased efficiency, and prospered. Deming is justifiably famous in Japanese industrial circles, but the manner in which his ideas were received and widely applied in Japan says more about that society than it does about Deming.

There are other important developments that have occurred in the postwar era. Japan has developed a more democratic form of government, and Western influences have fostered a greater interest in individuality. Japan has also developed a very efficient educational system. I suggested earlier that there is much in Japanese culture that points to an emphasis on feeling in preference of rationality, but I suggested in the preceding chapter that the kind of educational system we have created tends to enhance rational and analytical thinking. If the latter point is valid, we may well infer that the consciousness of the Japanese people is rapidly evolving in the direction of greater rationality, for their educational system is working better than ours in doing what ours is designed to do (U.S. Schoolchildren, 1984: also Cunningham, 1984). Several studies have shown that Japanese children tend to perform at a higher level than their American counterparts at various grade levels. The difference is most striking for mathematics but holds as well for such skills as reading comprehension. In many areas of learning, most American public schools function with only moderate efficiency, for many children go through a number of years of school in the United States without learning to read or mastering basic computational skills. This is much less likely to happen in Japan. The difference between the Japanese and American educational systems is also apparent in intelligence-test performance. One study found that Japanese and American educational systems is also apparent in intelligence-test performance. One study found that Japanese children taking translated versions of the tests commonly used in American schools scored eleven points higher in IQ on the average than American children at the same age levels.

We are accustomed to interpreting the deficiencies of American school children in terms of a failure on the part of our schools. There is some merit in this criticism, for some of our teaching methods are inefficient, but there are deeper reasons. Americans take public education for granted, but on the whole they have less respect for education and for teachers than do the people of most other modern nations. American children often do not take education seriously because their parents do not take it seriously. There are other cultures, including Japan, in which parents are more likely to provide informal instruction in language and arithmetic skills. The overall American attitude toward education is evidenced by the fact that teachers are grossly underpaid when compared with other professionals with the same amount of training. In no other modern nation would one find so great a discrepancy. The primary implication of all this for the evolution of consciousness would seem to be that those modes of conscious processing that are most stimulated by the common methods of public education, notably the rational and analytical modes, are undergoing little growth in the American population at present. Within the populations of Japan and perhaps a number of other nations, they have probably undergone considerable enhancement during the twentieth century.

In Japan, then, we see one more Asian country in which the predominant modes of experience reflected in the major streams of thought differ from those in our own society. Traditionally, there has been much more emphasis on feeling than on thinking, more concern with aesthetic issues than with questions of truth. There is a rationalistic stream embodied in Confucianism, but this tradition has much less to do with the experience of the mass of Japanese than does either Buddhism or Shinto. There is a strong mystical tradition in Japan, as there is in India and China, but in Japan it is more world-affirming in character. Japanese mystics have generally tended to be more interested in feeling completely at home in the world than in escaping from it.

Despite long cultural isolation prior to the middle of the nineteenth century, Japan has rapidly become the most Westernized country in Asia in the modern era. Rapid development in science, technology, and education is an obvious facet of this shift. There is reason to believe that this development has been accompanied by an increased emphasis on individuality and individual achievement and by a greater development of rational and analytical modes of consciousness on the part of the Japanese people in general. If Japan has in the past lagged behind our own society in the development of those modes of consciousness that reach their highest form of expression in science, it has long been ahead of our society in the cultivation of other modes of consciousness (e.g., those manifested in an awareness of the aesthetic properties of the environment). In Japan, as in India and China, the overall pattern of psychic development has followed a different course from that of Western culture.

6

Some Partial Views on Psychic Evolution

We have touched on a variety of theories that have a bearing on the evolution of consciousness. We turn now to theories concerned more with the overall course of psychic evolution. Some of these are rather global in character, and none of them provides the sort of specific detail we find in Heinz Werner's treatment of primitive thought. Furthermore, each one views psychic evolution from a limited perspective. In combination, they show us an array of possible interpretations that must all be taken into account in a more comprehensive account of psychic evolution.

A common feature of these theories is that each one assumes that the evolution of consciousness is closely tied to cultural evolution. Hence the theorists all make use of various kinds of cultural expression. The cultural development that one theorist regards as a sign of psychic progress, however, may be ignored by another or construed as a regressive movement. While these theorists differ in their views on the nature of psychic evolution, each one tends to consider a particular path as universally valid and to regard any deviation from the path as a temporary interruption or disruption of the natural process.

PROGRESSIVE RATIONALITY

Since the Enlightenment, Western thinkers have tended to view psychological development primarily in terms of a cultivation of the mode of efficiency, and in particular the cultivation of rational-analytical consciousness. This outlook is implicit in much of the theoretical work stimulated by Darwinian theory, and it is evident in Freud's treatment of ego development. It is more explicit still in the writings of Jacob Bronowski and Carl Sagan, both of whom tend to equate progress in human thought with successive stages in the historical development of science.

Bronowski (1973) says little about the origin of human thought, but he is concerned with the qualities that permit a uniquely human form of knowing, a form that reaches its highest expression in modern science. It rests on a combination of faculties that enable humans to rise above the immediate situation, to anticipate events and situations not yet present, and to be creative. Speech and other modes of symbolism are seen as providing a tool with which we can recall the past and explore both remembered and imagined events (Bronowski, 1970).

Bronowski (1964, 1977) speaks of both art and science as human pursuits that express a quest for freedom from the restrictions imposed by nature, that enable us to create, and that provide a kind of understanding. Yet he speaks more as a scientist than as an artist, for he regards imagination and creativity as an outgrowth of analytical and rational processes. He contends that analytical attention to the details of nature provides the essential foundation for imagination. He cites Michelangelo as an authority on this point and refers to Leonardo da Vinci as a supreme illustration of it. Great as the masters of the Italian Renaissance were, however, they fit Bronowski's argument a little too tidily. Perhaps some of the modern masters, such as Picasso, Chagall, or Klee, would not. Here we see more experimentation with the very mode of perceiving or apprehending reality.

Bronowski is not primarily concerned with conscious

experience as such. He focuses rather on the changing concepts and images in terms of which we seek to understand the world, but he occasionally spells out the implications of these for consciousness. He notes the contemporary shifts in the scientific picture of the universe, as well as our increased recognition of the impossibility of securing absolute knowledge and of the dependence of our understanding on our human modes of perception (Bronowski, 1978). Nonetheless, he believes that modern science has given us a fresh understanding of our relationship to the rest of the universe. It has given us "a real sense of unity with nature. We see nature not as a thing but as a process, profound and beautiful; and we see it from the inside. We belong to it. This above all is what science has given us: the vision of our age" (Bronowski, 1964, p. 108).

Thus, from the pen of the champion of rationality comes a remarkably sanguine portrayal of the role of science in contemporary human experience. What he is describing, however, borders on a mystical consciousness that requires more than a rational foundation. It is possible for scientific knowledge to support the sort of unitary outlook he is depicting, but it also requires intellectual habits that can stand in the way of a full appreciation of the unity. It is important to recognize two basic kinds of knowledge. Having lost the verb *to wit* in English, we are accustomed to using the words *know* and *knowledge* in a double sense, referring both the knowing of immediate, intimate acquaintance and to the knowing-about that depends on detached observation, abstraction, and the acquisition of facts. In German, one can readily distinguish between *wissen* and *kennen*; in the Romance languages, one can distinguish between *savoir* and *connaître*, *saber* and *conocer*, or *sapere* and *conoscere*. The word *science* is derived from Latin *scire*, and it refers to those intellectual disciplines that are concerned with the accumulation and organization of our knowledge about the universe. In both method and aim, science is concerned with abstract knowledge. It is for this reason that we call it *science*, rather than *cognoscence*, or in German, *Wissenschaft* rather than *Kennenschaft*. *Gnosticism* (a word derived from the Greek cognate of Latin *cognoscere*) refers to the quest for the kind of knowledge that science neglects. In accord with Bronowski, I would argue that science need not hinder the gnostic experience (unless we identify so closely with the role of scientist that we strive to be super-rational and super-analytic in all our waking moments), and under some circumstances it may even provide a useful springboard. I think Bronowski errs, however, in suggesting that the unitary sense is an automatic consequence of our modern scientific understanding. Bronowski has furnished some valuable insights into human psychic evolution, but his treatment of that evolution is really focused rather narrowly on the progressive changes that have occurred in our rational conception of the universe.

Bronowski's basic orientation is reflected in his treatment of religion, which he views primarily in terms of prescientific belief systems, ignoring its symbolic, mystical, and ethical sides. He also expresses alarm at the amount of contemporary interest in such things as Zen Buddhism and parapsychology, seeing in this a retreat from "knowledge" and a tendency to ask "falsely profound questions" (Bronowski, 1973, p. 437). Evidently, if the rational enterprise is to succeed, we must avoid exploring too many of our experiential capacities, and we must keep our imagination under careful control. Personally I suspect that if all scientists followed Bronowski's advice, science itself would stagnate.

Carl Sagan

Many of Bronowski's sentiments are echoed in a more recent work of Carl Sagan (1977). Sagan regards rational, analytical thinking as the distinctive feature of human thought, contrasting it with intuitive thinking, which he believes may go back to the origin of life. He views the mind as strictly the working of the brain and argues that we differ psychologically from our closest relative, the chimpanzee, primarily because we have larger brains and more highly developed frontal lobes. This anatomical development provides the necessary foundation for analytical ability, foresight, and (as an unavoidable corollary of foresight) anxiety.

Sagan recognizes that scientific work commonly requires an interplay of intuitive and rational thinking, the former providing most of our initial insights, which are then subjected to critical analysis and described by linear, rational arguments. Yet, for Sagan, as for Bronowski, rationality must have the last word. He, too, expresses alarm at the popularity of vague or erroneous doctrines that are too "mystical" or "right-hemisphere" and that betoken a lack of intellectual rigor and toughmindedness (Sagan, 1977, p. 247-48). His examples include astrology, the Bermuda Triangle "mystery," much of flying-saucer lore, pyramidology, the belief in ancient astronauts, Scientology, spiritualism, the doctrine of special creation by God or gods, and various beliefs pertaining to auras, Kirlian photography, the emotional lives of plants, flat and hollow earths, and astral projection. While his skepticism with respect to such intellectual fads is understandable, I would point out simply that the concern he expresses is that of a Western scientist who construes human psychic evolution primarily in terms of the progressive development of a rational understanding of the universe.

CHRISTIAN EVOLUTIONISM

The word of Pierre Teilhard de Chardin also reflects the spirit of Western science, but Western science combined with Christian tradition, for Teilhard was both a paleontologist and a priest of the Jesuit order. While he recognized the importance of rational consciousness, he conceptualized the perfection of consciousness more in terms of love than in terms of rationality. He thus expressed a mystical view that was distinctly Western in character, a mystical view emphasizing relatedness rather than transcendence.

Like Herbert Spencer, Teilhard (1959, 1964, 1970) sought to formulate a theory that would embrace evolutionary processes at all levels of manifestation. He believed one could identify a basic process of "cosmogenesis" operating in the evolution of matter at early stages in the development of the universe as well as in the development of various forms of life. Like Spencer's formula, Teilhard's basic law of "complexity-centricity" assumes two complementary processes of unification and diversification. By virtue of these processes, each stage in the evolutionary process is held to yield an entity more "complex-centered" than any prior entity, that is, an entity that is unified and at the same time more complex than its predecessors.

According to Teilhard (1959, 1970), matter is always accompanied by mind, consciousness, or "spiritual energy." He spoke metaphorically of consciousness as the "within" or "centricity" of all things, the physical form being the "without," and he contended that the "within" becomes increasingly important as forms become more complex. He rejected a strict Darwinian interpretation of evolution as a narrow position that stressed external determinants and chance and ignored the role of consciousness. While the Darwinian view might be adequate at lower levels of evolution, he felt that at higher levels there was a greater need for a Lamarckian or neo-Lamarckian view, which would recognize the urge toward greater consciousness as a relevant factor.

Given this outlook, it is not surprising that Teilhard attributed more goal-directedness to the evolutionary progression than most biologists would. Notwithstanding the proliferation of forms that evolution has yielded, Teilhard contended that there is a pervasive trend toward higher levels of consciousness and that a major physical counterpart of this is a progressive increase in the complexity of the nervous system. Teilhard believed, however, that we have finally approached the limit of sheer biological change and entered into a phase of evolution in which biogenesis is being superseded by psychogenesis. In purely biological terms, it was a small step from the common ancestor of anthropoid apes and humans to their present forms. By the middle of the last ice age, our ancestors had developed brains indistinguishable from ours, but a major development not reducible to sheer morphology has taken place since then. Teilhard spoke of this development in terms of *hominization*, the shift to a human level of consciousness.

Some might argue that in talking about a major transformation not dependent on morphological change, Teilhard was really talking about something in the realm of social or cultural evolution. In response, Teilhard would simply have noted that biological and cultural evolution are inseparable parts of a larger process. Biological evolution has yielded a species in which psychological progress cannot be separated from cultural change and in which the psychological growth of the individual is bound up with a process of socialization or education.

Teilhard characterized hominization as "the progressive phyletic spiritualization in human civilization of all the forces contained in the animal world" (Teilhard, 1959, p. 180). He also characterized the human realm as "a zone of continuous spiritual transformation, where all inferior realities and forces without exception are sublimated into sensations, feelings, ideas, and the powers of knowledge and love" (Teilhard, 1957, p. 114). One implication of this is that we are now embarked on a divine mission to transform nature by making it conscious. If so, what is there in human consciousness that renders it unique? What critical threshold have we crossed? According to Teilhard, the essential new feature that has appeared in the human is the power of reflection. Other animals are conscious and know, but only the human being achieves self-knowledge and knows that he or she knows. It is even clearer in Teilhard's original French that both forms of knowing are involved: "non plus seulement connaître, mais se connaître; non plus seulement savoir, mais savoir que l'on sait" (Teilhard, 1955, p. 181). At the human level, then, consciousness becomes self-consciousness. We may also speak of this in terms of the development of an ego. Teilhard spoke of it in terms of a process of *personalization*.

Having taken this step, according to Teilhard, we are now on the brink of yet another stage. As he saw it, the course of human development up to this point has produced a set of conditions that makes a further transition almost inevitable in the generations to come. Like other species, we have become racially and culturally diversified as we have spread over the globe, but we have now arrived at a point where further diversification and development in isolation are impossible. Advances in transportation and communication combine with a variety of economic, political, and intellectual developments to create a kind of geographic compression and ensure increasing cultural interpenetration.

According to Teilhard's basic theoretical formulation, at every level of cosmogenesis, diversification tends to be followed or accompanied by a unification or "in-folding" process in which the differentiated elements are combined into a more complex unity. For the human species, this would mean a shift from the development of individualized consciousoness toward a more collective process, which would yield a sort of "super-consciousness," a collective consciousness of spirit embracing all of mankind, or, if we think in terms of the noosphere, a unified spirit of the earth. In his writings, Teilhard used many different terms to characterize this process: the in-folding of mankind upon itself, the socialization of mankind, the collectivization of mankind, the planetization of mankind, the totalization of mankind, the unanimization of mankind, the social-scientific agglomerization of mankind upon itself, super-humanization, and the psychic in-folding of the earth upon itself.

This step is not totally inevitable, since we are sufficiently conscious to be able to exercise a great deal of choice over the path ahead. Teilhard noted three available sidetracks that would yield less desirable consequences: the path of isolation or individualism, the world-negating path of Hindu or Buddhist mysticism, and a totalitarian form of collectivization. The ultra-humanity that is now possible requires "a conspiracy informed with love." Teilhard believed that collectivization through love would be the most natural and, therefore, the probable ultimate common choice of humanity, for he regarded love as being as much a natural and universal principle as consciousness itself. In the collective union to which we were all drawn together by love, we would experience a new sense of species. At the same time, this union would heighten the sense of individuality—it would "super-personalize" individuals (Teilhard, 1964).

Teilhard's vision extended beyond the unification of humanity, for he referred extensively in his writings to the ultimate Omega point, the "apex of the cone of time," that point at which the universe achieves the highest possible degree of complex-centeredness. He equated Omega with God and with Christ and argued that this ultimate convergence is not only the goal of all present transformations but something already implicit in everything. Being already implicit, Omega operates as a guiding force, operating by the radiation of love-energy and drawing us toward the culmination of the evolutionary process. In theological terms, this idea corresponds to a view of God as both immanent and transcendent.

In terms of consciousness, Omega corresponds to a condition of super-consciousness, or hyper-personality, in which our individuality is fully realized, but at the same time consciousness becomes coextensive with the universe. Individual consciousness moves toward an ultimate union with the universal center of the converging universe, and this center, Omega, becomes a center of centers. This view has important theological ramifications, and Teilhard dealt with these in some of his writings, teasing out the implications for monotheism, as opposed to pantheism, and for such concepts as original sin, salvation, and incarnation (Teilhard, 1964, 1969).

Pierre Teilhard de Chardin was in many respects a

monumental thinker, perhaps one of the truly mythic thinkers of our time. In centuries to come, he may come to be regarded as the most profound religious visionary of his age. Among theorists concerned with the evolution of consciousness, he stands as the leading proponent of an evolutionary doctrine centering around the theme of relatedness and union, of humanity and between humanity and the divine, through love. It can be argued that his Christocentric orientation limits the breadth of his insights. He showed some awareness of other traditions, notably those of the Orient (Teilhard, 1976), but he made no satisfactory use of these in his own theorizing. Many readers are undoubtedly troubled by the vague and abstract quality of his writing, perhaps an inevitable result of his effort to provide a picture of cosmic scope, covering the total life of the universe.

I see Teilhard's position as basically unidimensional, and from my perspective it is thus limited in the same way that the position of Bronowski and Sagan is. Teilhard viewed one possible path as the necessary and, in some ways, inevitable future course for the evolution of human consciousness. What he foresaw as the one logical unfolding (by virtue of in-folding) of the human psyche, others will see as a tenuous inductive extrapolation from his interpretation of past evolution.

THE INTEGRATION OF THE PSYCHE

The work of Carl G. Jung has much in common with that of Teilhard de Chardin. It represents a blend of Christian tradition with scientific thought. It expresses an outlook that is essentially Western, though one informed by an awareness of Eastern thought. Furthermore, it is quite possible that Jung is destined to have a major influence on the future course of Western religion. If I am not mistaken, his current impact on the thinking of Christian theologians and clergy exceeds not only that of all other psychological theorists but that of Teilhard as well.

In many respects the ideas of Teilhard and Jung are

complementary, but there are many obvious differences between them. Jung had a much more elaborate psychological theory, but Teilhard had more to say about the future course of human consciousness. The theme of Christian love is central to Teilhard's work, but Jung had practically nothing to say about it. To be sure, he had a great deal to say about the processes that prevent our experience of it, but when his writings are addressed directly to the subject of love, it is usually the other forms of love. Jung's basic model of the psyche is that of an energy system with opposing contents and forces, and the goal depicted in this writings is an ultimate state of integration. Thus, the key to Jung's view of the aim of psychic evolution is not the mode of relatedness, but the mode of inner harmony.

The Course of Individuation

In most of his writings, Jung was concerned with the development of the psyche within a lifetime, with the course of individuation rather than the course of psychic evolution. For two basic reasons, however, all of his work has evolutionary implications. For one thing, he referred repeatedly to the biogenetic principle that ontogeny recapitulates phylogeny, and he insisted that emerging consciousness followed the same path in the infant as it had in the species. The second point is that Jung attached special importance to a layer of the psyche that he called the collective, or suprapersonal, unconscious, or in later years, the objective psyche. This is the inherited core from which everything else emerges in the course of a lifetime, and nearly all of it is assumed to be common to the entire species. Presumably there are levels of archetypal content within it that we share even more broadly with other primates, with other mammals, and with lower forms of life. Whether we regard the content of the collective unconscious as bearing the imprints of the experience of our ancestors (as Jung sometimes suggested) or as simply providing the blueprint that governed the nature of that experience, the symbols and images that express that content should furnish keys to the nature of early stages of psychic evolution.

Jung (1954, 1969a) believed that the infant lacks consciousness in the early months of life and that the movement from an unconscious animal state to consciousness involves a gradual turning away from a life based purely on instinct. He said that in the first stage of consciousness discernible in the infant there is nothing more than a recognition or "knowing" that is made possible when the infant can connect two or more psychic contents. Many other animals undoubtedly attain this level of consciousness. A major advance occurs in a second stage, in which the ego, or ego-complex, begins to form. With the emergence of the ego, the center of consciousness, the child acquires a feeling of subjectivity or "I-ness." Without an ego, according to Jung, there can really be neither conscious personality nor continuity of memory. Jung suggested that the ego-complex begins at the time when the child learns to use *I* to refer to himself or herself.

Jung believed that in the early years the child remains very much a psychic product of the parents, to the extent of dwelling with them in a state of *participation mystique.* He regarded adolescence as a time of "psychic birth," a point at which the psyche finally attains a condition of relative independence. The increase in psychic independence is accompanied by an awareness of inner tension. In earlier periods of life, the child experiences more of an inner unity but recognizes that external forces and limitations may oppose personal desires. Jung also believed that education plays a major role in the development of consciousness. Without schooling, children might be intelligent in an instinctual way but would lack consciousness of themselves and the world. An obvious implication of this position is that Jung tended to equate consciousness with the sort of rationality or conceptual operations fostered by Western educational practices.

We might dispute the special significance that Jung attaches to puberty or adolescence, since psychic independence must develop gradually, and any boundary line we draw between a stage of dependence and one of independence must be arbitrarily drawn. Jung, however, had little interest in identifying stages in childhood or in the total life cycle in any precise way. He was more interested in describing the nature of the progressions that occur in consciousness. As we have seen, these progressions include an increase in psychic independence, an increase in rationality, and an increase in self-awareness. Self-awareness includes the initial sense of "I-ness" as well as the later recognition of inner tensions. According to Jung, throughout the early years of life, both the conscious part of the psyche and the personal unconscious begin to form. The ego emerges and develops as a key system within the former, while several major subsystems develop from archetypal cores within the unconscious. These include the shadow and the animus (in the female) or the anima (in the male). To be aware of inner tensions is to be aware of conflict between contents and dispositions that have been integrated into the ego and those that have been denied or neglected in consciousness and incorporated into the relatively unconscious subsystems. We tend to project the content that we do not acknowledge consciously as a part of ourselves and perceive it only in other people.

To be aware of tension within, rather than just between oneself and the world without, is a step toward greater self-awareness, but we reach adulthood nonetheless in a very lopsided state. We have selectively developed only some of our potentials and neglected or suppressed the rest. We have moved in either an introverted or extraverted direction, we have cultivated one or two psychic functions, and we have developed only a few modes for relating to the world. We have disclaimed instinctual tendencies of which our society disapproves, as well as those modes of action and experience deemed more appropriate for the other sex. As awareness expands, however, we can recognize some of the elements in the shadow and anima or animus as parts of ourselves and integrate them into the ego.

According to Jung, the development of the ego, the willing and reflecting center of consciousness, is the task of the first half of life. In the middle years, there is a natural tendency for psychic energy to move from values and other qualities that have been dominant in consciousness to their opposites, which have remained unconscious. The task of the second half of life is to achieve wholeness, to permit expression of the total psyche, and this can only be partly accomplished by an expansion of the ego. There is a limit to what we can subject to conscious focus and control. Most of the unconscious realm is destined to lie forever beyond the reach of consciousness, but we can achieve a more harmonious relationship to it by becoming more attuned to the images and symbols that express that content. Jung spoke of the self as the center of the total psyche, and ego and self can never quite coincide. The goal of individuation is rather a balanced relationship between ego and self. The ego must retain responsibility for conscious decision but heed all the messages that come from the self in the form of images, impressions, sudden impulses, and so forth. In moving toward this goal, we must avoid two common pitfalls. One is the condition of psychic inflation, in which we presume to be the total masters of our being and seek to incorporate the self into the ego. The other is a loss or relinquishment of the ego; it appears to disintegrate or dissolve in the self. We see this in schizophrenic regression, and Jung (1969b) considered it a serious hazard in Eastern paths to enlightenment.

Cross-cultural Comparisons

In speaking of primitive peoples and of our own early ancestors, Jung described many of the same qualities that he saw in small children. He saw the primitive as having little or no ego development, and he viewed primitive thinking as largely undirected, nonverbal, associative, and dreamlike. He believed that it took the form of projected sense perceptions that are similar to the hallucinations of the psychotic. In a sense, the primitive does not really experience a thinking process; rather, thinking is experienced as something that happens, as a consequence of unconscious forces perceived as arising externally (Jung, 1970b). This view of primitive thought, of course, is central to the theory of the bicameral mind formulated at a later time by Julian Jaynes.

Jung also characterized the primitive consciousness as relatively undifferentiated, and he contended that the keen sense perception often attributed to primitive people is narrowly confined to familiar situations in their native surroundings where survival depends on it (Jung, 1970a). In describing primitives as in describing children, Jung invoked Lévy-Bruhl's concept of *participation mystique*, and he felt that this condition applied to the primitive's relationship to animals and objects as well as to others of the social group. Because of this, psychic contents are very generally projected, and no events are interpreted as just objective, physical events. Every happening is construed as a product of intention. The shift from a primitive to a civilized view of the world thus entails a despiritualization of the world. In the course of developing civilization and becoming more conscious, we have withdrawn our projections onto nature, moved away from a life governed by participation mystique, and introduced a distinction between the objective and the subjective. A collective shift of this kind first occurred when archaic mythic explanations were replaced by astrological ones. The basic consequence of the civilizing shift is that we experience ourselves as distinct individuals with individual intentions and a capacity for a deliberate use of thinking for various purposes.

Jung recognized much cultural variation in the patterns of psychic evolution. He attributed some of the features of the Western psyche to the fact that the natural course of psychic evolution for the people of Europe was interrupted by contact with the more advanced civilizations of the Mediterranean region (Jung, 1970d). As a result of the rapid spread of Hellenic culture northward, Europeans underwent a rapid transformation toward a higher level of consciousness for which they were not adequately prepared. This resulted in a rather extreme disassociation between the conscious and unconscious parts of the psyche. The Western individual suffers from a pronounced split between ego and shadow, and the Western male in particular suffers from a loss of touch with the feminine side of his psyche.

There is a pervasive tendency for Westerners to display an overdifferentiation of consciousness and of the intellect, while lacking any conscious connection with the vast realm of material that remains unconscious. This accounts for the seemingly paradoxical fact that the very societies that yield the most advanced forms of science and technology are capable of relapses into an appalling barbarity. Jung pointed this out with respect to the bombing raids and use of poison gas and barbed wire in World War I, but the massive slaughter and Nazi atrocities of World War II certainly illustrate the point even better. Today we are faced with the possibility of the ultimate barbarity: a nuclear war that can totally eradicate all higher forms of life on this planet. The very nations that engage most vigorously in an arms race that is inherently suicidal for all concerned are governed by people who suffer from the basic Western psychic split.

An individual who has struggled to live a life of conscious rationality and who has little awareness of the forces below the conscious level will tend to find the unconscious a source of great fear. As difficult as Westerners find it to deal constructively with the unconscious, however, they have sometimes found it a source of fascination as well as terror. Jung (1970b) traced an intense interest in the unconscious to the time of the French Revolution, when there was a major transition in Western thought and a decline of older values and accepted authority. A resurgence of such an interest, perhaps on a larger scale, seems to have begun in the nineteenth century and was reflected in a widespread interest in concepts such as animal magnetism, spiritualism, Theosophy, Eastern religions, Christian Science, and an assortment of mystery religions. Jung noted another upsurge of such interests in the wake of World War I, and Theodore Roszak (1975) described essentially the same phenomenon with respect to the 1960s and 1970s. In each of these periods in recent history that we have noted, there has been a loss of faith in established institutions as sources of guidance and spirituality, and people have searched for something to replace them. The development of psychology over the past century is a significant part of the whole process, and according to Jung (1970c), modern Western society is uniquely psychological. Whereas people of the past and of other civilizations have experienced the psyche on the outside, we have come to experience it on the inside. That is, people of other times and places have experienced the psyche through ideals, rituals, and symbols to which they could collectively relate, whereas our inner tensions have produced a more pronounced introspective quest.

This quest has often taken the form of turning to the Orient for enlightenment. Jung believed there was a great deal we could learn from various systems of Oriental thought, but he also noted a danger in simply adopting or imitating Eastern spiritual paths. Eastern yogic paths were designed for people who have grown up in the East and can be hazardous for Westerners. He argued that we need a Western form of yoga, and many of his followers believe that his work provides the essential foundation for this.

As Jung saw it, the psyche as it has developed in the West stands in sharp contrast to the kind of balanced orientation implied by the Chinese concept of *tao*, which points to a middle course that respects all opposing forces and tendencies. In India, as in China, Jung (1970d) saw a culture free from the kind of psychic split found in the West. He attributed this to the fact that India has enjoyed a more natural, continuous course of development from ancient times. For this reason, he said, the Indian has not been forced to repress, but remains in touch with, the primitive modes of experience that lie in the unconscious of the Westerner. As a result, there are some characteristic differences between the Indian and the Western individual in modes of thinking. Western thinking has a deliberate, analytical quality. It reflects an urge to rise above the natural realm and to control by "grasping" things in the mind. The Indian does not think as we do, but rather perceives his or her thoughts as the primitive does. This does not mean that the Indian is in fact primitive, for the primitive quality may be combined with a profundity that surpasses Western understanding. Indian thinking is generally less analytical and more concerned with allowing the whole to express itself.

Some Variations on the Theme

Jung's basic ideas have undergone further development at the hands of many of his students, one of the most brilliant and creative of whom was Erich Neumann. Neumann described a sequence of stages in psychic evolution and individual development in terms of characteristic patterns of symbolic expression in creation myths and great-hero myths, and his analyses of mythic themes are probably the most thorough ones to be found in the literature of analytical psychology. Like Jung, he conceptualized the goal of psychic development in terms of a harmonious relationship between conscious and unconscious, but the mode of creativity also played a role in his thinking. He saw the synthesis of conscious and unconscious as the source of creativity and stressed the role of the great individual, the culture-hero, who achieves such a synthesis and serves as a guide or revelator for the mass of individuals.

Like Jung, Neumann argued that ontogenetic development is a modified recapitulation of phylogenetic development. He assumed that the basic themes underlying both courses of development were evident in mythology, since myths are composed essentially of archetypal symbols. Yet he cautioned against reading the sequences in myths as a symbolic rendering of stages in history. He believed that the major archetypes underlying human experience were all present from the earliest stages in the development of our species, rather than being a product of ancestral stages. The mythic sequence must be understood as a representation of structural levels in the psyche, and these levels tend to produce corresponding sequences in individual and mass development, but in both kinds of development (of an individual and of a people) the same basic themes and stages are actually experienced a number of times. Thus, a mythic theme such as the dragon fight corresponds to more than one phase in the life cycle and more than one stage in history.

Some of Neumann's basic assumptions regarding the nature of consciousness have aroused considerable discussion. In his most monumental work, *The Origins and History of Consciousness* (Neumann, 1954), he said that consciousness, even in women, has a masculine character. He noted that, for this reason, men experience the ego and consciousness as clearly their own and view the "feminine" unconscious as alien, whereas women feel more connected with the unconscious. Other Jungians have regarded this rather blunt statement as disparaging of women, and James Hillman (1972) contended that it reflected a widespread tendency in our society to confuse consciousness with the rational, ordering mode of Apollonic thinking, while viewing the more free-flowing, feminine mode of Dionysian thinking with fear and suspicion. Although it is true that Neumann was using *consciousness* in a narrow sense in his controversial statement, in other writings he made essentially the same distinction as Hillman in terms of *patriarchal* and *matriarchal* consciousness. The concept of matriarchal consciousness was best developed in those writings in which he focused on the development of the female (Neumann, 1953, 1959, 1963). Neumann contended that in a patriarchal culture like ours, both men and women must develop a masculine, or patriarchal, consciousness, but that each of us really needs to develop both kinds to achieve wholeness.

Neumann presented his most comprehensive treatment of psychic evolution and development in *The Origins and History of Consciousness*, though he tended in that work to emphasize masculine development and patriarchal culture. He described there a grand sequence of mythic images and themes, beginning with the *uroboros*, or some equivalent image of an undifferentiated state. As a mythology unfolds, this image gives way to a succession of increasingly specific and humanized divine figures. These start with the Great Mother, which initially shows little differentiation and proceeds to a division into nurturing and devouring forms. The expansion of consciousness at this level of images is also expressed in a series of stages involving progressive separation from the Great Mother. Here we find heroes ranging from those whose unsuccessful struggle culminates in surrender, self-castration, or death, to those who successfully defy the mother. Early stages in the growth of consciousness may also be expressed in the theme of the separation of the world parents (e.g., Uranus and Gaea or Nut and Geb).

The splitting of images and the primordial separation symbolize the movement into a conscious world that contains fresh discriminations and dualities. In moving from the blissful state of unconsciousness, we are subject to a new sense of loneliness and suffering, and this is represented in various ways in creation myths. The familiar examples are the expulsion of Adam and Eve from the Garden of Eden and the torment of Prometheus, bound to a rock in the Caucasus.

As individual consciousness develops, the ego comes into being as a center of the conscious portion of the psyche, and Neumann describes several processes that contribute to its separate establishment: a "fragmentation of archetypes," the assimilation of unconscious content by abstraction and rationalization, and secondary personalization. He also ascribes importance to the gradual incorporation of unconscious tendencies that are initially experienced by the ego as destructive and threatening. These contribute to the power of the ego to analyze, discriminate, and defend itself.

The various stages evident in hero myths can all be understood psychologically in terms of the development of the ego. There are important motifs surrounding the basic nature and birth of the hero, and there are major heroic deeds that recur in various mythologies, as well as appearing in a succession of forms in any given mythology. In general, the hero must slay or overcome the negative form of the matriarchal image, and he must later overcome the Terrible Father, the negative form of the patriarchal authority. In the course of these deeds, new relationships with the feminine and masculine are represented in interactions with other mythic figures.

Neumann devoted particular attention to two late stages in the hero myth, which he viewed as stages in a transformation myth. The first concerns the accomplishment of the goal for which the dragon fight is undertaken. The goal usually takes the form of a virgin, captive, or treasure, and reaching it symbolizes the realization of the feminine in a more personal and desirable form. For the male, this represents an ability to relate more intimately to the feminine in an outer form (a woman) or a fresh realization of the feminine side of his own psyche. The second stage is described in terms of the dismemberment and resurrection of Osiris. Here we have a mythic theme that occurs subsequently in the myths of Dionysus, Orpheus, and Jesus, and it represents a movement toward the self or a union of ego and self. While the basic themes of the transformation myth have figured in the experience of the Western world for thousands of years, they still represent a phase of the individuation process that remains beyond the reach of most people in our society. Like Jung, Neumann contended that the people of the Western world suffer from an overdifferentiation of consciousness, a severe split between the conscious and unconscious parts of the psyche, which permits ample ego development but precludes successful accommodation to the self.

Feminine Development

In the writings in which Neumann focused on feminine development (Neumann, 1953, 1959, 1963), he contended that women go through essentially the same stages as men in individual development. In the initial uroboric stage, there is no discernible difference between the sexes. In the matriarchal and patriarchal stages, differences emerge. The girl experiences a closer identity with the mother in the matriarchal stage and a less compelling need for separation. In the stage that follows, she experiences the masculine as more alien than the boy does. Various systematic differences between men and women, with respect to the ways in which they relate to the masculine and feminine, are represented symbolically in hero myths.

In general, the stages of feminine development parallel those of masculine development, but according to Neumann, neither course of development is strictly confined to one sex. Each of us has both a masculine side and a feminine side, and each stage involves a characteristic relationship between these two sides. If we speak of the development of the male in terms of masculine development or of the female in terms of feminine development, this simply means we are focusing on the side that predominates in consciousness. A corresponding development occurs in the less conscious side. Ideally, the two sides move in the course of individuation from a state of unconscious nondifferentiation toward an ultimate state of androgynous integration.

Many other Jungians and "post-Jungians" have made additional contributions to our thinking about stages in psychic evolution and in the psychic development of the individual. Further thoughts about the development of women have been offered by M. Esther Harding (1970), Ann Belford Ulanov (1971), and Irene Claremont de Castillejo (1973). Edward C. Whitmont (1982) has written about the increasing role of the feminine in both male and female development. The evolutionary issue remains a primary focus of interest within the analytical-psychology movement. I have gained valuable insights regarding masculine and feminine development from lectures given by John Mattern at the C. G. Jung Institute in Zurich. The basic Jungian model of development still prevails within this movement: Development proceeds from undifferentiated wholeness toward integrated wholeness. In the intermediate stages, differentiation and selective utilization tend to yield a one-sided mode of functioning. The masculine-feminine split and an ultimate androgyny are generally regarded as an important aspect of the total sequence.

The basic approach to psychic evolution represented by Jung and his followers is far more inclusive than the others we have considered up to this point. Jung and Neumann dealt with many modes of conscious functioning, and they recognized more than one possible course of psychic development. Within the analytical-psychology movement, however, the goal of individual development and psychic evolution in general is understood in terms of overall integration or inner harmony, and this is always conceptualized in a way that reflects the essentially Western roots of the movement. The end-state requires a fully developed ego that embodies conscious individuality, but the emphasis is on the relationship of this ego to a larger whole that cannot be brought fully under its control.

A FEW STEPS TOWARD THE EAST

In comparison to Western traditions, Hindu and Buddhist traditions may be said to deemphasize individuality and to stress transcendence as a goal. There is variation within both these streams of Eastern thought with respect to the manner in which this goal and the steps leading to it are described. The goal may be regarded as the aim of a given lifetime or an end to be sought over a series of lifetimes, and the notion of reincarnation is sometimes cast in the form of doctrines that have clear implications for the evolution of both human beings and life in general.

In one school of Hindu thought, the doctrine of *advaita*, or nonduality, is interpreted very strictly. It is held that the only genuine reality is the brahman. Thus all the specific forms seen in the phenomenal world, including ourselves as individual beings, are strictly illusions. In other schools *advaita* is construed in a less extreme manner, and it is assumed that the brahman, as an eternal entity, can become a temporal reality. Thus, the individual in his or her true essence is still the brahman, but for the moment this essence has assumed a temporary form with a specific name. As a consequence of preoccupation with the desires and interests associated with a temporal existence, individuality may be sustained through a series of rebirths. In most streams of Buddhist thought, the sense of individual identity, or ego, is accorded a relative, or temporary, reality, but it is also understood as a kind of phenomenal construct (a product of the "five Skandhas"), having no reality apart from our ways of experiencing life and our ways of experiencing ourselves.

Sri Aurobindo

As a Hindu, Aurobindo accepted as the most fundamental reality a unitary and eternal self or consciousness, but his treatment of individuality and of evolution reflects a Western influence. He held that the temporal world of matter, physical objects, plants, animals, and individual human beings is created by an involution of the absolute Self (Aurobindo, 1970). The process of evolution operates in the reverse direction to reinstate the original unity. That unity is actually immanent in the multiform world that we now see, however, and evolution proceeds of necessity toward a predetermined end. Indeed, each form that emerges in evolution is assumed to exist implicitly in the form from which it emerges. Thus, matter per se contains life in veiled form, while life at its lowest levels is a form of veiled consciousness or mind. Aurobindo also saw the evolutionary process as twofold. On the one hand, there is a visible process of physical evolution, yielding a succession of forms of increasing complexity. At the same time there is an invisible process of soul evolution, in which the individual soul moves through a succession of rebirths toward higher forms of consciousness.

Aurobindo considered the human species to be at the forefront of the evolutionary process, being the sole representative of a stage in which soul evolution has moved from an unconscious to a conscious level of manifestation. Our present stage is a mental stage of development, in which we rely heavily on reason or intellect. Reason provides only a limited kind of understanding, and a higher stage is evident in a few people who have moved from mental to spiritual being. They retain the intellectual faculties of the mental person but possess greater intuitive understanding and are less bound by a narrow egoic identity.

There is still another level beyond spiritual being: that of supramental or gnostic being. According to Aurobindo, attainment of this ultimate goal requires a relinquishment of the intense investment in the individual ego, but there is no lack of individuality, uniqueness, or freedom. There is simply no sense of an individual will exerted in opposition to the world. One experiences the utmost freedom and spontaneity, but actions and experiences are so naturally ordered that they seem effortless. One is so identified with the universal Self that all actions are a direct expression of that Self. At this level, one does not experience a separative individuality; one individualizes the universe.

The gnostic individual represents a level of psychic evolution far beyond our present stage of mental being, and Aurobindo provided a variety of descriptions of the steps that will lead from our present level to that ultimate goal. He spoke, for example, of three phases of transformation—psychic, spiritual, and supramental—leading to the gnostic or supramental level. In the psychic phase, the individual soul comes forth into more direct expression, assumes greater direction over our lives, and promotes movement toward realization of the universal reality behind individual being by offering several images of the divine. In pursuing these images, one may follow any of three pathways, concurrently or in succession: the way of intellect or knowledge, the way of the heart or of emotion, and the way of will or of action. In the phases of spiritual and supramental transformation, there is increasing experience and realization of the universal Self.

Aurobindo also spoke of several stages of progression in the nature of understanding or intelligence that lead beyond our present mental level to the supramental level: higher mind, illumined mind, intuitive mind, Overmind, and Supermind. Higher mind, like ordinary mind, provides conceptual knowledge, but awareness arises more spontaneously, and we move beyond our present groping empirical and rational processing. Illumined mind involves the consciousness of the seer; it provides visions that cannot be totally reduced to thought. Intuitive mind provides a consciousness that goes beyond both sight and sound and beyond the forms of intuition found at lower levels. With Overmind, a sense of separate ego and individuality may virtually disappear, and one has glimmerings of the universal sense that appears in Supermind.

The higher stages are of such a nature that they cannot be fully grasped from a rational perspective. I must confess that I still depend too heavily on the processes of ordinary mind to comprehend them fully. With my present understanding of alternative modes of apprehension and conscious experience, I remain unconvinced that psychic evolution must necessarily follow the sequence indicated by Aurobindo. There is an admirable coherence to his account, however, and it is consistent with basic themes in traditional Hindu thought. In various ways, he described a progression from ordinary human consciousness to a condition in which we would be more open to the whole of our individual being, including all those parts we presently deny or that are inaccessible to conscious reason, and then a progression to a universal consciousness that transcends the bounds of our individual being.

From Eden to Atman

Like Aurobindo, Ken Wilber (1981) regards psychic evolution as the reconstitution of a unity that has become fragmented through a process of involution. The inevitable goal of atman-brahman operates as a guiding telos, or ultimate end, that affects both the nature and the rate of evolutionary change. As I noted in Chapter 1, Wilber offers the sheer rate of biological evolution in support of this view. He also regards what he calls the atman project as evidence that the true atman is an implicit goal of our present existence. The atman project consists of efforts to regain atman consciousness—a sense of all-important, wholeness, and immortality—in ways that actually preclude reaching that level of consciousness. Not realizing fully the nature of atman, we seek to gain and maintain its essential qualities through enhancement of our limited separate-self identity. We experience two basic drives in conjunction with the atman project. One is eros, the drive to perpetuate our separate existence. The other is thanatos, the urge toward death or dissolution of the separate self. So long as eros outweighs thanatos, we remain at a given level of development, and as a substitute for our own dissolution, we may convert thanatos into destructive actions directed toward others. We must let go of our present identity to move to a higher level of realization.

Wilber contends that we would not expend so much effort in an attempt to achieve a false immortality if we did not sense that our true nature is, in fact, the all-embracing, whole, eternal atman-brahman. This is not a matter of strict logical necessity, however, nor is it subject to empirical test. If we assume an atman telos, as Wilber does, the concept of the atman project is a useful way of explaining our tendency to become stuck at various way stations along the evolutionary route. Without that assumption, we are more likely to construe that tendency simply as a defense against any forces (including our own inclinations) that might draw us back toward our original state of unconsciousness.

The experience of atman-brahman is unitary, or non-dualistic, and Wilber equates this with an immediate, intuitive, or intimate mode of knowing. Western science, of course, rests on a mode of knowing that might be called conceptual, dualistic, analytical, symbolic, or abstract. While conceptual knowing is useful, only the unitary mode of knowing, according to Wilber, yields knowledge of Reality. We have moved away from Reality through a succession of dualistic splits, and according to Wilber (1977, 1979), it is possible to recognize a "spectrum of consciousness" composed of several levels defined by a cumulative succession of splits that lead away from unity consciousness. The splits are, first, between subject and object (or total organism and environment), then between life and death and between past and future, then between mind and body, and finally between persona and shadow.

Wilber offers some interesting speculations regarding the appropriateness of different forms of therapy for different levels in the spectrum, suggesting, for example, that psychoanalysis is appropriate at the level of the ego-body split, while Gestalt therapy may be appropriate at the level of the subject-object split. I see great heuristic value in this kind of speculation for the development of comprehensive treatment strategies, though I have many reservations about the levels Wilber describes and his specific assignments of therapies to them. He recognizes that his levels are a simplification, but I would question whether the spectrum of consciousness should even be viewed as a unidimensional hierarchy. There is probably much more individual variation in boundaries and levels of awareness than his scheme implies. It is questionable whether the splits necessarily occur in the sequence described and whether they are as independent as the stepwise succession implies. The personal qualities owned and rejected in the persona-shadow split tend to be linked to a mind-body dichotomy, while "good contact" with the body is possible even though a host of personal qualities—feminine modes of emotionality and expression, hostility, assertiveness, certain sexual impulses, etc.—are consigned to the region of the shadow. The pattern of splits that need to be healed surely varies from one individual to another, and it is doubtful whether any therapist can rely on a standard sequence of procedures.

Wilber's equation of reality with the non-dualistic knowing of unity consciousness is also debatable. The unity view, of course, is uniquely valid in the sense that it is the one view free of the illusions we create when we bisect reality. Any boundary we insert when we proceed to dualities is arbitrary and represents a structure we have imposed in the course of perceiving and conceptualizing. Unity consciousness is the most direct form of knowing in that it is free of such construction, but it is incommunicable. The moment we step far enough away from it to *call* it unitary, holistic, intuitive, or verbally ineffable, we have moved to a dualistic mode of thinking and speaking. Otherwise, we could not talk about it. To conceptualize a form of experience as unitary is to contrast it with a form that is dualistic or multiplex. To conceptualize the universe as a unitary continuum is to contrast it with a universe conceptualized as multiplex and particulate. Neither formulation is inherently better than the other, and for many purposes it is useful to have access to both views. Unity consciousness per se (as opposed to our conceptualization of it) is adualistic, but everyone who writes about it (including Wilber) presumes in doing so that there is value in a dualistic, conceptual mode of thinking.

I can agree with Wilber that it is desirable to have access to unity consciousness, and for anyone who has grown up in this culture, that requires letting go of dualities. It is less clear that the goal of psychic development must be conceptualized in terms of an achievement of the one true view of reality through unity consciousness, for it might make more sense to conceptualize it in terms of flexible access to alternative modes of consciousness, which would enable the individual to transcend the limited perspective of any one mode.

In presenting a system of states in psychic evolution, Wilber (1980, 1981) has done a masterful job of synthesis, blending ideas drawn from the developmental schemes offered by a great assortment of theorists and schools of East and West. One may question whether a common underlying system can properly be read into all those different schemas, but, if not, Wilber's derivative can stand on its own merits. There are many parallels in Western thought to the first half of his system. For the second half he has relied more heavily on Eastern thought.

Like Jung, Wilber regards the middle of the sequence of stages as a period of full ego development and maximal eccentricity, whether we think in terms of individuation or of phylogenetic evolution. For Aurobindo, this corresponds to the rational, mental stage. Wilber (1981) characterizes the principal stages as follows:

1. Nature (physical nature and lower life forms, pleromatic, material, uroboric-reptilian);
2. Body (highest bodily life forms, especially typhonic, magical);
3. Early mind (verbal, mythical, membership, paleological, bicameral);
4. Advanced mind (rational, mental-egoic, self-reflective);
5. Psychic (Nirmanakaya, shamanistic);
6. Subtle (Sambhogakaya, saintly);
7. Causal (Dharmakaya, sagely); and
8. Ultimate (Svabhavikakaya, absolute).

In the first stage there is a movement from an initial stage of nondifferentiation toward a rudimentary differentiation of self and uroboric other. In the second stage there is a clear differentiation of self and environment, but not of body and ego. The development of language is largely responsible for a shift to the third stage, and thinking becomes distinctly conceptual in the fourth stage. At this stage we have egoic self-consciousness, a complete split of body and ego, and considerable differentiation of shadow and persona qualities. Wilber contends that the Western world moved into the egoic stage, where it remains, between the second and first millennia B.C., but he distinguishes three principal historical periods within this stage. In the psychic stage, the separated parts of the organism—body and mind, shadow and persona—are brought into a higher-order integration, and consciousness is no longer identified with one part to the exclusion of others. There is a further healing of splits in the later stages, and in the ultimate stage there is a full realization of the formlessness, voidness, or non-separateness of all being.

Pre-egoic versus Trans-egoic Stages

An interesting feature of Wilber's system of stages is that some curious similarities are evident between pre-egoic and the trans-egoic stages. Wilber uses a number of paired descriptive terms to highlight both the similarities and the essential contrasts. Thus, the early stages are pre-verbal and pre-consensual, while the later ones are trans-verbal and trans-consensual. Body and ego remain undifferentiated at the typhonic level, and the result is impulsiveness. Having been differentiated, they are integrated at the psychic level, and the result is spontaneity. At both levels, the individual lives basically in the here and now, but the experience of time at the typhonic level is pre-sequential (hence, present-oriented awareness is the only possibility), while at the centauric level it is trans-sequential (and there is access to conventional extended time).

Wilber's terminological dichotomies reinforce the idea that he is presenting a unidimensional sequence of stages and help to dispel any suspicion that the stages form a purely cyclic sequence, but it is possible that his distinctions tend to exaggerate some of the pre-/trans- differences. He notes that the image of the Great Mother is important in the second and third stages, while the image of the Great Goddess belongs to the sixth stage. The same symbols and rituals may be used for both figures, but they are enacted literally for the Great Mother (e.g., in actual blood sacrifices), while they are enacted symbolically for the Great Goddess and serve to enhance consciousness. While Wilber's dichotomy serves a purpose, one could argue with equal justification that there is basically only one image or that there is a large number of distinguishable images. A maternal goddess image assumes importance at various points in human experience, undergoing transformation as our needs and understanding evolve. Thus, the image of a nurturing womb of nature gives way to a force that threatens to engulf us. After further modification and splintering of the image, it may emerge in a form that embodies a feminine guide in the further expansion of consciousness.

Wilber does not see a mother goddess as playing a role in the egoic stage, and it is certainly true that such images have been repressed during the many centuries of Western history that Wilber regards as belonging to this stage. One might ask whether the development of an ego demands repression of the matriarchal image—or whether, in Neumann's terms, it requires an emphasis on a patriarchal mode of consciousness and temporary neglect of the matriarchal mode. The difficulty with answering in the affirmative is that we would have to insist that the ego itself is strictly a Western phenomenon. The maternal-goddess image has never been so thoroughly repressed in India or China, and we do not find it separating neatly in those civilizations into pre-egoic and trans-egoic forms.

Recognizing a variety of East-West differences, Wilber suggests that mass concentration and fixation at the egoic stage is largely a Western phenomenon. The people of India thus developed the ego without the severe repression of mythic images, while at the same time developing techniques for transformation that permitted large numbers of people to advance to trans-egoic stages. In his brief discussion of India, however, Wilber suggests that basically, in contrast to this country, we would find more people still at pre-egoic stages, more at trans-egoic stages, and fewer arrested at the egoic stage in between. I believe we can interpret the underlying evidence in a somewhat different way if we relinquish the assumption of a universal sequence of psychic evolution. I would suggest that what Wilber considers the middle, egoic stage represents a mode of development in which the West has specialized to a greater extent than the East has. In the East, we see a different pattern of specialization and probably less exclusive emphasis on any particular mode of consciousness.

I see a problem in Wilber's treatment of shamanistic societies as well. He contends that such societies are typically at the second stage, where magical thinking abounds, while the gifted shaman who appears in these societies manifests a talent for telepathy, precognition, and healing—qualities that place him at the fifth stage. Granted that many, if not most, shamans merely pretend to have such abilities, it is remarkable that a leap from level 2 to level 5 should be a fairly common occurrence. Wilber makes the reasonable assumption that the exceptional individual of any society may advance two or three stages beyond the mass of individuals, but it seems odd that in shamanistic societies the characteristic leap places the shaman at the psychic level, rather than at the egoic level.

In response to Wilber, I would argue that the gifted shaman simply realizes to a higher degree certain qualities or modes of consciousness that are characteristic of his or her society. There is ample cause for believing that psi abilities are widespread in many societies that we view as "primitive." If so, it follows either that they do not presuppose the attainment of the fifth stage in psychic development or that the very notion of a single universal ladder of a mental ascent is inadequate. In any case, the sort of consciousness required for extrasensory abilities does not depend on the prior development of a high level of rationality or self-consciousness. A more obvious prerequisite is an access to nonrational modes of consciousness, and this may be present in an individual who is amply developed along many lines, in a schizophrenic, or in a child with little ego development. The concomitant presence of a high level of rational and analytical ability will obviously affect the way in which psi abilities are used, and it is likely to affect the way in which other people perceive the user.

Wilber once again deals with a contrast between the pre-egoic and the trans-egoic in dealing with fantasy and imagination.

In the early stages we have a primary-process experience of pre-verbal and pre-conceptual forms. At higher stages we have trans-verbal forms realized through vision-images, and the primary process is no longer involved. While this may be an improvement over the Freud-Kris view of creativity, I am not convinced that Wilber's sharp dichotomy is warranted. He arrives at it by interposing an egoic stage of verbal secondary-process mentation, which implies that fantasy subsides temporarily in the middle of the evolutionary sequence. Once again, I would argue that the intermediate stages represent development along a different dimension of consciousness. Egoic consciousness is not inherently incompatible with fantasy, but an emphasis on rational and analytical thought in our society, particularly in our school systems, tends to be accompanied by a suppression of the imaginal. The imaginal mode of consciousness, like psi ability, is really rather independent of rationality and egoic self-consciousness, and its natural course of development does not depend heavily on a concomitant development of egoic functions. The ability to evaluate and edit a creative production, of course, may call for nonimaginal modes of consciousness, and the interplay of modes may affect the final creative product. Under favorable circumstances, however, unencumbered by the usual instructional methods of our schools, the creative individual may start producing works in early childhood that bear the mark of "trans-verbal" fantasy.

7

A More Comprehensive View
of Psychic Development

Each of the theories considered in the preceding chapter assumes that there is one developmental goal of particular importance and a natural tendency for change to proceed along a universal pathway toward that goal. A more comprehensive theory would have to recognize that human adaptation and welfare are served by a variety of psychic attainments, that some of these attainments may be mutually incompatible, and that there are many possible developmental courses that can lead to any one goal, to different goals, or to various combinations and sequences of goals. To do justice to such possibilities, we must give more heed than other theorists have to the immense diversity of contents, qualities, and modes of processing that characterize human conscious experience.

DIMENSIONS OF CONSCIOUS EXPERIENCE

There is a vast range of possible conscious contents. Undoubtedly systematic changes in content characterize both individual development and psychic evolution, but for the most part the alternative contents do not form an obvious hierarchy of relative evolutionary achievement. It is not usually obvious that one content is preferable to another.

We can usually identify the focal content of our conscious experience as falling into one of three broad categories: external, internal, or cognitive/imaginal. If the content is external, attention is directed toward the realm surrounding the individual. Our perception of the environment may be governed by visual or auditory qualities or by qualities associated with the various tactile or chemical senses. We may rely heavily on one sense and ignore the information provided by another.

It is possible that our perception of the environment is affected by senses that are not widely acknowledged. The magnetic sense studied by R. Robin Baker (1981) apparently operates outside consciousness. It may affect our impressions of the environment, but we will not recognize anything in the way of a magnetic sensation as a component of our organized conscious perceptions. The same may be said of extrasensory perception. Unlike the magnetic sense, however, it probably does not operate by means of sensory information in the ordinary meaning of that term, despite the belief of some researchers that extremely-low-frequency electromagnetic radiation may be involved. In any case, when it yields valid information about the environment, the information comes to us in the form of images—visual, auditory, verbal, etc.—that correspond to the recognized senses. If the focal content of conscious experience is external, then, it consists of some combination of percepts and images whose component qualities correspond to those of the recognized exteroceptors.

If the focal content of consciousness is internal, attention is directed toward the body and its interior. Our impressions concern such things as movement, tension, pressure, pain, comfort, discomfort, heat, and cold. The sensory information may be broadly characterized as somesthetic. Several kinds of senses may be distinguished, but as in the case of external awareness, it is not clear that all the information involved can be reduced to input through well-defined sensory channels. Regardless of our anatomical knowledge, on a psychological level, internal awareness has never been understood very well in the Western world. The deeper understanding of adepts in a few yogic traditions affords them a sensitive awareness and control over a variety of internal states and processes. Their talents tend to baffle Westerners, but research investigations that have commenced in recent years in the United States and the Soviet Union may lead to a greater understanding of such yogic feats.

If the focal content of consciousness is cognitive or imaginal, attention is directed neither to the body nor to the immediate environment. The role of percepts arising from either somesthetic or exteroceptive sources is subdued, and images may assume greater importance. When the focus is actually external or internal, of course, our conscious experience usually reflects an interaction of images and concepts with sensory information, but when images are foremost our attention may be directed toward a realm that is remote in space or time or outside the bounds of ordinary reality. We may remember and reminisce about places and events of the past. We may anticipate a future event and perhaps engage in planning. We may picture places we have never seen and imagine places that could not exist. In dreams or fantasies, we may picture ourselves and the world in a realistic manner or in a manner that departs considerably from current reality, and we may employ images that correspond to any of the sensory modes involved in either external or internal perception. Abstract verbal concepts may also be employed. Vaguely imaged as sounds, visual forms, and speech movements, they will, at times, overshadow all other kinds of images.

It is obvious that our conscious experience, whatever its primary focus, contains a rich mixture of sensory, imaged, and conceptual ingredients. There are also a number of qualitative parameters in terms of which we might describe its overall character at a given time. One is the scope of the phenomenal field, the range of content to which one is attending. A second parameter is the clarity, articulation, or degree of definition of content. A third parameter is the complexity or amount of detail of the content. A fourth would be the orderliness, or degree of organization, of the content. A fifth would be the relative vividness or intensity of the content. A final parameter or set of parameters is the affective, or emotional, quality of the content. The most obvious modes of variation here would be the level of excitement and the hedonic tone (pleasantness vs. unpleasantness). The first of these (level of excitement or tension) undoubtedly shades into the vividness parameter to some extent.

Modes of Processing Content

Up to this point, we have been concerned essentially with the varieties and qualities of the content of consciousness. It is also possible to distinguish various modes of processing, ordering, or channeling content in consciousness. One possible distinction is that of Freud's primary and secondary processes, and there are numerous derivatives of this. Another is Carl Jung's (1971) system of four psychic functions: thinking vs. feeling and sensation vs. intuition. Guilford's (1967) structure-of-intellect model contains a classification of cognitive operations based on factor analyses of test performance, but the operation categories obviously correspond to distinguishable conscious processes. Guilford's operations include cognition (immediate discovery, awareness, or recognition), memory, divergent production, convergent production, and evaluation (comparing items of information and making judgments about correctness, identity, consistency, etc.). None of these categories is congruent with any of Jung's categories, but there are some obvious correspondences. Cognition comes closest to sensation. Both convergent production and evaluation are akin to Jung's rational functions. As measured, they both come closer to thinking than to feeling. Divergent production is the one category that permits the operation of intuition, but it is not strictly equivalent to that function as Jung defined it.

It is clearly possible to discern conscious processes that do not fit neatly into either of these systems. Guilford's model is limited to the components of those mental processes whose products can be graded with respect to intellectual worth. His memory category is concerned with the successful storage and retrieval of information, not the mere recollection of past events. In the academic world, we may not attach much value to states in which we merely dwell on the past, reviewing and reminiscing about events that have occurred. Nevertheless, this is a process in which we all engage frequently. We also engage in our inner rehearsal of events that have not occurred, and we daydream about events that are neither remembered nor anticipated. In each of these cases, we are living a story whose relationship to any external reality is subject to much variation. The content flow may take a totally different form. It may consist of a rational sequence of ideas, or it may consist of a more loosely associated series of impressions. In all likelihood, in everyone the latter takes place much more of the time than does the former. The character of the flow may depend a bit on the nature of the focus—in particular, whether the focal content at any instant is a very specific bit or a global pattern.

The flow of conscious impressions is also affected by mechanisms and strategies that serve to restrict the available content. A rational sequence of ideas is possible only to the extent that we have chosen at the moment to exclude any content that is not relevant to a particular purpose. Often we impose restrictions without any conscious decision to do so. Through denial, repression, or inattention we avoid content that might trigger anxiety, embarrassment, or some other unpleasant emotion. We may cultivate certain habits, such as silently humming a melody or reciting a verbal formula, as a means of blocking out unwanted ideas and memories. If we could secure a complete record of the stream of consciousness, we would find "screen" content of this sort recurrently invoked. There are things we can achieve in consciousness through learning to exert some control over the flow of impressions, and there are other possible aims that require a relaxation of control and an openness, or receptivity, to any available content.

STATES OF CONSCIOUSNESS

We commonly speak of different states of consciousness without giving much thought to the criteria by which we distinguish one state from another. The gulf between sleeping and waking seems so profound that few of us would hesitate to designate them as different states. Within sleep we may also distinguish a state of dreaming and a state of dreamless sleep. For the waking condition it has become popular to differentiate between ordinary (or "normal") consciousness and altered states.

For the most part, we make such distinctions because the various conditions we have identified as particular states "feel" different. To place their work on a firmer foundation, psychologists have often resorted to physiological criteria as a basis for making distinctions. This has sometimes led to absurd arguments. Thus, some have claimed that the hypnotic trance is a separate state, while others have insisted that it is not, since it is physiologically indistinguishable from ordinary waking consciousness. In recent years, it has become common to use eye movements and EEG waves as a basis for distinguishing between sleeping and waking and between dreaming and dreamless sleep. It is easy for some psychologists to forget that the physiological indices are useful in this case only because they correspond closely to certain psychological effects. If they did not, they would be irrelevant. The ultimate criteria for distinguishing between states of consciousness must be psychological in nature; they must involve variables of the sort that we have been discussing in this chapter. In the case of the hypnotic trance, physiological measures have not yielded much useful information. From a psychological standpoint, we can justifiably assert that hypnotic induction can provide a transition to one of more special states, but our precise formulation of this will depend on the specific psychological criteria we employ.

The basic issue underlying all of our questions about what states are different and about the number of possible states is one of taxonomy. There are no ultimate answers here. We classify states as different because it is convenient or useful to do so. There are those who would argue that it is counterproductive to make such distinctions because any such classification is artificial; any given state shades into others, since there is continuous variation along any pertinent psychological dimension. This is the same argument commonly given against the use of personality typologies, and there is obvious merit in it. Such classifications aid our thinking, however, so long as we remember that they consist of ideal conditions that individuals and conscious experience can only approximate. Surely we do not have to be reminded that no one is a pure introvert or cyclothyme, and we should be able to extend the same wisdom to our treatment of states of consciousness.

There is no one psychological dimension that provides an adequate basis for making the differentiations we most commonly make between states. The conscious experience of dreaming differs from that of most waking experience in terms of focal content, clarity, orderliness, the nature of the flow of events, our experience of control, and a variety of other variables, but no variable by itself provides a sufficient criterion for making a state distinction. If we want to distinguish systematically among a number of states, we need to employ a number of psychological dimensions. Any given state can be identified or defined in terms of a combination of positions on all the dimensions. We can consider two states different only if there is a difference between their patterns of positions. The total number of states we can distinguish will depend on the number of dimensions we employ and on our willingness to recognize fine distinctions in level. This basic view of state classification has probably been obvious to many investigators. Charles T. Tart (1975) has provided one of the most elaborate treatments of it. He proposes the concept of *discrete state of consciousness* as a designation for any "unique configuration or system of psychological structures or subsystems" for a given individual. He believes that if we assess any individual recurrently on a number of psychological dimensions over a period of time, noting the overall configuration of positions at each moment, we will find that the configurations will tend to fall into a number of distinguishable clusters. That is, there will be recurring patterns that have a certain coherence. Each of these represents a discrete state that has a certain stability and that the individual is likely to recognize as a condition that somehow "feels" different from the rest of his or her conscious experience.

It would be difficult to determine how many different states could be usefully distinguished. In practice, the ones that are distinguished usually depend on the biases of those who make the distinctions. To the extent that Western psychology, guided by the spirit of the Enlightenment, emphasizes realism and rationality, it has usually attached greatest value to ordinary consciousness. The various therapeutic movements based on the work of Sigmund Freud endeavor to eliminate the conflicts, fixations, and defensive patterns that interfere with the maximal operation of realism and rationality. For the most part, alternative states are viewed as lower in quality, since they entail a reduction in ego functioning. Religious conversion experiences and Eastern meditative states are classed with sleep and acute intoxication as conditions of severe regression to an infantile level of functioning.

Eastern traditions attach more importance to states that provide a kind of awareness not available to ordinary consciousness, and the Hindu and Buddhist literatures contain diverse descriptions of such states. The Upanishads describe a fourth state beyond waking, dreaming, and dreamless sleep. Dreamless sleep itself is regarded as a state closer to universal consciousness than are the waking and dreaming states, but this state is sharply separated from ordinary waking consciousness. It provides a blissful experience that we cannot remember when we awaken. The fourth state, *turiya*, is one in which the serene and universal consciousness is maintained constantly (cf. Rama, Ballentine, and Ajaya, 1976). In this state, one can carry total awareness through all phases of sleeping and waking.

It is well known that certain yogis of India and lamas of Tibet are able through meditation to develop an expanded awareness that they can carry into sleep (and into death, we are told, though that is a bit more difficult to verify). Such an individual may be fully aware during sleep of events in the immediate environment, as well as aware of events in the imaginal realm. Such an ability requires many years of training. Westerners can often augment their sleep awareness to some extent by paying closer attention to their dreams. Those who do this are more likely to experience lucid dreaming, a condition in which dream imagery is very clear and one is aware that one is dreaming and able to exert control over the process. Lucid dreaming, of course, is only a minute step in the direction of the awareness of *turiya*.

In some Eastern traditions a number of states higher than ordinary rational consciousness are distinguished. In the allegedly higher states one moves from rational consciousness toward a condition free from the illusions of ordinary consciousness. The illusions, or *maya*, are bound up in all the common ways of construing the world within our society. Strictly speaking, it is impossible to describe the world without being caught up to some degree in illusions contained in the consensual view of reality. Thus we progress toward states of pure awareness that cannot be verbally communicated to others and ultimately perhaps to *nirodh*, a state beyond awareness itself. Daniel Goleman (1975) has provided a description of some of the states recognized in Buddhist traditions as lying between that ultimate condition and ordinary consciousness.

ENDURING FEATURES OF
INDIVIDUAL CONSCIOUSNESS

A state of consciousness may be viewed as a configuration of variables that recurs in the experience of any individual. We can also discern configurations or patterns that are characteristic of particular individuals but largely absent from the conscious experience of other individuals. We tend to regard certain individual styles of consciousness as preferable to others, but, as with states, it is difficult to find a sound basis for any ultimate evaluative judgment on this matter.

Individual differences can undoubtedly be found in any psychic variable we might consider, and a number of such modes of variation have been stressed by one theorist or another. An individual may direct attention primarily to the external realm, to the body and its inner workings, or to the cognitive and imaginal realm. Jung conceptualized the dimension of extraversion vs. introversion in terms of something akin to the external vs. cognitive/imaginal contrast. Other theorists have shown much more interest in the somesthetic realm.

Within any of the three principal domains, our attention may vary in a number of ways. We may be oriented to people or to things, to fantasy or to abstract concepts, and so forth. Imagery types also represent a fundamental mode of variation in experience. The tendency to rely on visual or auditory imagery or to neglect either of these is obviously significant, but there is comparable variation in the use of kinesthetic, tactile, and other kinds of imagery. There is also variation in the qualities stressed within an imagery mode. Within the visual realm, variations in color and form orientation received considerable research attention at one time. Both verbal and musical imagery are usually auditory, and one may focus on either, neither, or both. Emphases and preferences in imagery obviously parallel emphases and preferences in perception. The individual who stresses visual or auditory imagery will also depend heavily on the same sense in the perceptual realm. An obvious exception is the individual who has lost the use of a sense that was once highly developed. Ludwig van Beethoven, who was deaf in his later years, is a case in point.

There are many additional variables that may constitute major dimensions of individual variation. One is temporal focus, whether the individual is oriented primarily to the past, present, or future. Another is the inclination to perceive analytically, focusing on details, or globally. The affective character of consciousness has been a topic of theoretical speculation since Galen proposed a system of temperament types based on the four humors of Hippocrates. The typology of Carl Jung (1971) is a still more elaborate typology designed to capture major patterns of conscious functioning.

Self-experience

A much different way of approaching individual differences in conscious experience is in terms of the major attitude-belief systems that govern much of our perception and understanding of ourselves and the world. We may think of these in terms of three basic categories: the self-concept, the weltanschauung (or world-view), and the system of other-person concepts. The three categories are quite interdependent, and to some extent they represent merely different vantage points from which we may examine some of the same issues (see Coan, 1983).

The one aspect of self-experience that was received the greatest amount of attention from psychologists in recent years is the level of self-acceptance or self-esteem. While this variable lends itself fairly readily to crude assessment and research manipulation, there are other aspects of self-experience of more fundamental importance. The advent of self-awareness as such, the experience of oneself as a conscious being with an individual viewpoint and an individual sense of will and decision, may be the most important step along the path of psychic evolution and the path of individual psychic development.

Self-awareness implies the emergence of a concept of personal identity. We may think of the available contents of this identity in terms of three main components of self-experience: the material self (the body, physical attributes, and closely related objects and possessions), the psychological self (oneself as a being that experiences, a being that thinks, feels, senses, intuits, dreams, imagines, etc.), and the interactive self (oneself as a social being, with a certain status and certain roles, who interacts in various ways with others). Each of us has some awareness of all three components, but the self-concept tends to focus selectively on certain ingredients of each component. For some people, it may focus almost entirely on just one component. Whatever the primary focus, the self-concept is also subject to the sorts of variation we noted earlier for any conscious content: in scope, clarity, elaborated detail, and so forth.

A self-concept that is very comprehensive is bound to contain some internal inconsistency, since we all have some conflicting needs and predispositions. A somewhat different issue is what we might call the integrity or coherence of self-experience, the extent to which all parts of one's being seem to be parts of one integrated whole. One instance of low integrity is the basic split between the "true self" and the "false self" that R. D. Laing (1965) found in the schizoid individual. Internal fractionation can take many different forms. There may be a lack of temporal coherence, that is, a lack of continuity with respect to self-experience at different moments in time. The multiple personality is a dramatic illustration of this situation. In a profound psychotic breakdown, the sense of identity may become thoroughly splintered, and the loss of experienced identity and organization is accompanied by a loss of a sense of will, or personal control.

To be sure, nearly all of us suffer to some degree from deficient integrity, since we are alienated from some parts of our total being. Some of these parts, bound up with instinctual or emotional qualities that we do not acknowledge consciously, operate as subpersonalities of which we are only dimly aware. We most often experience them in a projected form, seeing them only in other people who excite us in either a positive or a negative way. In the multiple personality, a subpersonality may usurp control of consciousness for a period of time. In the schizophrenic, it may be experienced as a hallucinatory voice that appears to lead a life of its own. The condition we deem "normal" in this society is not so much a matter of true integrity as it is a matter of effective repression, which serves to banish the unwanted voices from waking consciousness. To achieve greater integrity, we would need to heed the voices, acknowledge them as an unknown part of our being, and come to terms with them. Whether the ultimate denouement of such a course would be a sense of inner unity is debatable. Presumably Jung would say so, but James Hillman (1971) contends that our true psychic nature is multiform, like "stars or sparks or luminous fish eyes." If this is so, then to experience it as unitary might be considered an illusion. On the other hand, one could argue that there is such a thing as unity in diversity and that such a unity results from a gradual process of inner accommodation and reconciliation.

From an Indian perspective, the view of the individual self as a separate entity, unitary or otherwise, is an illusion, albeit an illusion that may be appropriate at a certain stage of development. Be that as it may, this is certainly an important aspect of self-experience: the extent to which one is held to be a distinctly separate entity as opposed to being a part of a larger whole—at the extreme, not even a part but rather inseparable or indistinguishable from the whole, the universal consciousness. On various grounds, one might argue that either view is the correct one or that the two views are different ways of looking at the same issue, neither being the ultimate answer to the riddle of human consciousness.

The Experience of Others and the World

Other-person experience and other-person concepts present many parallels to self-experience and self-concepts. We can view other people in terms of the same kinds of content that are important in self-experience, attending primarily to physical characteristics, to their modes of thinking and feeling, to patterns of social interaction, to roles and status, etc. Our concepts of others are also subject to variation with regard to scope of content, clarity, complexity, internal consistency, and overall integrity.

Much of the variation in our experience of other people is highly dependent on our self-experience. We may be relatively open to the actuality of the other, open to whatever is being expressed by the other at a given moment, or we may impose constructs that limit our receptivity to fresh information. The construct or image that we project onto the other person may contain content that we have denied in ourselves. This sort of projection, i.e., defensive projection, serves to enhance our own comfort, and at the same time it creates a sense of distance or separation between ourselves and the other. Broadly speaking, perception nearly always involves a projection of available images or schemata, and it need not all be defensive in character. Much of it is naive, or assimilative, projection, in which we merely assume that the other experiences things the same way we do. As a consequence of defensive projection, we may view the other as a thing, so alien as to lack human qualities. Such an attitude may enable a soldier to kill the "enemy" without any qualms. A similar detachment, assumed with greater control and less defensive projection, may be put to more constructive use by a surgeon. Assimilative projection provides the basis for a sympathetic concern or even an empathic understanding of the other. Most of our projection onto others, however, serves to maintain separation, and when it ceases, the barrier between self and others dissolves. We may experience the other as a part of our own being, a part that happens at the moment to appear in a different place, but a part whose feelings, emotions, and thoughts we know from within as experiences lying within our own totality.

Just as we experience various degrees of closeness, or even oneness, with other people, we can experience either alienation from or connectedness with the world in general. At the extreme, connectedness would amount to a sense of oneness with the world, and something like this is undoubtedly a part of the experience of many Chinese mystics, certain native American cultures, and a few Westerners like Saint Francis. On the whole, the progressive deanimation of nature seen in Western culture tends to yield a sense of alienation from nature. To some extent, the basic variations in our experience of nature are reflected in such metaphysical positions as materialism and spiritualism. A related aspect of our experience is reflected in the perennial cosmological question as to whether the universe is essentially a plenum, an uninterrupted whole, or a vast assemblage of separate things, each of which in turn is composed of separable, if not separate, particles.

There are individual differences in the experience of many additional aspects of matter and space, as well as in the experience of time and causality. We noted earlier in this work the possibility of construing time in terms of either a linear or a cyclic progression. There is also obvious variation among individuals in the apparent speed of time, in temporal direction (whether one is oriented to past, present, or future) and temporal extension (the span of time with which one is typically concerned—the moment, the current year, a generation, etc.). The infant seems to lack an awareness of passing time, and our remote ancestors probably lived a pretemporal existence. With development, awareness of passing time and temporal extension both increase. Once this has happened, a present orientation may betoken either a rich experience of the moment or a defensive avoidance of thoughts about the past and future.

In Eastern traditions, full enlightenment, the goal of psychic evolution, is often described in terms of timelessness, immortality, eternity, or the eternal now. This is not the timelessness of the infant, but a fresh way of experiencing the passage of time. If the ultimate reality is held to be an unchanging reality, then all the multiplicity, differences, and changing appearances that we perceive are part of the illusion or lesser reality of maya. The enlightened individual is simply attuned to the underlying eternity that is present within each moment through which the transient world moves.

In an unchanging world, causality is not an issue. In the world as we ordinarily perceive it, causality may be construed in several ways. We noted that the experience of will was an important aspect of self-experience. In the world in general, events can be seen as governed by human intention, divine will, chance, or natural laws and forces that are totally indifferent to our needs or wishes. Chance implies event sequences that lack regularity and predictability, whereas natural law implies sequences that are regular and inherently predictable. It is also possible to construe natural events as governed by an inherent non-chance pattern, which we might call the tao, that cannot be fully known and expressed in the form of laws. It is not altogether clear that psychic evolution necessarily requires consistent movement toward one of these views, though there has been a historical trend in Western culture toward increasing emphasis on natural laws and their elucidation by the methods of science. Most accounts of the movement from "primitive" to more advanced thinking hold that so-called primitives naively project human intentions onto the natural world and that this tendency is elaborated in the early mythologies. The implication is that psychic evolution entails a restriction of the idea of human intention to its proper sphere. Even within the sphere of our own behavior and private experience, it seems important to distinguish between what we can personally own (the actions and thoughts governed by conscious intention) and what arises independently of any choice we are aware of making. Some would contend that even where a personal will seems most clearly in control, this is actually an illusion and that we must turn to other modes of explanation. Most of those who so maintain—B. F. Skinner, for one—must be counted among the ranks of the deanimators of the universe. They often see themselves at the forefront of science. Yet there are a few voices in modern science who believe that deanimation has gone too far. Morris Berman (1984) calls for a "reenchantment" of the world. One of the most eminent of modern astronomers, Fred Hoyle (1984), believes that much of what goes on in the universe, including human biological evolution, is governed by a cosmic intelligence that lies beyond our present understanding.

ARE THERE TWO BASIC PATTERNS?

Many theorists have held that there are two fundamental modes of awareness, of knowing, or of viewing the world, and that the variation we have just noted can be largely understood in terms of one basic dimension or polarity. Our willingness to accept such a generalization probably depends somewhat on our own preferred pattern of conscious functioning—whether it favors a concern with broad patterns or attention to the specific details that are not reducible to these patterns. Carl Jung (1971) contended that the dimension of introversion vs. extraversion is so basic to our experience that even the major disputes in Western philosophy since the time of Plato and Aristotle are expressions of this contrast. William James's (1907) characterization of the basic split in philosophy in terms of tenderminded and toughminded types is closer to the mark, though his description of these contains a few ingredients (such as dogmatism and optimism) that seem only marginally relevant.

On the basis of my own research on patterns of theoretical orientation in psychology, I have concluded that there is a general dimension, which I have called fluid vs. restrictive orientation, that runs through psychology, philosophy, and a variety of other disciplines (Coan, 1979). In all likelihood, it is the dimension that most basically separates people drawn to the arts and humanities from people drawn to the natural sciences on the basis of their preferred modes of experience. The restrictive mode found expression in the Enlightenment of the eighteenth century, and this was followed by a resurgence of the fluid mode in Romanticism. The dominant Anglo-American movements in philosophy and psychology from Locke on have emphasized the restrictive orientation, whereas the dominant movements on the European continent following Leibniz have leaned more toward idealism and stressed the fluid orientation. In contemporary psychology, these two traditional paths find expression in the movements we broadly characterize respectively as behavioristic and humanistic. *Restrictive* and *fluid* may be equated with *toughminded* and *tenderminded*, but we could not simply adopt the latter terms without revising James's definition of them.

I chose the terms *fluid* and *restrictive* because they capture, as well as any words I can think of, the basic contrasts in ways of perceiving, thinking, and understanding. I have characterized the two alternative paths in psychology as follows:

> The psychologist whose orientation is basically fluid tends to be concerned with conscious experience, to employ concepts pertaining to mind or consciousness, to favor dealing with wholes in both theory and research, to attempt to understand people as totalities, to favor the content and methods of the humanities, and to be willing to employ relatively loose and informal methods. The psychologist of restrictive bent, on the other hand, is more inclined to confine his attention to overt behavior, to favor more strictly behavioral terminology, to favor the sort of precision that comes with the systematic pursuit of

fairly circumscribed problems, to prefer
dealing with processes or structures
abstracted from people, and to favor
the content and methods of the natural
sciences (Coan, 1973, p. 325).

This description captures the most salient features of the
two orientations as they are expressed in a choice of methods
and content in psychology. Many additional features could be
added to the description, since the fluid-restrictive dimension
has been demonstrated in the analysis of questionnaire responses
of contemporary psychologists, as well as in the analysis of
descriptive ratings of major theorists. In the questionnaire realm,
the fluid-restrictive dichotomy is represented by a general factor
of subjectivism vs. objectivism. In a refined questionnaire that I
have developed, the Theoretical Orientation Survey, this general
factor is scored by the summing of scores for five more specific
factors. Thus, as I measure it, *objectivism* embraces an impersonal
view of causality, behavioral content emphasis, elementarism,
physicalism, and quantitative orientation. *Subjectivism* embraces
the use of concepts of personal will, experiential content emphasis,
holism, and de-emphasis of physicalism and quantification.

The questionnaire has been administered to hundreds of
psychologists, and numerous correlates have been established
(Coan, 1979). There is a slight tendency for female psychologists
to be more subjectivistic than male psychologists, but there is an
even clearer association between this dimension and what might
be called masculinity-femininity of interests and values. We may
summarize many of the findings by stating that objectivists tend
to display more interest in the physical sciences and in research,
while subjectivists display more interest in the arts, in people,
and in human-service activities. There is some evidence of a
pervasive difference in cognitive style. Subjectivists are inclined
to be more open to varied experience, and they tend to perceive

and conceptualize people in terms of a richer and more complex set of characteristics. Correlations with available measures of Jungian types indicate that objectivists tend to emphasize the thinking and sensation functions, while subjectivists emphasize feeling and intuition.

It appears that the major patterns of orientation in psychology are rooted in the two alternative modes of experiencing life and the world that I have called restrictive and fluid. To claim primary credit for discovering a major dimension of human experience, however, is a bit like getting burned and announcing to the world that one has discovered fire. My dimension corresponds rather well to the toughminded-tenderminded dichotomy of William James. For Nietzsche, it was the contrast between the Apollonian and the Dionysian. We see it again in Neumann's distinction between patriarchal and matriarchal modes of consciousness.

Many differences in experience that have been characterized in terms of masculine and feminine modes apply here. There is Jung's distinction between the logos and eros principles. In Chinese thought, the parallel distinction is between yang and yin. Roger Sperry's research with "split-brain" patients has inspired a fresh spate of related speculation regarding a contrast between "left-hemisphere" and "right-hemisphere" modes of consciousness. The former is said to be linear and analytical, while the latter is holistic and intuitive. Similar distinctions have been offered in recent years by many writers, using a variety of terms.

We need not review all the terminological distinctions that have been proposed, but it is important to get some sense of all the ingredients embraced by these various contrasts that all appear to hover about a common fundamental duality in human consciousness. Some of the ingredients have to do with ways of perceiving or apprehending. In this case, the contrast is essentially between the analytical and focused on the one hand and the global and diffuse on the other. The individual whose orientation is restrictive, patriarchal, and toughminded would attend more to the immediate contents of experience (Jung's sensation function), would give more heed to specific details, would focus more sharply and would pay more attention to form in the visual field. The individual whose orientation is fluid, matriarchal, and tenderminded would attend more to meanings and possibilities in the given situation (Jung's intuition function), would perceive wholes at the expense of details, would perceive more diffusely, and would attend more to colors and emotional qualities in the sensory realm.

A number of differences have been suggested in the realm of cognitive processes. In Jungian terms, the restrictive orientation would favor thinking over feeling, that is, the use of judgments concerned with issues of truth rather than issues of value. The fluid orientation would favor feeling over thinking. The restrictive orientation would tend to emphasize convergent thinking—i.e., rational thinking aimed at deduction of a single correct result— while the fluid orientation would tend to emphasize divergent thinking. We might expect the thought processes of the restrictive individual to be more ordered, linear, or sequential, while those of the fluid individual would probably reflect the same global concern evident in immediate perception and would less often evince an orderly progression from one detail to another.

Ways of Knowing and Perceiving

There are some related differences with respect to knowledge, meaning, and conceptualization. In terms of Joseph Royce's (1970) ways of knowing, we might expect the restrictive orientation to be expressed in rationalism and empiricism, while the fluid orientation would be expressed in metaphorism, and my data largely bear this out (Coan, 1979). We would also expect the restrictive individual to be more concerned with signific or literal meaning (meaning that can be articulated in terms of specifiable referents), while the fluid individual would have a greater appreciation for symbolic meaning. According to Jung, the symbol, as opposed to the sign, provides a link to an unconscious realm of meaning, and we can best deal with symbolic meaning through intuition. It is possible that the restrictive orientation generally favors meanings that can be successfully expressed verbally. My data also indicate that it favors the kind of knowing associated with the ideal of the detached observer, while the fluid orientation has more room for empathic understanding. Perhaps the detached mode of verbalized understanding depends on the knowing (or "knowing about") of *sapere, savoir,* and *wissen,* while the fluid orientation might stress the direct knowing of *cognoscere, connaître,* and *kennen,* a knowing that cannot be mediated by words.

The focal attention and orderly cognitive habits of the restrictive individual would seem to limit the kinds of information that can be processed. For this reason, there may be various kinds of apprehension and understanding that are available only to individuals of more fluid orientation. The kinds of insight and understanding sought by mystics, which can never be fully expressed verbally, are an obvious example. Aesthetic experience offers other examples. Extrasensory perception, which rests heavily on impressions whose character and source are usually unclear, would also appear to lie more within the province of the fluid orientation. (For this reason, people in our rationally oriented society learn, as they grow up, not to use it.)

There are also differences in ways of viewing and experiencing self, others, and the world that we should consider, and some of these may follow from differences we have already considered. Presumably the restrictive, patriarchal, or toughminded orientation attaches importance generally to discrete things and to separations and differences. To an individual of this orientation, it would be important to experience a separate and well-defined individuality. The contrasting orientation would be more open to the experience of unity with, or relationship to, a larger whole. To experience oneself as separate from others is to experience others as separate from oneself, and an accentuation of differences can lead at the extreme to a depersonalization of others, or a view of people as objects. The fluid outlook would deemphasize differences and stress the personal qualities of others. The restrictive view is conducive to a view of relationships in terms of power, while the fluid outlook would favor a view of relationships in terms of love, harmony, relatedness, or union. At the extreme, this would amount to a dissolution of the boundary between self and other and a recognition of the essential oneness of the two. One would see the other, in a sense, as a part of oneself that just happened at the moment to occupy a different body and a different set of circumstances.

Many of the same ideas apply to views of the world in general. The individual of fluid outlook should feel more connected with the world at large, perhaps inseparably united with it. The restrictive orientation would favor an inanimistic and mechanistic view of nature, while the fluid orientation would favor an animistic and vitalistic view. The restrictive individual would tend to stress the multiplicity of things and their ultimately discrete, particulate character, while the fluid individual would view the world in terms of continuity or cosmic unity. In the cosmological view of such an individual, the universe is a unitary plenum. Experiencing time as he or she experiences space, the restrictive individual would see constant change, or transience, while the fluid individual would be more concerned with an eternal, unchanging reality.

I believe that all the ingredients I have now suggested for the two allegedly basic patterns of experience have been described in one form or another by various writers. The terms most often used in delineations of the patterns are *rational* and *analytical* on one side and *holistic* and *intuitive* on the other. If we construe these words very broadly, they capture many of the specific perceptual, cognitive, and conceptual tendencies I have just discussed. I believe it is reasonable to think in terms of a broad general dimension of conscious experience that corresponds to the two basic patterns we are now considering. At the same time,

I would insist that we cannot adequately describe all individual differences in consciousness by assigning people to positions along this single dimension. It is definitely possible for one to be restrictive with respect to some of the variables I have noted and fluid with respect to others.

If we could adequately assess the conscious experience of a large number of people and subject it to a factor-analytic study, I am confident that we would find the general dimension. It is not clear whether we would find well defined component factors corresponding to selected parts of the general dimension, since this depends on regularities of subpatterns that would run through the total sample of subjects. Within individuals we can undoubtedly find various combinations of fluid and restrictive characteristics, and some of these combinations serve important purposes. Indeed, the psychologist who would seek to make systematic sense of both the restrictive and the fluid, the patriarchal and the matriarchal, the toughminded and the tenderminded, must at the same time be able to appreciate the diffuse and global view of the latter while engaging in a good deal of rational analysis. Here at least I find myself in the distinguished company of William James and Carl Jung.

It is important to recognize that some areas of expression of either orientation can be fairly independent of other areas of expression. Thus, the self may be perceived and understood in a restrictive manner, the individual having a clear sense of a separate personal identity, while much of the experience of the world at large is experienced in a manner more characteristic of a fluid individual, with more reliance on global perception and intuition. Apart from overall perception and conception of the self, it is possible for experience of the inner, or subjective, realm to be processed differently from experience of the outer, objective realm. Directed outward, the fluid orientation may be expressed in a sense of being-at-one-with-others or in an intuitive understanding of other people. Directed inward, it may be expressed in an intuitive apprehension of one's own feelings, images, fantasies, and dreams. These need not go together. Directed outward, the restrictive orientation may be expressed in an analytical concern with specific facts, a tendency to see the world in terms of inanimate things, and a clear sense of others as separate from oneself. Directed inward, it may be expressed in a rational concern with abstract ideas. Again, inward and outward modes of expression may be somewhat independent. In addition, the body may be experienced as fairly separate from the rest of one's personal being. In this case, it may be experienced as a sort of alien vessel, or it may be almost totally ignored in consciousness. Given such a split, there may be a considerable difference between the mode of consciousness manifested in the experience of the body and the mode manifested in a psychological realm of unembodied ideas, feelings, and images. At this point, we do not know for certain to what extent all the possible expressions of either basic mode of consciousness covary within the general population. This is an empirical issue that merits further examination. We do know that the covariation is not perfect, for it is not difficult to find individuals who operate at the fluid or restrictive extreme in some respects and not in others. My own data on psychologists show such patterns for the expression of these modes of consciousness in psychological theory.

A FRESH LOOK AT POSSIBLE EVOLUTIONARY GOALS

In Chapter 2, we considered some of the possible goals of psychic evolution. In Chapter 6, we noted the positions taken on this matter by a variety of significant theorists. We must now reconsider the matter in the light of our more detailed examination of the variations in human consciousness. The question of evolutionary goals is of fundamental importance, for we cannot describe evolutionary progress up to this stage in human experience, and we cannot forecast future developments without having some notion of the kinds of change we would consider progressive, the kinds we would consider regressive, and the kinds we would consider merely digressive.

The mode of efficiency, as I earlier described it, is concerned with the cultivation of all our psychological capacities and with their effective use in coping with the various problems of life. The capacities that are cultivated are subject to fashions that vary between cultures and over time. Some of the capacities are sensory—our awareness and ability to make effective use of visual, auditory, tactile, kinesthetic, or other sensory information. The development of corresponding imagery modes is presumed to be closely tied to this. There are also sensitivities, notably intuition and extrasensory perception, that do not involve well-defined sensory channels.

A closely related class of attainments is the skills that depend on a coordination of sensory information with appropriate somatic adjustments. Some of these adjustments take the form of the accomplished movements of the dancer, mime, gymnast, or musician. Others take the form of the bodily self-regulation that enables an individual to deal inwardly with stress, avoid or overcome psychosomatic ills, and maintain optimal functioning in the cardiovascular, respiratory, and digestive systems. Our neglect of most of the capacities I have just noted has become more obvious as a result of increasing contact with people from other cultures. For this reason, we have been hearing a lot in recent years about the benefits of Gestalt therapy, sensory-awareness exercises, biofeedback, and a variety of yogic practices and body therapies. If what we are concerned with is the level of sheer awareness of various kinds, we can add to this list an assortment of meditative techniques and methods for working with dreams and fantasies.

The many additional ways of processing the information gathered by our senses are also a concern of the mode of efficiency. We may include here all the ways of judging and knowing that I noted earlier, as well as the intellectual factors that we have attempted to assess psychometrically. There are modes of processing information that we have failed to measure and modes that have been generally ignored in our culture. We have stressed successful adaptation to the environment, and we have usually regarded rational thinking and reality contact (the qualities of the Freudian ego) as the psychological basis for adaptation. In Western rationalistic traditions, reality has generally been equated with the current-science model of the universe. In recent times, this has been a materialistic, mechanistic, and inanimistic model that assumes our separateness from a world of separated things. While modern physicists have begun to abandon this model, it is still the one that prevails in our society, and most of my colleagues in psychology cling to it as fervently as any nineteenth-century physicist did. In general, the stress on this model has been accompanied by an emphasis on a literalistic, sign-mediated form of understanding.

Self-awareness is an important aspect of overall awareness. *Self-awareness*, of course, has come to mean a number of things, including agreement between self-concept and organismic experience, agreement between self-concept and behavior, agreement between self-concept and social image (how one is perceived by others), and attention to all one's sensations, images, dreams, and fantasies. In addition, the term often implies the mere possession of an elaborate self-concept, a clear picture of one's individually distinctive qualities. This last notion goes with the contemporary Western emphasis on individual separateness and personal control.

The mode of creativity is akin to the mode of efficiency in so far as it involves the cultivation of certain capacities, but the capacities are ones less directly required for most of our adaptation to the world, and they are capacities less valued in Western society. While we often value the products of creativity, we tend to disparage and discourage the process that yields those products. The individual who chooses a life of creativity may have to accept the role of a misfit, one whose habits are at odds with the surrounding social milieu. Perhaps comforts may have to be sacrificed, and we know of many instances in which a creative artist accepted a great deal of torment for the sake of the work. In one of his letters, Vincent van Gogh once wrote that "man is not on this earth merely to be happy [but rather] to realize great things for humanity." Even within psychology, the creative process has been eyed with suspicion, as a process entailing a regression to an infantile mode of consciousness. While I may decry this position as the narrow-minded view of mainstream psychoanalysis, the Freudian outlook itself is merely one expression of the rationalism that pervades Western science.

The mode of creativity, like the mode of efficiency, would seem to require attention to various kinds of sensory input and imagery, but there may be a difference in emphasis. Much of what we have prized in the realm of efficient adaptation depends on analytical observation of clearly represented content. The individual who is bent on creative action or production may tune out the clearest and most obvious content and attend to bits that are unclear, unexpected, and perhaps so faint that they might readily escape notice. At least part of the time, attention is likely to be more diffused than focused. The content gathered may be subjected to processes that are less orderly and rational than those often required for the achievements associated with the mode of efficiency. They may take forms we could characterize as discursive, narrative, or imaginal. The result will be a more novel and less predictable product than rational processing would yield.

To the extent that creativity implies an openness to the novel and unanticipated, we may expect novel features in the individual's view of self and world. There may be more freedom to entertain views of the world and all its contents that depart from the conventional picture. The self-concept, too, may assume a somewhat different form from the usual, perhaps emphasizing a much different kind of content from that which appears central for most people. The self-concept may also be less fixed or static, the individual experiencing himself or herself less as a person with a set of fixed traits than as a process that is ever-changing, a process of continual discovery.

The mode of inner harmony has no clear implications for modes of perception or information processing. At its highest levels, it presupposes a general acceptance and reconciliation of contents, in particular those contents involving what we might call self-experience. A likely effect of this would be a prevalence of states we could describe in terms of tranquility or serenity. If inner harmony is to be profoundly realized, self-awareness must be extensive; one must attend fully at times to all the varied self-referent contents that enter consciousness. The more common condition, of course, is one in which we selectively attend to contents, neither recognizing the extent to which they contradict one another nor permitting a reconciliation of conflict.

Many systems of psychological thought seem to agree that the dividing line between self-experience and other-experience is rather arbitrary and ill-defined. Even if we do not accept the idea that individuality is, indeed, only an illusion, we must still wrestle with the paradoxical fact that the quest for the most intimately personal and individual parts of our being always leads to a ground that proves to be universal. The more we move from those features of our experience that are linked to the peculiarities of our present life situation and its contemporary social setting, the more we encounter features that simply link us to a far broader community because we share them with people of other times and cultures. From a Jungian perspective, this would mean that we move from the remnants of our personal history to a level of experience that expresses more directly the contents of the collective unconscious. The same essential discovery has been made countless times and expressed in many other ways. William James (1960) conjectured that the separateness of our psyches is more apparent than real and that they are like islands projecting individually above the surface of the ocean but joining in one great common land mass below the surface. Whatever metaphor one chooses for rationalizing our inherent connectedness, one clear implication is that an inner harmony resting on extensive self-awareness will tend to imply as well a respect for and harmony with a whole that extends beyond anything we can strictly call individual. Under various circumstances, we might want to speak of that whole in terms of the self (in Jungian terms), nature, the tao, humanity, or universal mind or consciousness. Perhaps this means that at its more profound levels, inner harmony will tend to merge with the modes of relatedness and transcendence.

The mode of relatedness is defined primarily in terms of an experience of union, harmony, or connection with other beings. Individual self is experienced as self-in-relation or self-at-one-with-others. Formulations of this mode usually focus on our relationship to other humans, but the inclusive whole may extend beyond humanity to include all other living things or the whole of nature, animate and inanimate. The whole of nature may be viewed as animate. In some traditions, such as those involving bhakti yoga, one's love for other beings is viewed as a natural consequence of a more fundamental love for the deity or for the divine of which we all partake.

With respect to modes of perception and cognitive processing, relatedness implies a sensitivity to the thoughts, feelings, and consciousness of the other, and an awareness of the other that is both accurate and emphatic. It implies an openness to the other that requires an absence of defensive projection and an absence of the critical mode of observation that is designed to maintain a clear boundary between self and other. When we relax the critical attitude and allow our sense of separateness to dissolve, the natural effect is love for the other person and a recognition of the other as part of a larger self. An autobiographic comment of Thomas Merton captures the effect: "In Louisville, at the corner of Fourth and Walnut, in the center of the shopping district, I was suddenly overwhelmed with the realization that I loved all those people, that they were mine and I theirs, that we could not be alien to one another even though we were total strangers" (Merton, 1966, p. 140). The experience transcends cultural boundaries. It is represented in Christian culture by St. Francis of Assisi and by Mother Teresa, in Hindu culture by Gandhi, and in Islamic culture by Badshah Khan. Despite our Christian tradition, this experience is difficult to achieve in a society that over-values individuality. Often, as we sense our boundaries dissolving, before we can be overwhelmed by love, we are overwhelmed by a fear that we shall lose our integrity and be swept into the abyss of psychotic formlessness.

The mode of transcendence implies a still more radical departure from our usual experience of a separated self. In the mystical traditions of both East and West, the separated self is regarded as an illusion, a false image, or an idea we have constructed in an effort to enhance our sense of individual worth. The more basic reality is held to be a self that is either closely linked or identical to universal mind, God, or the ground of all being. Movement along the path defined by the mode of transcendence would be movement toward an experience of non-separateness, and from a sense of egoic identity toward a radical self that is the perfect image of God (Cashen, 1981), toward a transcendental "I" or atman, or toward a realization of identity with the brahman. All action is increasingly experienced as an expression of universal will, or of the basic flow of all nature, rather than as a product of personal decision.

In general, the modes of awareness that are held to be most characteristic of the mode of transcendence are those sought in mystical traditions. There are many descriptions of these modes of awareness, and I noted earlier the valuable accounts provided by such authors as Goleman (1975) and Chaudhuri (1975). To the extent that movement toward identity with universal consciousness entails a transcendence of all dualities and a oneness with an absolute reality beyond all forms and all change, the ultimate state to be attained may even be described in terms of transcendence of consciousness itself.

FLEXIBILITY AND THE INTERACTION OF MODES

In earlier work I stressed the importance of flexibility as both a precondition of personal growth and a consequence of growth (Coan, 1974). Experiential flexibility might well be considered an appropriate goal of psychic evolution. It is obvious that our lives will be richer if we are able without difficulty to shift from one kind of awareness, perception, or knowing to another. We can be more broadly aware if we have full use of all the senses and corresponding forms of imagery; if we can direct attention either into the body, toward our physical surroundings, or toward the cognitive and imaginal realms; if we can attend to various kinds of content; if we can attend analytically to detail or more diffusely to total patterns; and if we can view the world with either empathic involvement or objective detachment. We can also be more broadly aware if we have access to all the alternative modes of judging, knowing, and understanding that we have noted. I believe the desirability of flexibility is also evident with respect to our basic views of self, others, and the world, and access even to those views that have been labeled inferior or pathological can be valuable.

A corollary of this argument is that there are problems in being confined to limited modes of consciousness. The skilled therapist can choose to experience personal fragmentation, but the schizophrenic is trapped in that experience. Something is lost if we are stuck in either a concrete or an abstract mode of thinking. Both the imperialism of Western rationality and the imperialism of cosmic unity (the insistence that either view is the one true view) can lead to a sterile existence. The psychotic who claims to be God, identifying his separateness with the cosmic to ward off fragmentation, is caught in a rigid blend of the egoic and the mystical.

I would argue that within any of the five modes of fulfillment, the highest levels of attainment require flexible access to alternative forms of awareness. To some extent, this means access to forms of awareness central to other modes of fulfillment, and an important implication is that at higher levels the paths leading to the alternative goals of psychic evolution may converge. We cannot regard them as merging completely, however, so long as we are concerned with distinctive features of the alternative goals.

Flexibility and the Mode of Efficiency

Of the five modes, the one most concerned with understanding and knowledge is the mode of efficiency. In the West, the goal of efficiency is most often equated with highly developed rationality, but the most comprehensive kind of understanding and world-view requires a perspective that rests as well on the experience of nonrational states and nonrational forms of information processing. The limitations of sheer rationality are particularly evident in the field of psychology, where we often see efforts to interpret the experience yielded by nonrational states in terms that make no reference to the qualities of those states. Thus, such phenomena as romantic love, aesthetic rapture, and mystical experiences are reduced to stimulus-response sequences, reinforcement contingencies, physiological tensions, and analogs of computer processes. Anxiety, hallucinations, and the schizophrenic loss of identity are rendered no more intelligible by such language. The problem is not that the formulations are incorrect, but that they represent a partial view achieved in a state different from the ones in which the phenomena are experienced. A psychologist can say many things about the perceptual and imaginal processes involved in romantic love, but the metaphoric language of the poet may preserve, by connotation, a quality that is absent in our more rational utterances. The wise poet knows, of course, that he is grasping at a vapory sprite that can never quite be caught in a net of words.

The folly of seeking the one true formulation has always been recognized by mystics and has been more widely noted in the

Orient, where it is well known that "the tao that can be spoken is not the tao." We come closest to a comprehensive picture of reality when we base the picture on the varied experience of different states and modes of awareness. Yet our varied experience yields a picture which to the intellect seems contradictory and which can be rendered most faithfully in words in the form of paradoxes. At the core of our conscious experience of ourselves and the world lies a set of existential polarities that permit opposing ways of experiencing and conceptualizing. Thus, the universe can be viewed as unitary or manifold, and the same may be said of the individual self. Life may be viewed as a very serious and tragic affair or as comic. Whatever we regard as most sacred can also be seen as the core of a great cosmic joke. Anything to which we attach importance can also be seen as inconsequential, and our own lives may be regarded with either pride or humility. I may view myself as a separate individual or as part of a whole. I may view myself as a willing agent or as one who acts in strict accordance with fate, divine will, or the impersonal causality of natural forces. It evidently serves a human purpose to express our understanding in words—at any rate, the effort to do so is certainly one of our species characteristics. It is vain to hope, however, that the product of this effort will always consist of simple, logically coherent, and directly testable statements. At times, we must be content to let our words point to a mystery that is destined to lie beyond the reach of our intellect.

There are various kinds of awareness and self-regulation that require an ability to shift easily from one mode of consciousness to another. The meditative practices of the Orient serve to enhance this ability, while the characteristic emphasis on personal control, or will, in the West tends to inhibit it. We must be willing to let go of controlled and organized thinking in order to experience all the effects of meditation. To achieve control of many physiological processes (e.g., to divert blood flow away from the head to overcome a vascular headache), we must replace efforts at active control with "passive volition" (Green, 1973). To receive information telepathically or clairvoyantly, we must allow images not under our control to arise, turning off analytical attention and rational ordering at least for a moment. Receptivity of this kind does not require a high level of psychological development, but effective use of it does. We must be able to shift between states at the appropriate moment and discriminate between valid impressions and those generated by memory or imagination (Targ and Harary, 1984).

Flexibility and Creativity

A high level of creative production in the artistic or intellectual realm requires an ability to move between a form of consciousness that is ordered, rational, and restrictive and one that is more fluid and intuitive. There is a growing body of research evidence indicating that the more creative people in the arts and sciences have access to both "primitive" and organized forms of thinking and are open perceptually to both the "outer" and "inner" worlds (Dellas and Gaier, 1970). An individual with such tendencies is able to let go of an existing order, permitting novel insights to arise, and is then able to make productive use of the insights.

Jan Ehrenwald (1984) has argued from life-history and life-style information that many outstanding geniuses have displayed a one-sided overdevelopoment of the right cerebral hemisphere. He contends that a few creative geniuses, like Pablo Picasso and Leonardo da Vinci, have shown a balanced access to both hemispheres. At the same time, he cites Beethoven, Nietzsche, Mozart, and Einstein among the lopsided cases, but too much depends on the evidence one chooses to look at. Beethoven may have been a clumsy man and poor speller, and Mozart may have been a bit child-like and unable to handle money very responsibly, but no one can doubt that both men achieved a rare balance of inspiration and craftsmanship. The essential flexibility was evident in their work. Even if their lives lacked an optimal balance, the greatest works of Beethoven, Mozart, Nietzsche, and

Einstein were possible because these people were able consistently to shift to an ordered, Apollonian, "left-brain" form of thought at the crucial moment.

The key to a generally creative lifestyle may be a facility for flexible access to different modes of perception and awareness in all phases of living. It may be important to be able to view both oneself and one's world in a variety of ways, assuming at times a "realistic" perspective and at other times a more imaginal perspective. Both James Hillman (1972) and Mary Watkins (1976) have advocated the cultivation of the "imaginal ego" as a foundation for personal growth.

Inner Harmony, Relatedness, and Transcendence

The mode of inner harmony requires even more clearly an access to various views of oneself. It requires the acknowledgment and mutual reconciliation of all parts of our nature, including those tendencies that are unflattering, socially unacceptable, or inconsistent with our personal aims—all those potentials that we readily attribute to other people but fail to see in ourselves. With respect to our total sets of behavioral, cognitive, and emotional tendencies, it can be argued that each of us is both masculine and feminine, both child and adult, both animal and angel, both good and evil, both intelligent and stupid, both tidy and messy, both strong and weak, both outgoing and indwelling, both noisy and quiet, both kind and cruel, both dependent and independent, both loving and hostile, and both generous and selfish. Some of these qualities we have cultivated on a conscious level and learned to express in an organized way, while others are qualities of which we are only dimly aware. We may express them unwittingly or go to great lengths to avoid expressing them. Some of us who are psychologically sophisticated develop a knack for confessing all our latent attributes, but this is often just an intellectual game. To gain the awareness needed for inner resolution, we must depend less on verbal manipulation. We must work with various states of consciousness, and we must attend to our "accidental" actions, to tensions in our muscles, to changes in internal organs, and to the fleeting images that appear in our fantasies and dreams.

Realization of the aims of the mode of relatedness also requires a similar flexibility with respect to self-experience and experience of others. We cannot fully experience ourselves in a condition of relationship, harmony, or union with others so long as we are either lacking in self-awareness or too intent on maintaining a clear sense of separate identity. We must attend both to the qualities that we share with others and to the qualities that make us different. To attend fully to both, we must be aware of the content that we project onto others to maintain distance and be willing to accommodate more to the actuality of the other. Then we can recognize in our difference a shared potential that is simply expressed more amply in one of us. Therein lies the possibility of a full meeting between persons.

The goal of transcendence, as it is usually understood, requires access to more than one state and more than one form of awareness. The mystic seeks an experience of unity that dissolves both the sense of individuality and the discrete "thing-ness" of the universe itself. While this experience is not possible in a state of rational-analytical consciousness, the typical mystic has already cultivated the rational state and retains full access to it. A natural consequence of flexible access to such different states might be an ability to appreciate two contrasting world-views— one of a rationally ordered and constructed world and one of cosmic unity. In the Orient, of course, enlightenment is generally understood to involve a realization that the rationally ordered world of separate things is maya. If we construe maya as the illusion of a playful and arbitrary reality, enlightenment can be interpreted as a second stage of reflection in the course of psychic development. Through the first reflection we become aware of ourselves as beings that possess awareness, thus separating ourselves from the animal kingdom, and we proceed to develop an image of ourselves as individual persons. The second reflection amounts to a recognition of the process of self-reflection and self-construction. A realization of the arbitrary nature of the picture we have assembled on the basis of selective memories, perceptions, and identifications makes possible a more flexible attention to total self-experience with all the changes through which it passes as we move from one phase of our existence to another.

IMPLICATIONS FOR A THEORY OF PSYCHIC EVOLUTION

It is obvious from the preceding discussion that for each mode of fulfillment higher and lower levels of manifestation can be distinguished. The mode of efficiency is realized at a low level in the sensory intelligence of the animal, in a capacity for making the perceptual discriminations that result in the most adaptive responses to the immediate environment. Given keen senses and efficient sensory-motor coordination, further development depends on the ability to abstract and generalize. Self-reflection, contemplation of the past, planning for the future, and rational thought then become possible. Achievement of a more comprehensive understanding and a world-view that encompasses a variety of perspectives requires, in addition, an access to different states and different modes of awareness.

Imaginal thought is of particular importance for the mode of creativity, and we may distinguish levels with respect to its use. At the lowest level, it is confined to the primary-process thinking of the infant. With further development, there is a growing capacity for choosing states, and there is evidence of this growth in the make-believe play of the child. At a higher level, it is possible to a still greater extent to let images flow when one wishes—and even to seek a particular kind of imaginal content. It is even possible to cultivate a very active kind of imaginal thought (which, indeed, Jung labeled "active imagination") in which one achieves an interplay between a deliberate, rational, egoic part of the psyche and a more spontaneous, imaginal, free-flowing side that yields unanticipated content. The highest forms of creative production require a capacity for this kind of interplay. The vivid image that comes unbidden is experienced as a hallucination. The vivid image that is sought and welcomed is a vision that can provide the foundation for artistic, religious, or intellectual insights. In the Western world, the distinction has often been obscured, because both the church and science have mistrusted the imaginal realm, disparaging dreams and visions as unworthy of serious attention. The fresh products of the imagination, of course, often pose a challenge to ideas derived by other means. Thus they can threaten the authority of dogma, the supremacy of rational thought, and an empiricism that relies heavily on sense data as a direct source of information about concrete reality. When imaginal thinking is developed to its highest level, however, the individual should have a well developed capacity for distinguishing between the imaginal reality and the ordinary consensual reality and should be able to combine imaginal thought effectively with rational thought and analytical observation.

We can also speak of inner harmony at many levels of consciousness. In the state of undifferentiated awareness, or preconsciousness, of the newborn infant or the simpler organism, there is inner harmony in the sense that there is as yet no basis for conflict. There is total spontaneity, for there is no separation between impulse and action, and there is no internal restraint or suppression of impulses. With the development of more organized consciousness and self-reflection, certain parts of the total set of psychic potentials receive focal attention, and the individual identifies with them. Other potentials remain unrecognized or undergo repression. So long as the repression is effective, one may experience inner harmony, but it is a superficial harmony dependent on limited self-awareness. As its highest level, the mode of inner harmony requires comprehensive self-awareness and reconciliation of contrasting elements within the psyche.

In considering the mode of relatedness, we move from

harmony within to harmony of self and other, and in some respects the levels distinguishable for the one mode are parallel to those distinguishable for the other. At a low level of consciousness, there is no experienced separation between self and other and no differentiation within the psyche between the personal and the collective. Here we have the relatedness of non-separateness and participation mystique. A further step in consciousness is necessary for the experience of separateness or difference. With partial self-awareness, we selectively own certain psychic contents, while the contents we repress are viewed as alien and perceived as a property of the other. Various contents may be attributed to other members of the family and immediate community while the contents viewed as least compatible with one's evolving self-image may be projected beyond the community to the "enemy" outside the perimeter. There may be only a limited sense of individuality: One may still be largely identified with the immediate community while experiencing sharp separation from the group without. Increasing emphasis on individuality would seem inevitably to lead away from the goal of relatedness, but this depends on the extent to which projection is employed to reinforce repression and to bolster a sense of separateness and uniqueness. A respect for the uniqueness of the other goes hand in hand with an acceptance of one's own undeveloped potentials. With extensive self-awareness, projection is less and less likely to serve a defensive purpose, and we inevitably recognize our commonness, our inner community with others. We see the other as basically like ourselves with just a different pattern of manifest potentials. At the highest level of realization of this mode, we experience a oneness with all other beings based on comprehensive self-awareness.

The goal of transcendence is also possible at various levels of consciousness. In early infancy, we experience unity with all being in the same sense that we experience total relatedness: There is as yet no sense of separation from anything else. There is no experienced individuality, no *me* distinguishable from a *not-me.* Self and universe are one great undifferentiated mass. This is not true transcendence, of course, for there is no individual ego to be transcended. The ultimate goal differs psychologically from the initial condition by virtue of the fact that there is a full capacity for the experience of separateness, individuality, and diversity underlying the experience of unity with all being. If that capacity is lost, we have only schizophrenic regression, not the transcendence of the mystic.

Universal Features and Superordinate Goals

It is possible, then, to recognize a progression of levels with respect to each mode of fulfillment. At the highest levels, the modes are not altogether independent of one another, and we can probably make a case for some superordinate goals toward which the five modes converge. Some of the higher levels I have just described depend on the development of flexible awareness, on the possession of ready access to alternative states of consciousness and alternative modes of perception, knowing, and processing information. A related quality is the ability to deal with both literal, or signific, and symbolic kinds of meaning. Also related is a capacity for higher levels of reflection, which permits access to differing views of oneself, life, and the world.

On similar grounds, it can be argued that the truly primitive condition is one of restricted viewpoint and inflexibility with respect to modes of awareness. The lack of flexibility is to a great extent a function of a failure as yet to make distinctions that are important at more advanced levels of consciousness. We miss this basic point when we simply label the thinking of the presumed primitive as concrete, literal, or mythological. The primitive cannot deal with either literal or symbolic meanings as we might, since a distinction between the literal and the symbolic has not yet been made. Similarly the concrete and the imaginal have not been distinguished, and the experienced world remains a rich mixture of things and spirits interfused. Radical materialism and literalism become possible once some of these basic splits have occurred, and they represent a loss or denial of a choice that has already emerged in the course of psychic evolution.

Just as we may be able to recognize some superordinate goals toward which psychic evolution tends, we may be able to identify some universal features of the evolutionary process. The one obvious feature of this sort is discrimination. Movement from the primeval state, whether in the development of individual consciousness or in the evolution of the mass of people depends on certain basic distinctions. As William James (1961) noted, each of us must early in life make one grand splitting of the universe into two parts, the *me* and the *not-me*. We must proceed from there to make additional distinctions between people, between things, and between aspects of ourselves: body parts, feelings, thoughts, social roles, etc. There are some fundamental distinctions that may be universally made. One concerns the body-mind split, and there is a host of additional distinctions that may be viewed as loosely related to this: between matter and mind, concrete and abstract, literal and symbolic or figurative, etc. The distinction between male and female and between the masculine and the feminine is also universal. The manner in which this is elaborated is subject to cultural variation, but there are some underlying features that are more or less constant.

The most widely recognized formula for evolutionary progression is a three-stage sequence: an initial state of nondifferentiation, followed by a differentiation of parts or aspects, followed by a higher-level integration in which the parts are brought together into a new whole. We can undoubtedly argue that psychic evolution has proceeded by a process of discrimination or differentiation in all parts of the world, but there is much variation among individuals in psychic development and much variation among cultures in psychic evolution. Both the similarities and the differences between cultures are important.

Richard W. Coan

Cultural Variations

As we have noted, the Western world has proceeded along a line that is strongly materialistic and literalistic, tending in recent centuries to reject as unreal anything that cannot be clearly grasped with the recognized senses, particularly vision. In the process, we have deanimated the world; having made a split between the animate and the inanimate, we have tended to view more and more parts of the world as lifeless. We have tended also toward a sharp division between subject and object and toward a rejection of participant consciousness, preferring knowledge by abstraction and by concepts based on "detached" observation.

There are major cultural divisions within the Orient, but the Orient on the whole has never made such a radical split between the rational and the mystical, the animate and the inanimate, or the abstract-literal and the symbolic. Of course, we can find East-West parallels. The transition from mythic thinking to the philosophy of the early Brahmins in India resembles the transition that occurred in Greece around the same time. There are some similarities between early Buddhism and early Christianity, and perhaps we can liken the medieval alchemists of Europe to the Taoists of China. Divergences appeared early, however, and have been accentuated in recent centuries. The philosophy of the Brahmins, like that of the classical Greeks, provided a foundation for both a rational path and a mystical path, but the mystical path gained ascendance in India and neighboring countries. In Greco-Roman culture, the mystical path was followed by the early Christians, but it was subverted at an early point in the development of Christianity. The quest for individual enlightenment has always been important in Hindu and Buddhist culture, but from about the third century on, the Christian church began to demand strict adherence to dogma, and this required the suppression of the unregulated mystical path. The individual who experiences and thinks too freely is always a potential heretic. The authoritarian role of the church was counterbalanced to some extent during the Middle Ages by a few great mystics, such as Saint Francis, and by the beginning of a secular quest for individuation. Late in the Middle ages, the church took a distinctly rational turn under Thomas Aquinas, and this element has been prominent in Catholicism ever since. The Renaissance, the Enlightenment, and the rise of modern science and technology in the West have all added to the rational thrust of Western thought and have tended to shape the quest for individual fulfillment along lines that stress the rational and the material. In twentieth-century America we have adopted a view of the ideal condition of "mental health" or "normality" that rests on the model of the ideal scientific observer, one who is thoroughly rational and realistic, *realism* in this case being defined in terms of the outlook of a materialistic science.

The psychic evolution of the West might be viewed as an experiment in the concentrated cultivation of the ego. It has yielded some notable accomplishments in science and technology, and it has yielded a heightened sense of individual separateness. The Orient, on the other hand, has produced more sophisticated philosophical systems and an "inner" technology unmatched by anything in the West. For obvious reasons, many Westerners now feel a need to learn from Eastern culture, just as many people of Asia feel a need to learn from the West. It would be foolish to argue that either broad culture is more advanced than the other, but each serves to highlight the deficiencies of the other. In each culture, there is a need to develop forms of consciousness or psychic capacities that have been neglected. In the West, where efficiency has been so strongly emphasized, further development of consciousness is likely to place greater emphasis on the imaginal, the extrasensory, and the modes of relatedness and transcendence. In some parts of the Orient, there may be a need to develop aspects of the mode of efficiency that have long been stressed in the West. The modes of creativity and relatedness have yet to reach their highest development in either part of the world. In the case of relatedness, the need has become quite urgent, for the survival of our species into the next century may depend on the widespread development of a "global consciousness," a greater awareness on the part of people in all walks of life, particularly people in positions of leadership, of our common species identity, of our psychic interdependence, and of our mutual belongingness.

Given the recognized historical differences between East and West and the obvious current difference in needs for further development, it seems odd that many writers would insist on a universal sequence of psychic evolution. Often the key idea in the scheme is that the marked egoic development we see in the West represents an intermediate stage and that the ultimate goal is one of transcendence, or union with the brahman. This represents an Eastern reading of Western evolution, but it is possible to find Eastern systems in which such a sequence is viewed as universal. The chakra system of kundalini yoga, for example, can be interpreted according to a sequence in which different modes of psychic fulfillment form an ascending hierarchy. Compassion, creativity, intuitive knowledge, and universal consciousness are said to be governed by the heart, throat, third-eye, and crown chakras respectively (Rama, Ballentine, and Ajaya, 1976). If we equate the development of consciousness with the ascension of kundalini from the root chakra to the crown chakra, we could argue that the goals of relatedness, creativity, and transcendence lie at successively higher stages of development. The most obvious facts of individual development and cultural history do not support any such sequence. Any of these modes can be emphasized to the very virtual exclusion of the others, and each is subject to realization on a number of levels in and of itself.

THE OVERALL COURSE OF EVOLUTION

What can we now say about the course of psychic evolution as a whole? I have described a variety of views on this matter. One possible position is that there is one universal sequence leading to one universal goal. The sequence may be described either in terms of an increasing manifestation of just one desired quality, such as rationality, or it may be regarded as leading through intermediate stages (e.g., an egoic stage) involving qualities that contrast sharply with the ultimate goal. I consider all the major formulations of this type to be inadequate. In most of them, the goal corresponds either to the mode of efficiency or to the mode of transcendence. If I am offered a choice between the Western scientific god of rational-analytical consciousness and the Eastern god of Brahmanic unity, I can do nothing but declare myself a polytheistic heathen.

A second possible position, which has a little more merit, is that there are several alternative pathways leading to different goals. The possible goals might be identified with the five modes of fulfillment, but there is room for some variation in choice within each of the modes. A third position is that there are alternative pathways leading ultimately to one common goal. In the form in which I have suggested such a position in this chapter, this position actually embraces the second one as part of the total evolutionary process. It assumes that evolutionary development may proceed initially toward a limited goal, perhaps one defined in terms of rationality, relatedness, or transcendence. Once development has proceeded far in this direction, however, further development may concentrate on the cultivation of potentials of a much different nature. If there is one ultimate common goal in the evolution of human consciousness, I believe that the goal must be understood as the maximal realization of all our potentials for perceiving, understanding, and judging, and that maximal realization requires having ready access to all these potentials. It means being able to choose the states of consciousness and modes of awareness that best meet our needs at any time.

Alternative Pathways

It is likely that in any individual and in any cultural group, development will tend initially to emphasize certain potentials to the neglect of others. The initial path might be aimed toward any of the five modes. Perhaps we could usefully encompass the major possibilities by classifying in terms of two broad possibilities corresponding to the basic patterns we considered earlier. Thus, in some cases, the initial course of development might be characterized as restrictive, Apollonian, masculine, or rational-analytical. In other cases, it might be characterized as fluid, Dionysian, feminine, or holistic-intuitive. Most of the goals embraced by the mode of efficiency require the former course, while the goals embraced by the modes of relatedness and transcendence require the latter course. The mode of creativity may emphasize either course but requires both for maximal realization. The mode of inner harmony also requires both.

There are other ways in which we might characterize some of the more specific paths that lie within the range of these broad categories. The Apollonian way would include a path directed outward toward the world of material things, with an emphasis on accumulation of objective facts and on analytical understanding and control of the objective realm. It would also include an inward path that emphasizes abstraction and the rational processing of ideas. The Dionysian way would also include both inward and outward paths. The outward path in this case would be concerned more with relationship than with analysis. This might be expressed in a concern with a relationship either to be whole of nature or to other people and perhaps a concern with an intuitive-feeling understanding of people. The inward path would focus more on the inner realm of feelings, images, fantasies, and dreams. The inward path could be directed toward transcendence. In this case, the universal whole would be understood as all-embracing spirit. In a more outward path, the goal of transcendence would be understood more clearly as including the natural, material world. Telepathy and clairvoyance also fall within the Dionysian domain, and the form these assume may depend somewhat on whether the basic direction of the path is outward or inward.

The body may be of focal interest or it may be largely ignored with either an Apollonian or a Dionysian orientation. The Apollonian paths would tend to favor a sharp mind-body, or ego-body, split, and the body, if it receives attention, would be viewed as something to be mastered or controlled. The Dionysian paths would favor a greater sense of oneness with the body, with desired effects experienced in terms of this oneness, rather than in terms of dominance of mind over body. Perhaps this contrast is the key to some basic differences between Western approaches to body-building and health management, on the one hand, and the yogic practices and martial arts of the Orient on the other.

A predominant trend in either the Apollonian or the Dionysian direction yields a one-sided development in consciousness, and the subsequent cultivation of the neglected potentials will result in a condition that is more balanced or androgynous. Perhaps development at any one time will tend to focus selectively, favoring some potentials over others. It is possible, however, for development within a given individual or a given culture to proceed in a fairly balanced way, so that at any one level along the way there is an androgynous access to both the rational and the intuitive, the Apollonian and the Dionysian, and, for that matter, both the inner and the outer. Certainly it is not necessary for every culture to pass through the extremely Apollonian, or patriarchal, egoic phase of consciousness that characterizes modern Western culture. This condition, like its mystical opposite, is one possible step along one of the paths of psychic evolution. Movement beyond that step should lead ultimately to a condition of more balanced realization of all psychic potentials.

The idea that evolution can proceed along alternative routes implies, obviously, that while progress is occurring with respect to one mode of consciousness, there may be no change with respect to other modes. A reasonable corollary is that evolution as such is not inevitable. Indeed, our assumption that psychic evolution has been steadily taking place over the past so many thousand years probably reflects a tacit faith in the myth of progress, rather than a conclusion that can be safely drawn from available evidence. Even the facts I noted in Chapter 4 for the historical period from classical Greece to the modern era provide an ambiguous picture. If we are looking merely at the high points represented by the most exceptional individuals of our society, it is not clear that the modern era has advanced beyond classical Greece with respect to rationality and creativity. With respect to relatedness, it is not clear that we have advanced beyond the level represented long ago by Jesus of Nazareth or Francis of Assisi. With respect to transcendence, it is not clear that we have moved beyond the level represented in ancient times by Jesus, Paul, Pythagoras, the Orphic cult, of the gnostics. In each of these modes, we find significant models within our culture as long as 2,000 or 2,500 years ago.

It is possible, of course, to argue that the exceptional individuals of long ago were more exceptional at that time than they would appear to be if they lived now—that the average level of the mass of people has moved upward, closer to the level represented by those individuals. We lack direct evidence for this, however; we must point to changes in institutions and social systems as pertinent data. At least for certain expressions of the mode of efficiency, the spread of education and literacy provides a relevant argument. We can point to the many marvels of the modern world as proof of our psychic growth. Yet above all these looms the undeniable fact that we are caught up in a nuclear arms race that can easily culminate in the unraveling of millions of years of biological evolution. Here our actions reflect an inability to find either rational or creative solutions to our problems, a lack of inner harmony, a lack of love for our fellow beings, and a tendency to keep projecting our unrecognized psychic potentials onto the world around us. In the face of this situation, I feel no great assurance that the people of Western culture or of the world as a whole have undergone a great deal of psychic evolution over the past few thousand years. It is evidently in our nature to seek greater awareness, but it is also in our nature to avoid awareness, and the balance of these two tendencies is subject to fluctuation. I am not certain that further psychic evolution is inevitable, but I firmly believe it is possible. We must do everything we can to protect that possibility against the threat of a global nuclear disaster that can destroy it forever. In that possibility we can find meaning in our present struggle and a hope for a future that stretches far beyond the reach of our present vision.

NEEDED RESEARCH

Our understanding of psychic evolution remains limited. The best anyone can do is suggest reasonable interpretations on the basis of available evidence. We can also seek new information to augment our understanding. We need more knowledge of patterns of conscious activity that can provide a more adequate foundation for taxonomies of states, modes of consciousness, and experiential types of people. At present, we have an abundance of useful information of a very selective nature. We have personal accounts of religious experience, psychotic experience, and drug experience. We have studies of hypnotic and meditative procedures, sensory deprivation, and sleep and dreams. We also have the observations based on a few studies in which the thought of subjects have been sampled in an ordinary waking state (see, for example, Klinger, 1978; Pope and Singer, 1978).

States of Consciousness

For the most part, we rely on a priori classifications of states, making minor modifications on the basis of selective observations of the types I have just noted. If our aim is a more adequate taxonomy of states, the ideal method would be some form of multivariate analysis, such as factor analysis, of a comprehensive set of psychological indices applied to experiences in a large and varied assortment of situations. The situations or occasions must vary in such a way that they can be assumed to encompass all the experiences in which we are interested, and there are two major strategies we might adopt in selecting them. We could either select moments by some random procedure over a long period of time or select them by a systematic procedure that would ensure coverage of all circumstances that are assumed to relate significantly to important psychological effects (e.g., such circumstances as sleep, alcoholic or drug intoxication, organized mental labor, etc.).

Ideally, at each moment sampled we would want an elaborate phenomenological report of ongoing experience, or else responses to a questionnaire covering all variables of interest. The variables should include every aspect of experience that may provide a key to important state differences. Thus, we would need to ask about the degree to which attention is focused, the width of the attentional span, the organization or orderliness of the experience, the extent to which percepts or concepts are clearly differentiated, the locus or nature of the focal content (whether concrete or abstract, external or internal, etc.), the sensory or imagery modes involved, the experience of control (whether the individual feels in control, is the victim of unwanted controlling forces, or experiences trust in a benign power), the intensity of the experience (intensity of sensations, images, or emotions), the predominant hedonic tone (pleasant or unpleasant), the experienced meaningfulness of the events, and their communicability (or ineffability). We would be interested as well in the experience of time (its apparent speed of passage, the sense of continuity of the present with the past and future, the span of the experienced present, and the extent to which the individual is oriented to present, past, or future). Above all, we would want to know about the nature of self-experience—in particular, the sense of separateness (vs. unity or merging with a larger whole or with another being), the sense of personal integrity (as opposed to fragmentation or inner splitting), the sense of personal embodiment (as opposed to depersonalization, deanimation, or mechanization), and level of self-esteem or self-satisfaction.

In all likelihood, the ideal experiment as I have described it cannot be executed. There are obvious difficulties in the way of obtaining all the desired information at all the desired times. We could come closest to the ideal by resorting to retrospective reports from highly trained and sophisticated subjects. Other compromises might be necessary, such as relying partly on the use of experimenter ratings and piecing together the total picture from incomplete sets of information gathered at different times.

There are additional considerations, regarding the research design and method of analysis, that have a bearing on the nature of the patterns we are able to identify. If we are seeking a classification of states of consciousness, we might employ a P-technique form of analysis. (For a discussion of P, R, and other techniques, see Coan, 1961, and Cattell, 1966.) In this method, we analyze covariation of psychological variables over a series of occasions for an individual subject. If the occasions are meaningfully identifiable in terms of events (such as sleeping, meditating, or intoxication) that have an obvious relevance to states, then we might employ O-technique, analyzing the covariation of occasions with respect to the associated psychological data. To the extent that we find essentially the same patterns in more than one subject, we will be able to move toward a classification of states applicable to people in general.

Individual, Developmental, and Cultural Patterns

We may need additional forms of research to illumine other kinds of patterns. To find out more about experiential types and about modes of psychological processing, we need research that highlights individual differences. I have already acknowledged that conventional R-technique factor-analytic studies of intellectual performance, as in the work of J. P. Guilford, can furnish information that bears on patterns of cognitive processing. There are additional kinds of information that require introspective accounts of the processes by which various problems are solved. There are inherent limitations, of course, to an experimental task that calls for the one correct response. We need more work with situations that permit the individual to respond in a wide array of possible ways. The traditional use of the Rorschach test is a crude example of the kind of research that might be used to illuminate styles of perception, cognition, and imagination. Traditional Rorschach scoring takes into account the features of the stimulus to which the subject responds, the extent to which the subject focuses on details or on the whole, the organization of the response, and the way in which the immediate impression is subjected to imaginative elaboration. Valuable as inkblots may be as a projective stimulus, however, they are only one type of stimulus material. We can gain a more adequate picture of the individual's basic style of conscious functioning by examining responses to a great variety of visual, auditory, and conceptual stimuli.

If we conduct the kind of research I have described with adult subjects, we can secure a better understanding of the patterns of conscious experience prevalent in the general adult population. If we want a comprehensive picture of possible patterns, however, we may need to select subjects from other populations. It may be important to do intensive research with subjects from various select populations—subjects with various psychotic conditions, people who have engaged in intensive meditative practices, people who practice mediumship or have frequent paranormal experiences of other sorts. To gain a better understanding of developmental changes in experiential patterns, we must work with children and with people of various adult age groups.

We would need a time machine to study evolutionary changes in consciousness directly, but ontogenetic changes are more accessible to us and undoubtedly bear some relationship to phylogenetic changes. Much more work is needed to illuminate the experiential patterns that are actually characteristic of children at various age levels. Most of the relevant work with children so far has been research in the Piagetian tradition. For the most part, this work has been designed to identify changes in cognitive processing, and it has not been sufficiently phenomenological in nature to cast much light on the raw experience of the child. The primary aim of Piagetian research has been to identify the points at which the individual acquires or manifests various adult modes of perceiving, judging, or conceptualizing. Piaget (1976) spoke of the development of consciousness (in French, *conscience*) in his writings, but he equated this with the development of conceptualization and abstraction.

Much of the research in this tradition has been guided by an underlying expectation that cognitive development consists of the gradual emergence of the "realistic" and "rational" view of the world favored in Western culture, and changes of any other kind have been generally overlooked. Even the major shifts in self-conception have received little attention from cognitive researchers. They have been of more focal concern within a broad movement, variously known as ego psychology and self psychology, that is rooted in the psychoanalytic tradition. In the writings of such people as René Spitz, Margaret Mahler, Melanie Klein, Erik Erikson, and Heinz Kohut, we find various formulations of such concepts as self and ego but a consistent interest in the developing relationship between me and other. Their work complements that of the non-psychoanalytic cognitive researchers in important ways, but it still does not furnish the comprehensive view we might like of the shifting stream of conscious experience from infancy to adulthood.

Thus, more work needs to be done with children both within our own society and in other societies. We must develop observational methods that permit ready application cross-culturally, not merely to study child development in other settings but also to examine more systematically the differences that exist between adults who have grown up in different cultural milieus.

It would be valuable to gather data in India, China, and Japan, but we may obtain some unique insights into possible evolutionary pathways by studying people in third-world societies that have developed largely outside the sphere of influence of either Western or Oriental culture.

Flexibility

In this book and elsewhere I have stressed the idea of flexibility as one key to individual development and psychic evolution. There is a need for new methods for assessing flexibility and for subsequent investigation of the relationship of flexibility to various kinds of development. I regard my own efforts to assess openness to experience as an initial venture into the assessment of flexibility (Coan, 1972, 1974). My primary contribution here, however, is a set of questionnaire scales, and self-description can go only so far.

Thorough assessment of flexibility would be a very complex operation. We need to examine many forms of flexibility and determine their interrelationships. One form would be simply the ability to shift deliberately from one conscious content to another, to shift attention to different objects, aspects of objects, tasks, subject matters, and so forth. The scope of focal content that can be handled in a differentiated way at a given time might be another facet of flexibility. Related to these would be the ability to shift from one mode of perception or imagery to another.

Perhaps a more profound form of flexibility would be the ability to shift readily from one state to consciousness to another. Akin to this would be the ability to shift from one mode of processing, ordering, or channeling conscious contents to another mode. An important form of conceptual flexibility would be the ability to entertain alternative ways of viewing or conceptualizing oneself, other people, and the world.

As far as possible, we should attempt to develop methods for assessing flexibility that can be applied across a wide spectrum of individuals differing in age, current mode of psychological functioning, and cultural background. We need to investigate the relationship between flexibility and psychological development in general—at least ontogenetic development if phylogenetic development is to remain beyond our reach. Perhaps the overall relationship is not monotonic. Flexibility may not increase continuously in the course of development. If Jung, Neumann, and Wilber are correct, the first half of development may yield a one-sided, ego-centered condition. In some ways, this condition would be characterized by inflexibility. Flexibility need not be a unidimensional trait, of course; hence, some forms of flexibility may increase while others decrease. It would be useful to determine what course each form of flexibility follows throughout the life cycle.

I have argued in the preceding pages that flexibility is a key to more advanced levels of development within each of the basic modes of fulfillment, and the connections I suggested should be studied in greater depth. Thus, we should determine the role of flexibility in its various forms in the development of bodily self-control, psi abilities, creativity, and various forms of understanding. Likewise, we need to learn more about the role of flexible access to various psychic contents and flexible use of different ways of perceiving and conceptualizing in the development of inner harmony and relationships with others. If the pathways leading to different fulfillment goals tend ultimately to converge, as I have suggested, this convergence probably requires a reconciliation of values that may have seemed earlier to be incompatible. We need to learn more about the forms of flexibility that permit or generate this kind of reconciliation and make possible generally the achievement of advanced levels in a combination of pathways.

A more direct examination of actual evolutionary changes in consciousness would require a sampling of moments in time to which we have no access. We can only infer features of the consciousness of our ancestors from their symbolic, conceptual, and literary products. If we leave an adequate record of our own experience, a comparison of our experience with that of our remote descendants will be a possible task of future science. If sufficient evolutionary change has occurred when that comparison becomes possible, science as we now know it may no longer exist.

Bibliography

Arieti, Silvano. *Creativity: The magic Synthesis*. New York: Basic Books, 1976.

Aurobindo. Sir. *The Life Divine*. Pondicherry, India: Sri Aurobindo Ashram, 1970.

-----. *The Essential Aurobindo*. New York: Schocken, 1973.

Baker, R. Robin. *Human Navigation and the Sixth Sense*. London: Hodder & Stoughton, 1981.

Berman, Morris. *The Reenchantment of the World*. Toronto: Bantam, 1984.

Blofeld, John. *Taoism: The Road to Immortality*. Boulder, Colorado: Shambhala, 1978.

Boas, Franz. *The Mind of Primitive Man*. New York: Macmillan, 1921.

Boone, John Allen. *Kinship with All Life*. New York: Harper, 1954.

Bronowski, Jacob. *Insight*. New York: Harper & Row, 1964.

-----. "The Creative Process." In John D. Roslansky (ed.), *Creativity: A Discussion at the Nobel Conference*. Amsterdam: North Holland Publishing Company, 1970.

-----. *The Ascent of Man*. Boston: Little, Brown & Company, 1973.

-----. *A Sense of the Future: Essays in Natural Philosophy*. Cambridge, Massachusetts: MIT Press, 1977.

-----. *The Origins of Knowledge and Imagination*. New Haven: Yale University Press, 1978.

Bury, J. B. *The Idea of Progress: An Inquiry into Its Origins and Growth*. New York: Dover, 1960.

Campbell, Joseph. *The Masks of God: Occidental Mythology*. Harmondsworth, England: Penguin, 1964.

-----. *The Masks of God: Creative Mythology*. New York: Viking, 1968.

-----. *The Masks of God: Primitive Mythology*. New York: Viking, 1969.

-----. *The Masks of God: Oriental Mythology*. New York: Penguin Books, 1976.

-----. *The Way of the Animal Powers, Volume 1, Historical Atlas of World Mythology*. London: Summerfield Press, 1983.

Capra, Fritjof. *The Tao of Physics*. New York: Bantam, 1975.

Cashen, Richard Anthony. *Solitude in the Thought of Thomas Merton*. Kalamazoo, Michigan: Cistercian Publications, 1981.

Cattell, Raymond B. "The Data Box: Its Ordering of Total Resources in Terms of Possible Relational Systems." In Raymond B. Cattell (ed.), *Handbook of Multivariate Experimental Psychology*. Chicago: Rand McNally, 1966.

Chaudhuri, Haridas. "Yoga Psychology." In Charles T. Tart (ed.), *Transpersonal Psychologies*. New York: Harper & Row, 1975.

Claremont de Castillejo, Irene. *Knowing Woman: A Feminine Psychology*. New York: G. P. Putnam's Sons, 1973.

Coan, Richard W. "Basic Forms of Covariation and Concomitance Designs." *Psychological Bulletin*, 1961, Vol. 58, 317-24.

-----. "Measurable Components of Openness to Experience." *Journal of Consulting and Clinical Psychology*, 1972, Vol. 39, 346.

-----. "Toward a Psychological Interpretation of Psychology."

Journal of the History of the Behavioral Sciences, 1973, Vol. 9, 313-27.

-----. *The Optimal Personality: An Empirical and Theoretical Analysis*. London: Routledge & Kegan Paul, 1974.

-----. *Hero, Artist, Sage, or Saint? A Survey of Views on What Is Variously Called Mental Health, Normality, Maturity, Self-Actualization, and Human Fulfillment*. New York: Columbia University Press, 1977.

-----. *Psychologists: Personal and Theoretical Pathways*. New York: Irvington, 1979.

-----. *Psychology of Adjustment: Personal Experience and Development*. New York: Wiley, 1983.

Cunningham, Susan. "Cross-Cultural Study of Achievement Calls for Changes in Home." *APA Monitor*, September 1984, Vol. 15, No. 9, 10.

Dellas, Marie, and Eugene L. Gaier. "Identification of Creativity: The Individual." *Psychological Bulletin*, 1970, Vol. 73, 55-73.

Drury, Nevill. *The Shaman and the Magician: Journeys Between the Worlds*. London: Routledge & Kegan Paul, 1982.

Ehrenwald, Jan. *Anatomy of Genius: Split Brains and Global Minds*. New York: Human Sciences Press, 1984.

Eliade, Mircea. *The Myth of Eternal Return*. New York: Bollingen, 1954.

Erikson, Erik H. *Gandhi's Truth: On the Origins of Militant Nonviolence*. New York: W. W. Norton, 1969.

Ferguson, Marilyn. *The Aquarian Conspiracy: Personal and Social Transformation in the 1980s*. Los Angeles: J. P. Tarcher, 1980.

Frankl, Viktor E. *Man's Search for Meaning: An Introduction to Logotherapy*. New York: Washington Square Press, 1963.

Freud, Sigmund. *Moses and Monotheism*. New York: Vintage, 1939.

Goldstein, Kurt. *Human Nature in the Light of Psychopathology.* New York: Schocken, 1963.

Goleman, Daniel. "The Buddha on Meditation and States of Consciousness." In Charles T. Tart (ed.), *Transpersonal Psychologies.* New York: Harper & Row, 1975.

The Gospel According to Thomas, translated by A. Guillaumont, H.-Ch. Puech, G. Quispel, W. Till, and Yassah 'Abd Al Masih. New York: Harper & Row, 1959

Green, Elmer, et al. *Autogenic Feedback Training.* Topeka, Kansas: Menninger Foundation, 1973.

Greenway, John L. *The Golden Horns: Mythic Imagination and the Nordic Past.* Athens, Georgia: University of Georgia Press, 1977.

Guilford, J. P. *The Nature of Human Intelligence.* New York: McGraw-Hill, 1967.

Guilford, J. P., and Ralph Hoepfner. *The Analysis of Intelligence.* New York: McGraw-Hill, 1971.

Guthrie, W. K. C. *In the Beginning: Some Greek Views on the Origins of Life and the Early State of Man.* Ithaca, New York: Cornell University Press, 1957.

Haberstam, David. "Yes We Can!" *Parade Magazine*, July 8, 1984, 4-7.

Halifax, Joan. *Shaman: The Wounded Healer.* London: Thames and Hudson, 1982.

Harding, M. Esther. *The Way of All Women: A Psychological Interpretation.* New York: C. G. Jung Foundation for Analytical Psychology, 1970.

Harner, Michael. *The Way of the Shaman.* New York: Harper & Row, 1980.

Hillman, James. "Psychology: Monotheistic or Polytheistic?" *Spring*, 1971, 202.

-----. *The Myth of Analysis: Three Essays in Archetypal Psychology.* Evanston, Illinois: Northwestern University Press, 1972.

Hoyle, Fred. *The Intelligent Universe: A New View of Creation and Evolution*. New York: Holt, Rinehart and Winston, 1984.

Huizinga, Johan. *Homo Ludens: A Study of the Play-Element in Culture*. Boston: Beacon Press, 1955.

James, William. *Pragmatism*. London: Longmans, Green, 1907.

-----. "The Final Impressions of a Psychical Researcher." In Gardner Murphy and Robert O. Ballou (eds.), *William James on Psychical Research*. New York: Viking, 1960.

-----. *Psychology: The Briefer Course*. New York: Harper & Row, 1961.

Jaynes, Julian. *The Origin of Consciousness in the Breakdown of the Bicameral Mind*. Boston: Houghton Mifflin, 1976.

Jones, Alexander (ed.). *The Jerusalem Bible*. Garden City, New York: Doubleday, 1966.

Jung, C. G. "Child Development and Education." In C. G. Jung, *Psychology and Education*. Princeton, New Jersey: Princeton University Press, 1954.

-----. Foreword to *The I Ching*, translated by Richard Wilheim, rendered into English by Cary F. Baynes. Princeton, New Jersey: Princeton University Press, 1967.

-----. "The Stages of Life." In *The Collected Works of C. G. Jung, Volume 8, The Structure and Dynamics of the Psyche*. Princeton, New Jersey: Princeton University Press, 1969a.

-----. *The Collected Works of C. G. Jung, Volume 11, Psychology and Religion: West and East*. Princeton, New Jersey: Princeton University Press, 1969b.

-----. "Archaic Man." In *The Collected Works of C. G. Jung, Volume 10, Civilization in Transition*. Princeton, New Jersey: Princeton University Press, 1970a.

-----. "The Role of the Unconscious." In *The Collected Works of C. G. Jung, Volume 10, Civilization in Transition*. Princeton, New Jersey: Princeton University Press, 1970b.

-----. "The Spiritual Problem in Modern Man." In *The Collected Works of C. G. Jung, Volume 10, Civilization in Transition*.

Princeton, New Jersey: Princeton University Press, 1970c.

-----. "What India Can Teach Us." In *The Collected Works of C. G. Jung, Volume 10, Civilization in Transition.* Princeton, New Jersey: Princeton University Press, 1970d.

-----. *The Collected Works of C. G. Jung, Volume 6, Psychological Types.* Princeton, New Jersey: Princeton University Press, 1971.

Kalff, Martin. "The Negation of Ego in Tibetan Buddhism and Jungian Psychology." *Journal of Transpersonal Psychology,* 1983, Vol. 15, 103-24.

Kierkegaard, Søren. *Concluding Unscientific Postscript to the Philosophical Fragments,* Princeton, New Jersey: Princeton University Press, 1941.

-----. *Either/Or.* Princeton, New Jersey: Princeton University Press, 1944.

-----. *Fear and Trembling and the Sickness unto Death.* Garden City, New York: Doubleday, 1954.

Klinger, Eric. "Dimensions of Thought and Imagery in Normal Waking States." *Journal of Altered States of Consciousness,* 1978, Vol. 4, 97-113.

Kris, Ernst. *Psychoanalytic Explorations in Art.* New York: International Universities, 1952.

Kuhn, Thomas S. "The Structure of Scientific Revolutions." *International Encyclopedia of Unified Science,* Vol. 1, No. 2. Chicago: University of Chicago Press, 1970.

Laing, R. D. *The Divided Self.* Harmondsworth, England: Penguin, 1965.

Legge, James. "Was Taoism Older than Lao-tze?" In *The Texts of Taoism, Part I,* translated by James Legge. New York: Dover, 1962.

Leonard, George B. *The Transformation: A Guide to the Inevitable Changes in Humankind.* New York: Delacorte, 1971.

Lévy-Bruhl, Lucien. *Primitive Mentality.* New York: Macmillan, 1923.

-----. *The "Soul" of the Primitive.* New York: Praeger, 1966.

Maslow, Abraham H. *Motivation and Personality.* New York: Harper & Row, 1970.

Merton, Thomas. *Conjectures of a Guilty Bystander.* Garden City, New York: Doubleday, 1966.

Morris, Colin. *The Discovery of the Individual: 1050-1200.* New York: Harper & Row, 1972.

Motoyama, Hiroshi, with Rande Brown. *Science and the Evolution of Consciousness: Chakras, Ki, and Psi.* Brookline, Massachusetts: Brookline Press, 1978.

The Nag Hammadi Library in English, translated by members of the Coptic Library Project of the Institute for Antiquity and Christianity. San Francisco: Harper & Row, 1977.

Needham, Joseph. *Science and Civilization in China, Volume 2, History of Scientific Thought.* Cambridge, England: Cambridge University Press, 1956.

Neumann, Erich. *Psychologie des Weiblichen.* Zurich: Rascher Verlag, 1953.

-----. *The Origins and History of Consciousness.* Princeton, New Jersey: Princeton University Press, 1954.

-----. "On Psychological Stages of Feminine Development." *Spring*, 1959, 63-97.

-----. *The Great Mother: An Analysis of the Archetype.* Princeton, New Jersey: Princeton University Press, 1963.

Nisbet, Robert. *History of the Idea of Progress.* New York: Basic Books, 1980.

Pagels, Elaine. *The Gnostic Gospels.* New York: Random House, 1979.

Parrinder, Geoffrey (ed.). *World Religions from Ancient History to the Present.* New York: Facts on File, 1981.

Piaget, Jean. *The Child's Conception of the World.* New York: Harcourt, Brace, 1929.

-----. *The Grasp of Consciousness: Action and Concept in the Young Child.* Cambridge, Massachusetts: Harvard University Press, 1976.

Pope, Kenneth S., and Jerome L. Singer (eds.). *The Stream of Consciousness: Scientific Investigations into the Flow of Human Experience.* New York: Plenum, 1978.

Rama, Swami, Rudolph Ballentine, and Swami Ajaya. *Yoga and Psychotherapy: The Evolution of Consciousness.* Honesdale, Pennsylvania: Himalayan International Institute of Yoga Science and Philosophy, 1976.

Reich, Charles A. *The Greening of America: How the Youth Revolution Is Trying to Make America Livable.* New York: Random House, 1970.

Reynolds, Terry S. "Medieval Roots of the Industrial Revolution." *Scientific American,* 1984, Vol. 251, No. 1, 122-130.

Rogers, Carl R. *On Becoming a Person.* Boston: Houghton Mifflin, 1961.

Roszak, Theodore. *Unfinished Animal: The Aquarian Frontier and the Evolution of Consciousness.* New York: Harper y Row, 1975.

Royce, Joseph R. *Manual: Psycho-Epistemological Profile.* Edmonton, Canada: Department of Psychology, University of Alberta, 1970.

Russell, Bertrand. *Wisdom of the West.* London: Crescent Books, 1959.

Sagan, Carl. *The Dragons of Eden: Speculations on the Evolution of Human Intelligence.* New York: Random House, 1977.

Schwaller de Lubicz, R. A. *Symbol and the Symbolic: Ancient Egypt, Science and the Evolution of Consciousness.* New York: Inner Traditions International, 1981.

Skinner, B. F. *Walden Two.* New York: Macmillan, 1948.

Spencer, Herbert. *The Principles of Sociology, Volume 1.* New York: D. Appleton and Company, 1898.

-----. *First Principles.* New York: D. Appleton and Company, 1912.

Story, Ronald. *The Space-Gods Revealed: A Close Look at the*

Theories of Erich von Däniken. New York: Harper & Row, 1976.

Suzuki, Daisetz Teitaro. *Introduction to Zen Buddhism.* New York: Causeway Books, 1974.

Tao Teh King. In *The Texts of Taoism, Part I,* translated by James Legge. New York: Dover, 1962.

Targ, Russell, and Keith Harary. *The Mind Race: Understanding and Using Psychic Abilities.* New York: Villard Books, 1984.

Tart, Charles T. *States of Consciousness.* New York: E. P. Dutton, 1975.

Teilhard de Chardin, Pierre. *Le Phénomène Humain.* Paris: Editions du Seuil, 1955.

-----. *Le Milieu Divin: An Essay on the Interior Life.* London: Collins, 1957.

-----. *The Phenomenon of Man.* New York: Harper and Brothers, 1959.

-----. *The Future of Man.* New York: Harper & Row, 1964.

-----. *Christianity and Evolution.* New York: Harcourt Brace Jovanovich, 1969.

-----. *Activation of Energy.* London: William Collins, 1970.

-----. *Toward the Future.* London: Collins, 1975.

The Texts of Taoism, Part I, translated by James Legge. New York: Dover, 1962.

Toffler, Alvin. *Future Shock.* New York: Random House, 1970.

Ulanov, Ann Belford. *The Feminine in Jungian Psychology and in Christian Theology.* Evanston, Illinois: Northwestern University Press, 1971.

Ullman, Montague, and Stanley Krippner. *Dream Telepathy.* New York: Macmillan, 1973.

U.S. School Children Behind Japan, Taiwan, Study Shows. *Arizona Daily Star,* July 17, 1984.

van der Post, Laurens. *The Dark Eye of Africa.* New York: William Morrow, 1955.

-----. *The Lost World of the Kalahari*. London: Hogarth Press, 1958.

-----. *A Mantis Carol*. London: Hogarth, 1975.

von Däniken, Erich. *Chariots of the Gods?* New York: Bantam, 1971.

Wallas, Graham. *The Art of Thought*. New York: Harcourt, Brace, 1926.

Watkins, Mary M. *Waking Dreams*. New York: Gordon and Breach, 1976.

Watson, Lyall. *Lifetide: The Biology of the Unconscious*. New York: Simon & Schuster, 1979.

Watts, Alan W. *The Way of Zen*. New York: The New American Library, 1957.

Werner, Heinz. *Comparative Psychology of Mental Development*. New York: Follett, 1948.

Whitmont, Edward C. *Return of the Goddess*. New York: Crossroad, 1982.

Wilber, Ken. *The Spectrum of Consciousness*. Wheaton, Illinois: Theosophical Publishing House, 1977.

-----. *No Boundary: Eastern and Western Approaches to Personal Growth*. Los Angeles: Center Publications, 1979.

-----. *The Atman Project: A Transpersonal View of Human Development*. Wheaton, Illinois: Theosophical Publishing House, 1980.

-----. *Up from Eden: A Transpersonal View of Human Evolution*. Garden City, New York: Anchor Press/Doubleday, 1981.

Wilhelm, Richard. Introduction to *The I Ching*, translated by Richard Wilhelm, rendered into English by Cary F. Baynes. Princeton, New Jersey: Princeton University Press, 1967.

Index